Readings

FAITH & RACE IN AMERICA
The Native American Religious Experience

VOL 1

Second
Edition

EDITED BY
JON R. STONE

with Suggestions by Gabriel Estrada and Carlos R. Piar

Kendall Hunt
publishing company

For my former graduate students both here and abroad, including:

Angelo Anagnos, Jordan Almanzar, Henry Bens, Angela Chompff,
Jennifer Dick, Antonio Dillehunt, Philippe Duhart, Jonathan Friedmann,
Javier Gonzalez, Heather Mackey, Jennifer Hoddevik, Shafiel Karim, Daniel Majors,
Ethan Quillen, Jessica Rehman, Vanessa Soriano, Timothy Vizthum, Nikolas Xiros,
and Suzette Zazueta.

Cover image © Shutterstock.com
Heebe-tee-tse of the Shoshone Nation. Ca 1899.

Kendall Hunt
publishing company

www.kendallhunt.com
Send all inquiries to:
4050 Westmark Drive
Dubuque, IA 52004-1840

Published in the United States of America

Contents

Chapter Sources for Volume 1: The Native American Religious Experience

Chapters 1–3: Richard Erdoes and Alfonso Ortiz (eds.). *American Indian Myths and Legends*. New York: Pantheon Books, 1984.

Chapters 4–6: Morris Edward Opler. *The Myths and Tales of the Jicarilla Apache Indians*. New York: American Folklore Society (v. 31), 1938.

Chapter 7: Frank Hamilton Cushing (Jesse Green, editor). *Zuñi: Selected Writing of Frank Hamilton Cushing*. Lincoln, NE: University of Nebraska Press, 1979.

Chapters 8–9: Selwyn Dewdney. *The Sacred Scrolls of the Southern Ojibway*. Toronto: University of Toronto Press, 1975.

Chapters 10–13: Robert Oswalt. *Kashaya Texts*. Berkeley: University of California Press, 1964.

Chapter 14: Jaime de Angulo. *Indian in Overalls*. San Francisco: City Lights Books, 1990.

Chapter 15: John G. Neihardt. *Black Elk Speaks: Being the Life Story of a Holy Man of the Oglala Sioux*. Lincoln, NE: University of Nebraska Press, 1961.

Chapter 16: Louise Erdrich. *Tracks*. New York: Henry Holt & Co., 1988.

Chapter 17: Leslie Marmon Silko. *Ceremony*. New York: Penguin Books, 1986.

Chapter 18: Vine Deloria, Jr. *Custer Died for Your Sins: An Indian Manifesto*. New York: Macmillan, 1969.

Chapter 19: Nancy Auer Falk and Rita M. Gross. *Unspoken Worlds: Women's Religious Lives*. New York: Wadsworth, 2001.

Chapters 20–22: James Treat (ed.). *Native and Christian: Indigenous Voices on Religious Identity in the United States and Canada*. New York: Routledge, 1995.

Other Volumes in This Series

THE AFRICAN AMERICAN RELIGIOUS EXPERIENCE

1. A Thanksgiving Sermon 1808 [Absalom Jones]
2. A Dialogue between a Virginian and an African Minister [Daniel Coker]
3. Ethiopian Manifesto [Robert Alexander Young]
4. Appeal to the Colored Citizens of the World [David Walker]
5. Narrative of the Life of Frederick Douglass, an American Slave [Frederick Douglass]
6. Religious Experience and Journal of Mrs. Jarena Lee [Jarena Lee]
7. Religious Instruction [Peter Randolph]
8. Pastor and Flock [from *Lay My Burden Down*]
9. Count the Stars through the Cracks [from *Lay My Burden Down*]
10. The Chanted Sermon [Albert J. Raboteau]
11. Of the Faith of the Fathers [W.E.B. DuBois]
12. Religion in the South [W.E.B. DuBois]
13. Jesus Christ in Georgia [W.E.B. DuBois]
14. Letter from a Birmingham Jail [Martin Luther King, Jr.]
15. Black Man's History [Malcolm X]
16. God in Black Theology [James H. Cone]
17. Womanist Theology: Black Women's Experience as a Source for Doing Theology, with Special Reference to Christology [Jacquelyn Grant]
18. Women in Islam [Aminah Beverly McCloud]

THE LATINO/A AMERICAN RELIGIOUS EXPERIENCE

1. Hymns, Prayers, and Other Religious Verses [Aurelio M. Espinosa and J. Manuel Espinosa]
2. The Penitente Brotherhood [Cleofas M. Jaramillo]
3. Holy Week at Arroyo Hondo [Cleofas M. Jaramillo]
4. Noche Buena and Religious Dramas [Cleofas M. Jaramillo]
5. Saints' Holy Days [Cleofas M. Jaramillo]
6. The Felicity of Mexico in the Wonderful Apparition of the Virgin Mary, Our Lady of Guadalupe (1675) [Luis Becerra Tanco]
7. Theological Significance [Jeanette Rodriguez]
8. India [Richard Rodriguez]

THE ASIAN AMERICAN RELIGIOUS EXPERIENCE

Foreword to the Second Edition of This Series

The need to renew the copyright permissions for most of the selections in these volumes now occasions the publication of a second edition. Since first appearing in 2007, the selections in these four volumes of *Readings in American Religious Diversity* (originally published as one hefty quarto tome!) have been changed only modestly. For the 2012 revised edition, I added only two or three readings to volumes one and two, ones that helped fill-in some of the instructional gaps in the course material. For this second edition, my colleagues and I have decided (reluctantly) to drop several readings—ones that our faculty have tended not to assign—in favor of several newer and fresher ones. In terms of size and substance, the most noticeable additions have been to volumes three and four, which our faculty had deemed a little lean as compared to the first two volumes. And for this second edition, as the editor, I have also taken this opportunity to revise and reword a number of the discussion questions in each volume as well as update the introductory material in each volume to reflect the changes in content (with thanks to Professors Gabriel Estrada, Bradley Hawkins, Sophia Pandya, and Carlos Piar for contributing helpful suggestions).

As I had noted in the *Foreword* to the first edition, it has become a commonplace to speak of America as a religiously diverse nation. From its origins, dating well before the arrival of European settlers, the American continent contained a great variety of peoples, languages, cultures, and religions. The native groups that came to inhabit this vast and varied landscape were of many types, from pueblo dwelling peoples, to those living in the woodlands, prairie, mountain, and coastal regions. During the period of European exploration and colonial expansion, the Americas soon became home to English, French, Spanish, Portuguese, and Dutch settlers. And, after slavery was introduced into the New World, peoples of African tribal descent added their own cultural and religious expressions to the growing ethnic and racial diversity of the land. From many peoples there emerged one nation; from one nation there arose many religious voices. The long conversation—and the spirited debate—over issues of religious and cultural identity continues to this day. What does it mean to be an American? What does it mean to be part of an ethnic or racial community in America? In what ways have religious beliefs and traditional cultural practices informed that meaning or helped shape that identity?

This four volume series presents to students of American religion a collection of primary source materials that serves to illustrate the ethno-racial dimensions of religion in America beyond its usual European expressions. The ethno-racial religious communities featured in this anthology broadly include Native American, African American, Asian American, and an array of Latino communities. A unique feature of these volumes is that their readings come from within the communities themselves, rather than from researchers commenting upon these communities from the outside. Thus, students reading these selections will come to hear the voices and sense the deeply-felt passion, sorrow, frustration, hope, and joy of those individuals who were or are still part of the important conversations at the heart of these four ethno-racial communities' ongoing dialogue and debates within themselves.

More specifically, these primary-source readings are designed to complement the religious and historical materials of the junior-level interdisciplinary capstone course, "American Religious Diversity," which is offered every semester at California State University, Long Beach. For this course, students are required to read religious literature produced by women and men from within at least two of the four ethno-racial communities mentioned above. While many of our instructors have assigned works of fiction, such as short stories or novels, we have found that fictional literature has tended to give our students only a partial picture of the religious dimensions of these communities and the difficulties these groups have experienced in their attempts to maintain traditional beliefs and practices in a predominantly "white" and Protestant culture. Thus, in addition to works of fiction, we have discovered that the diversity of religious experience as well as responses within these communities to discrimination, social dislocation, and loss of traditional culture could be "read" within other types of literature. These include folktales, sermons, letters, speeches, essays and addresses, autobiographies, oral histories and published interviews, as well as immigrant community histories, scholarly treatises, and ethnic denominational self-studies.

Because the course for which these four volumes are designed is taught each semester by six full-time and part-time faculty members, I do not believe that it has been my role as the lead editor of this anthology to instruct my colleagues in how to use these selections. At the same time, because not all of our faculty work in the area of American religious and ethnic history, I think that it is important to provide an outline of themes that emerge from these readings, especially as they show both the similarities as well as the differences in the experiences of these four ethno-racial communities and the role that religious ideas and practices have played within each. Thus, despite differences in their origins and in their specific experiences in the Americas, the literature produced by persons within the Native American, African American, Asian American, and Latino communities share a number of themes which students and instructors can reflect upon and fruitfully discuss. Among these themes is the experience of being outsiders, of social and cultural "otherness," of dislocation, disorientation, and uprootedness, of turning to tradition and relying upon religious institutions for personal and communal support, of the importance of family and the larger ethnic community, of striving after the recognition of basic rights and of one's human worth, of resistance to assimilation and the struggle against the secularizing influences of modern social and cultural life, and of drawing upon mythologies to strengthen one's sense of self and importance in the world.

Owing to all these difficulties and other personal and social experiences, it is profound that, beyond everything, people have continually turned to religion and to traditional expressions of community life for their remedy. There are those who seek succor within a religious community as well as those who adapt themselves and their traditions to meet the exigencies of life as immigrants, as sojourners or as outsiders, in a world where one's experiences are constantly defined by harassment, discrimination, and unrelenting assaults upon one's dignity. But also, and perhaps more importantly, people's experiences have likewise been defined by family, faith, community, friendship, religious mystery, wonder, thankfulness, laughter, and the renewal of the human spirit in the face of adversity.

Of course, while these themes predominate, one can also discern from these readings many lesser and many more contrasting themes. From this quartet of ethno-racial communities, a *discors concordia* or discordant concord can also be heard. The themes and variations that play throughout the pages of this anthology intersect in grand fugal style, and bear witness to the resilience of the human spirit, the signal significance of community, and the central role that religion plays in defining one's place in the world. Religion has been the tie that has bound individuals to their communities, has strengthened those same communities by renewing members' commitments to long-standing traditions, even as those traditions are transformed by the challenges that these and other like communities have had to face.

With respect to the selections themselves: originally it had been the hope of our faculty to include at least 25 readings per volume. But, due to obvious page limitations and higher than expected copyright costs, we have had to limit the number of selections in each volume to about 17–22. Despite these constraints, but not because of them, we decided that it was important to reprint the selected chapters, speeches, essays, and articles in their entirety, unedited, and as they originally appeared in print—coarse language and all. To understand and appreciate the positions and views being advanced or expressed, students need to read these selections *in toto*—two notable exceptions being the journal of Mrs. Jarena Lee and the lengthy chapter from Leslie Marmon Silko, both of which I felt obliged to condense by some 25–30 original printed pages.

Additionally, because the aim of these volumes is to highlight the various types of religious literature produced by members of these four ethno-racial communities, it is evident that not all communities produce the same varieties of literature, neither in the types nor in the same quantity. This difference is most evident in the volume on the Asian American religious experience, in which, to maintain some balance of material among volumes, I have had to include more scholarly and historical types of literature.

Lastly, while this primary-source anthology is primarily intended to meet the interdisciplinary and human diversity requirements of a specific course at Long Beach State, my colleagues and I are also aware of its potential instructional value outside Southern California. Recognizing that instructors and their students at other colleges and universities throughout the United States might likewise find these selections of interest, the volumes are designed to appeal more generally to faculty teaching similar courses in the fields of history, religious studies, ethnic studies, American studies, rhetoric, and comparative literary studies. To help familiarize readers with the four ethno-racial religious communities that comprise this anthology, I have also provided a brief preface or "foretaste" for each volume, along with several suggested questions to help facilitate class discussion. And so that those using this reader may be encouraged to explore further the histories and literatures of these communities, at the beginning of each volume I have included a list of recommended sources for both instructors and students to consult (with credit to Carlos Piar for Volume 3).

Notwithstanding these limitations, my colleagues and I have sought to create an anthology that allows a variety of voices within these communities to be heard, in many cases for the first time under the same cover. Indeed, this text represents a true celebration of the religious diversity that defines the American nation.

Vox manet—the Voice remains (Ovid).

—Jon R. Stone, Ph.D.
Long Beach, Calif.
May 2015

An Addendum to the new title:
Faith and Race in America

Since 2007, when *Readings in American Religious Diversity* was first published as one large volume of primary source readings, the course for which it was designed has undergone a number of changes. Broadly conceived in 1994 as an upper-level interdisciplinary capstone course examining the multifaceted varieties of religious experiences in the United States, by 2006 this course shifted its focus more directly on the key ways by which religion helped define and preserve the traditional cultures and customs of America's four main racial and ethnic communities: Native American, African American, Latina/o, and Asian American. The course's original unwieldy title, "Religious and Social Ethical Dimensions of American Diversity," was then shortened to "American Religious Diversity." The course reader that accompanied this new focus captured the spirit of that change by giving voice to women and men from within those very communities. But, by 2015, the focus of the course evolved even further by adding greater emphasis on issues of racial justice and gender equality in the United States. With the recent change in the course title to "Faith and Race in America," it seemed natural, if not necessary, to change the title of the course reader as well. But notwithstanding the new title, the essential aim of this collection of readings remains unchanged: diverse voices whose many faiths both affirm communal and inspire individual aspirations to seek after something higher as a nation that is, to quote Ronald Takaki, "peopled by the world."

"Let justice roll down like waters and righteousness like a mighty stream."
(Rev. Martin Luther King, Jr., April 1963, after Amos 5:24)

—Jon R. Stone
Long Beach, Calif.
July 2020

Sources and Selected General Works in American Religious History

Ahlstrom, Sydney E. *A Religious History of the American People.* New Haven, CT: Yale University Press, 1972.

Albanese, Catherine L. *America: Religions and Religion,* 3rd ed. Belmont, CA: Wadsworth, 1999.

Alba, Richard, Albert J. Raboteau, and Josh DeWind (eds.). *Immigration and Religion in America: Comparative and Historical Perspectives.* New York: New York University Press, 2009.

Barkan, Elliott Robert (ed.). *Immigrants in American History: Arrival, Adaptation, and Integration,* 4 vols. Santa Barbara, CA: ABC-CLIO, 2013.

Becker, Penny, and Nancy Eiesland (eds.). *Contemporary American Religion: An Ethnographic Reader.* Walnut Creek, CA: AltaMira Press, 1997.

Butler, Jon, Grant Wacker, and Randall Balmer. *Religion in American Life: A Short History.* NY: Oxford University Press, 2003.

Carroll, Bret E. *The Routledge Historical Atlas of Religions in America.* New York: Routledge, 2000.

Corrigan, John, and Winthrop S. Hudson. *Religion in America,* 7th ed. Upper Saddle River, NJ: Prentice-Hall, 2004.

Ebaugh, Helen, and Janet Chafetz. *Religion and the New Immigrants: Continuities and Adaptations in Immigrant Congregations.* Walnut Creek, CA: AltaMira Press, 2000.

Eck, Diana L. *A New Religious America.* San Francisco: HarperSanFrancisco, 2002.

Gaustad, Edwin S (ed.). *A Documentary History of Religion in America,* 2 vols. Grand Rapids, MI: Eerdmans, 1982–1983.

_____. *A Religious History of America,* rev. ed. San Francisco: Harper & Row, 1990.

Goff, Philip, and Paul Harvey (eds.). *Themes in Religion and American Culture.* Chapel Hill, NC: University of North Carolina Press, 2004.

Hackett, David G. (ed.). *Religion and American Culture: A Reader.* New York: Routledge, 1995.

Handy, Robert T. *A History of the Churches in the United States and Canada.* New York: Oxford University Press, 1977.

Hemeyer, Julia Corbett. *Religion in America,* 5th ed. Upper Saddle River, NJ: Prentice-Hall, 2005.

Lippy, Charles H., Robert Choquette, and Stafford Poole. *Christianity Comes to the Americas, 1492–1776.* New York: Paragon House, 1992.

McDannell, Colleen (ed.). *Religions of the United States in Practice,* 2 vols. Princeton, NJ: Princeton University Press, 2001.

Neusner, Jacob (ed.). *World Religions in America,* 3rd ed. Louisville, KY: Westminster/John Knox Press, 2003.

Porterfield, Amanda (ed.). *American Religious History.* Oxford, UK: Blackwell Publishers, 2002.

Warner, R. Stephen, and Judith G. Wittner (eds.). *Gatherings in Diaspora: Religious Communities and the New Immigration.* Philadelphia: Temple University Press, 1998.

Williams, Peter W. *America's Religions: From Their Origins to the Twenty-first Century,* 3rd ed. Urbana: University of Illinois Press, 2008.

_____ (ed.). *Perspectives on American Religion and Culture: A Reader.* Oxford, UK: Blackwell Publishers, 1999.

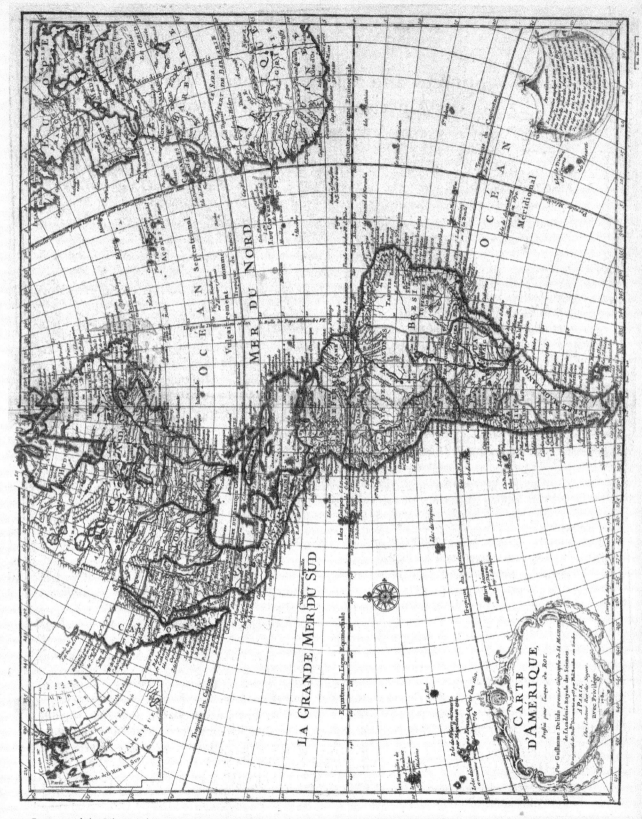

CARTE
D'AMERIQUE,
Dressée pour l'usage du ROI,
par Guillaume Delisle premier géographe de sa Majesté
de l'Academie Royale des Sciences
A PARIS.
Chez l'Auteur Rue des Sapins
Avec Privilege
1780.

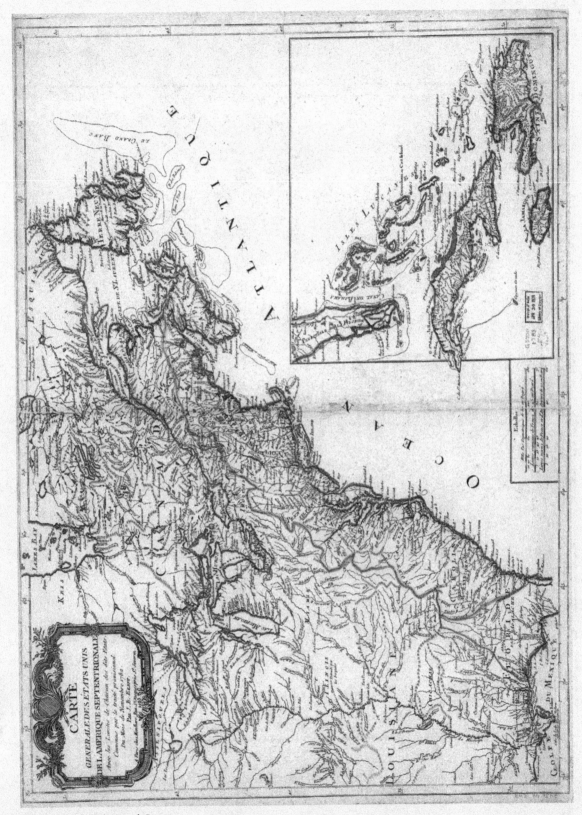

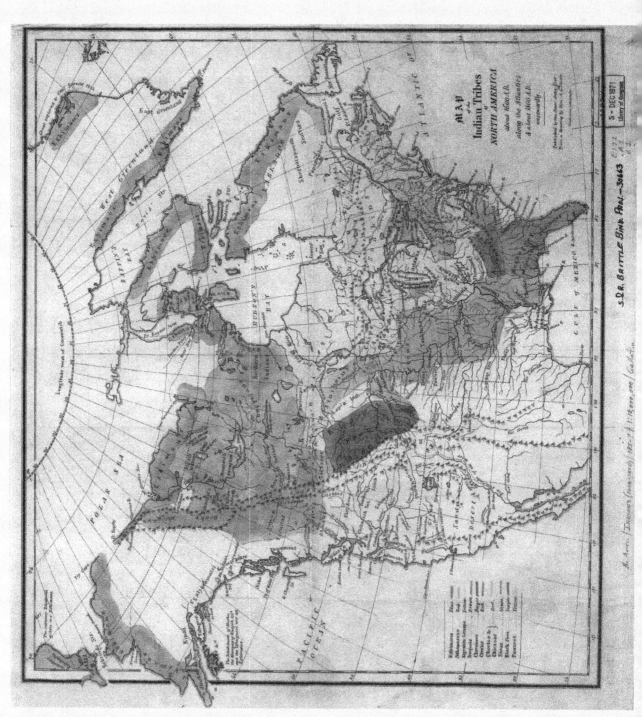

Courtesy of the Library of Congress

ELEVENTH CENSUS OF THE UNITED STATES.
ROBERT P. PORTER, SUPERINTENDENT.

INDIANS.

MAP OF
LINGUISTIC STOCKS
OF
AMERICAN INDIANS
chiefly within the present limits of the United States.
From Annual Report of Bureau of Ethnology Vol. 7.
by J.W. POWELL.

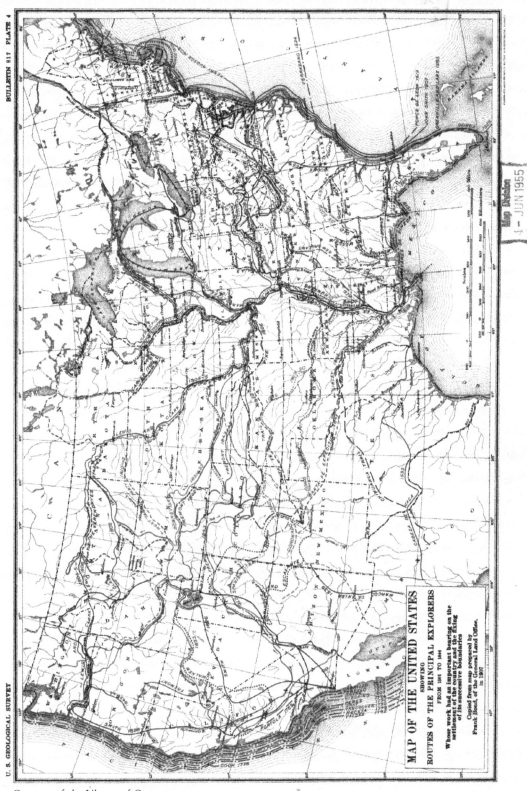

MAP OF THE UNITED STATES
SHOWING
ROUTES OF THE PRINCIPAL EXPLORERS
FROM 1501 TO 1844

Whose work had an important bearing on the
settlement of the country and the fixing
of its successive boundaries

Copied from map prepared by
Frank Bond, of the General Land Office,
in 1907

Readings in Native American Religious Traditions: A Foretaste

Sometime between 30,000 and 40,000 years ago, it is believed that nomadic tribes from Northeast Asia began to migrate into what was later to be called the North American continent. These hunting groups followed game southward, depositing themselves in various locations along the way. While some continued to wander eastward across the continent, by 8000 BCE, others began to settle in Central and South America, building various kinds of shelters, such as wood lodges or rock hewn dwellings, depending upon the terrain. These later tribes developed the means for growing modest amounts of corn, beans, and squash; learned to prepare acorns; dug for roots; and gathered pine nuts, wild grass seeds, and an assortment of berries.

Not surprisingly, the religions of these two types of subsistence tribes—hunting and gathering, planting and harvesting—developed myths and rituals associated with their primary food source and its growth and renewal. The sacred came to denote that which was essential and indispensable to the maintenance of life and of the group. The religious worldview of these native tribes related closely to the rhythms of nature, viewing all living beings in the natural world as interconnected. True, while for many of these tribes there was a creator deity—such as Wakan Tanka and Tam Apo—all things within that created world were seen as sacred or participating in and sharing divine power. Wolf, bear, coyote, buffalo, eagle, badger, spider, and even rock possessed sacred power and became the subject of folktales and legends passed down through stories—an oral tradition that continues to this day.

Along with stories, Native peoples of North America also incorporated actions such as ritualized dances, many in imitation of the movements of sacred animals and beings. Among them included the sun dance, buffalo dance, and, later, the ghost dance. Many of these dance rituals were borrowed or shared among dozens of tribes living across the northern and central plains and into the Great Basin. In one account of the central role the sun dance continues to play in the ritual life of the Sioux, Tahca Ushte, a medicine man known also as John Fire/Lame Deer, explains that "[t]he sun dance is a prayer and a sacrifice. One does not take part in it voluntarily but as the result of a dream, or a vision." The ritual follows a prescribed process, a process that is both physically and spiritually demanding. As Lame Deer relates further, "[i]nsights gained at such a price are even greater than those that come to a man on a hilltop during his vision quest; they are truly *wakan*—sacred" (Fire & Erdoes 1972:199–200).

Though belonging to a tribal group, individuals within the tribe were encouraged, even expected, to seek power as well as guidance from the spirit world. Typical among these types of rituals of spirit contact was the vision quest. The individual, usually an adolescent boy, would leave the community and set out alone or with other boys his age in search of a spirit guide or other channel of sacred power. During the period of the quest, the boy would open himself to the spirit world, expecting contact from an animal spirit or some other type of spirit that would choose him as worthy of sharing in that spirit's sacred power. According to Sam Gill, among the Ojibway, "visions commonly took the form of a journey into the world of the spirits. During this journey the visionary was shown the path on which his life should proceed. He was associated with one or more spirit beings who would serve as his guardians and protectors throughout life" (2005:72). But among other native tribes, vision quests were not limited only to puberty rituals. Åke Hultkrantz notes that among the Plains Indians, "warriors repeatedly withdrew into the wilderness to seek spirits" and "may therefore have a variety of guardian spirits, each of which is good for a different purpose" (1987:31).

The arrival of European settlers in the sixteenth and seventeenth centuries proved disruptive to thousands of years of cultural continuity. Adaptation by native tribes became difficult, even as Christian missionaries revised traditions and, in many cases, eradicated longstanding rituals and the mythologies that informed them. The story of the Native encounter with Europeans—the Spanish, French, English, and others—can be summarized in one word: loss. It was not so much a clash of peoples as of religions and ways of life. The Native view of land as sacred did not square with the Western Christian belief in a fallen world—a world to be conquered, dominated, and eventually redeemed.

In this volume of readings, I have selected varying types of literature that show these Native traditions likely before and after contact with European ideas. The first several readings are of tribal tales taken from various peoples within North America, such as Plains Indians, Pueblo Indians, and those dwelling in the northern woodlands and along coastal California. Some of these tales have been passed down through oral repetition and elaboration. Others, notably from the southern Ojibway, have been preserved on birch bark scrolls. For comparative purposes, I have also included a less formal mid-twentieth-century rendition of a creation myth, as recorded by the unconventional anthropologist, Jaime de Angulo.

The history of Native peoples since the mid-twentieth century has been one of recovery of Native traditions, of renewed connections to community, and of the rediscovery of lost identity. Thus there are readings that document this aspect of Native Indian history as well. For instance, the middle three selections record issues of religious identity as presented in an autobiographical recollection (Black Elk) and two fictional reflections on the importance of Native traditions to the continuing survival of Native peoples. The last five selections document more recent attempts by Native peoples to reclaim lost traditions, even among those embracing the teachings of Christ. The late Vine Deloria, Jr., himself a Christian theologian, notes that "the credal [sic] rhetoric of Christianity filled the vacuum it had created by its redefinition of religion as a commodity to be controlled." But, despite this, "Indian beliefs have always retained the capacity to return from their exile because they have always related to the Indian's deepest concern" (1969:102). During the 1960s, Deloria began to notice that "[t]he impotence and irrelevancy of the Christian message has meant a return to traditional religion by Indian people. Tribal religions are making a strong comeback on most reservations" (1969:112). He cites the sun dance, mentioned above, as one such example, and the growing membership in the Native American Church as another. In response, Deloria calls upon his fellow tribesmen and women to "return to their older religions wherever possible," believing that "an Indian version of Christianity could do much for our society" (1969:124).

Not all individuals were comfortable abandoning long-held Christian beliefs in favor of returning to Native religious practices. In the selection by Rev. Laverne Jacobs, one finds an Ojibway Christian struggling over the problem of holding dual identities. In this case the cognitive rub is over his desire to participate in the sweat lodge ceremony. With Jacobs, one discovers Native peoples being awakened to long dormant traditions, and finding that Christianity and Native religious traditions are not necessarily at odds, but, as Jacobs came to see it, "the sounds of many voices . . . together sing the praises of God the Creator and Jesus the Son in one great symphony of creation. In the midst of that glorious sound rings the phrase 'this is you—both Native and Christian.' The meaning of that phrase will be a lifelong dialogue with self" (Jacobs, in Treat 1997:240).

Thus, in all these readings, one gains a greater understanding, not only of the heroic struggles of the Native peoples of North America, but of the resilience of their religious and cultural traditions.

Sources and Selected Works in Native American History, Literature, and Religions

[*indicates works of fiction]

Archambault, Marie Therese, Mark G. Thiel, and Christopher Vecsey (eds.). *The Crossing of Two Roads: Being Catholic and Native in the United States.* Maryknoll, NY: Orbis Books, 2003.

Blaisdell, Bob (ed.). *Great Speeches by Native Americans.* New York: Dover Publications, 2000.

Brown, Joseph Epes. *The Spiritual Legacy of the American Indian.* New York: Crossroad, 1982.

Calloway, Colin G. *First Peoples: A Documentary Survey of American Indian History,* 2nd ed. New York: Bedford/St. Martin's Press, 2004.

Capps, Walter Holden (ed.). *Seeing with a Native Eye: Essays on Native American Religion.* San Francisco: Harper & Row, 1976.

Carrasco, Davíd. *Religions of Meso-America.* San Francisco: Harper & Row, 1990.

Cornell, Stephen. *The Return of the Native: American Indian Political Resurgence.* New York: Oxford University Press, 1990.

*Craven, Margaret. *I Heard the Owl Call My Name.* Garden City, NY: Doubleday & Co., 1973.

Crawford, Suzanne. *Native American Religious Traditions.* Upper Saddle River, NJ: Prentice Hall, 2006.

*Crow Dog, Mary. *Lakota Woman.* New York: Harper & Row, 1990.

*Deloria, Ella Cara. *Waterlily.* Lincoln, NE: University of Nebraska Press, 1988.

Deloria, Philip J., and Neal Salisbury (eds.). *A Companion to American Indian History.* Oxford, UK: Blackwell Publishing, 2004.

Deloria, Vine, Jr. *Custer Died for Your Sins: An Indian Manifesto.* New York: Macmillan, 1969.

_____. *For This Land: Writings on Religion in America.* New York: Routledge, 1999.

_____. *God Is Red: A Native View of Religion.* New York: Dell Publishing Co., 1973.

DeMallie, Raymond J., and Douglas R. Parks (eds.). *Sioux Indian Religion: Tradition and Innovation.* Norman, OK: University of Oklahoma Press, 1989.

Dillehay, Thomas D. *The Settlement of the Americas: A New Prehistory.* New York: Basic Books, 2000.

*Dorris, Michael. *A Yellow Raft in Blue Water.* New York: Warner Books, 1988.

Erdoes, Richard, and Alfonso Ortiz (eds.). *American Indian Myths and Legends.* New York: Pantheon Books, 1984.

_____ (ed.). *American Indian Trickster Tales.* New York: Penguin Books, 1998.

*Erdrich, Louise. *Love Medicine.* New York: Bantam, 1987.

*_____. *Tracks.* New York: Henry Holt & Co., 1988.

Feldmann, Susan (ed.). *The Storytelling Stone: Traditional Native American Myths and Tales.* New York: Dell Publishing, 1965.

Forbes, Jack D. *Native Americans of California and Nevada,* rev. ed. Happy Camp, CA: Naturegraph Publishers, 1982.

Gill, Sam. *Native America Religions,* 2nd ed. Belmont, CA: Wadsworth, 2005.

Grounds, Richard A., George E. Tinker, and David E. Wilkins (eds.). *Native Voices: American Indian Identity and Resistance.* Lawrence, KS: University of Kansas Press, 2003.

Gutiérrez, Ramón A. *When Jesus Came, the Corn Mothers Went Away: Marriage, Sexuality, and Power in New Mexico, 1500–1846.* Stanford, CA: Stanford University Press, 1991.

Hagan, William. *American Indians,* 3rd ed. Chicago: The University of Chicago Press, 1993.

Harrod, Howard L. *Becoming and Remaining a People: Native American Religions on the Northern Plains.* Tucson, AZ: University of Arizona Press, 1995.

_____. *Renewing the World: Plains Indian Religion and Morality.* Tucson, AZ: University of Arizona Press, 1987.

Hausman, Gerald. *Tunkashila: From the Birth of Turtle Island to the Blood of Wounded Knee.* New York: St. Martin's Press, 1993.

Heizer, Robert F., and M.A. Whipple (eds.). *The California Indians: A Source Book,* 2nd ed., rev. & enl. Berkeley, CA: University of California Press, 1972.

Hirschfelder, Arlene B., and Paulette Molin. *Encyclopedia of Native American Religions: An Introduction,* updated ed. New York: Facts on File, 2001.

Holler, Clyde. *Black Elk's Religion: The Sun Dance and Lakota Catholicism.* Syracuse, NY: Syracuse University Press, 1995.

Hoxie, Frederick E., Peter C. Mancall, and James H. Merrell (eds.). *American Nations: Encounters in Indian Country, 1850 to the Present.* New York: Routledge, 2001.

Hultkrantz, Åke. *Native Religions of North America.* San Francisco: Harper & Row, 1987.

Hunt, Edward Proctor. *The Origin Myth of Acoma Pueblo.* New York: Penguin Classics, 2015.

_____. *The Religions of the American Indians.* Berkeley, CA: University of California Press, 1979.

Jackson, Robert H., and Edward Castillo. *Indians, Franciscans, and Spanish Colonization: The Impact of the Mission System on California Indians.* Albuquerque, NM: University of New Mexico Press, 1996.

Josephy, Alvin M., Jr. (ed.). *America in 1492: The World of the Indian Peoples Before the Arrival of Columbus.* New York: Vintage Books, 1993.

_____. *500 Nations: An Illustrated History of North American Indians.* New York: Alfred A. Knopf, 1994.

Kehoe, Alice Beck. *The Ghost Dance: Ethnohistory and Revitalization,* 2nd ed. Long Grove, IL: Waveland Press, 2006.

Kelley, David. *Tradition, Performance, and Religion in Native America: Ancestral Ways, Modern Selves.* New York: Routledge, 2014.

Kidwell, Clara Sue, Homer Noley, and George E. Tinker. *A Native American Theology.* Maryknoll, NY: Orbis Books, 2001.

Fire, John/Lame Deer, and Richard Erdoes. *Lame Deer Seeker of Visions.* New York: Simon and Schuster, 1972.

Kroeber, Karl (ed.). *Native American Storytelling: A Reader of Myths and Legends.* Oxford, UK: Blackwell Publishing, 2004.

Leeming, David, and Jake Page. *The Mythology of Native North America.* Norman, OK: University of Oklahoma Press, 1998.

Lobo, Susan, and Kurt Peters. *American Indians and the Urban Experience.* Walnut Creek, CA: AltaMira Press, 2001.

Lobo, Susan, and Steve Talbot (eds.). *Native American Voices: A Reader,* 2nd ed. Upper Saddle River, NJ: Prentice Hall, 2001.

Lopez, Barry. *Giving Birth to Thunder, Sleeping with His Daughter: Coyote Builds North America.* New York: Avon Books, 1990.

Loftin, John D. *Religion and Hopi Life in the Twentieth Century.* Bloomington, IN: Indiana University Press, 1991.

Mancall, Peter C., and James H. Merrell (eds.). *American Encounters: Natives and Newcomers from European Contact to Indian Removal.* New York: Routledge, 2000.

Maroukis, Thomas C. *The Peyote Road: Religious Freedom and the Native American Church.* Norman, OK: University of Oklahoma Press, 2012.

Mintz, Steven (ed.). *Native American Voices: A History and Anthology,* 2nd ed., enl. St. James, NY: Brandywine Press, 2000.

Mooney, James. *The Ghost-Dance Religion and Wounded Knee.* New York: Dover Publications, 1973 [reprint of 1896 edition].

Nabokov, Peter (ed.). *Native American Testimony: A Chronicle of Indian-White Relations from Prophecy to the Present, 1492–1992.* New York: Penguin Books, 1992.

Nagel, Joane. *American Indian Ethnic Renewal: Red Power and the Resurgence of Identity and Culture.* New York: Oxford University Press, 1997.

Neihardt, John G. *Black Elk Speaks.* Lincoln, NE: University of Nebraska Press, 1961.

*Niatum, Duane (ed.). *Harper's Anthology of Twentieth Century Native American Poetry.* San Francisco: Harper & Row, 1988.

Nies, Judith. *Native American History: A Chronology of a Culture's Vast Achievements and Their Links to World Events.* New York: Ballantine Books, 1996.

Olson, James S., and Raymond Wilson. *Native Americans in the Twentieth Century*. Urbana, IL: University of Illinois Press, 1986.

Ostler, Jeffrey. *The Plains Sioux and U.S. Colonialism from Lewis and Clark to Wounded Knee*. New York: Cambridge University Press, 2004.

Page, Jake. *In the Hands of the Great Spirit: The 20,000-Year History of American Indians*. New York: The Free Press, 2003.

Parman, Donald L. *Indians and the American West in the Twentieth Century*. Bloomington, IN: Indiana University Press, 1994.

Porter, Joy, and Kenneth M. Roemer (eds.). *The Cambridge Companion to Native American Literature*. New York: Cambridge University Press, 2005.

Powell, Joseph F. *The First Americans: Race, Evolution and the Origin of Native Americans*. Cambridge, UK: Cambridge University Press, 2005.

Powers, William K. *Oglala Religion*. Lincoln, NE: University of Nebraska Press, 1977.

_____. *Sacred Language: The Nature of Supernatural Discourse in Lakota*. Norman, OK: University of Oklahoma Press, 1992.

Pritzker, Barry M. *A Native American Encyclopedia: History, Culture, and Peoples*. New York: Oxford University Press, 2000.

Rawls, James J. *Indians of California: The Changing Image*. Norman, OK: University of Oklahoma Press, 1984.

Richter, Daniel K. *Facing East from Indian Country: A Native History of Early America*. Cambridge, MA: Harvard University Press, 2003.

Rushforth, Scott, and Steadman Upham. *A Hopi Social History*. Austin, TX: University of Texas Press, 1992.

*Silko, Leslie Marmon. *Ceremony*. New York: Penguin Books, 1986.

Smoak, Gregory E. *Ghost Dances and Identity: Prophetic Religion and American Indian Ethnogenesis in the Nineteenth Century*. Berkeley, CA: University of California Press, 2005.

Stewart, Omer C. *Peyote Religion: A History*. Norman, OK: University of Oklahoma Press, 1987.

Sullivan, Lawrence E. (ed.). *Native American Religions: North America*. New York: Macmillan Publishing Co., 1989.

_____ (ed.). *Native American Religions of Central and South America: Anthropology of the Sacred*. New York: Continuum, 2002.

Tinker, George E. *Missionary Conquest: The Gospel and Native American Cultural Genocide*. Minneapolis, MN: Augsburg Fortress, 1993.

Treat, James (ed.). *Native and Christian: Indigenous Voices on Religious Identity in the United States and Canada*. New York: Routledge, 1995.

Tyler, Hamilton A. *Pueblo Gods and Myths*. Norman, OK: University of Oklahoma Press, 1964.

Underhill, Ruth M. *Red Man's Religion*. Chicago: The University of Chicago Press, 1965.

Utter, Jack. *American Indians: Answers to Today's Questions*, 2nd ed. Norman, OK: University of Oklahoma Press, 2001.

Weaver, Jace (ed.). *Native American Religious Identity*. Maryknoll, NY: Orbis Books, 1998.

Wilson, James. *The Earth Shall Weep: A History of Native America*. New York: Grove Press, 2000.

Some Suggested Questions for Discussion

1. What do the various myths and tales in this volume teach us about the Native American understanding of the sacred world and their relationship to it? In what noticeable ways do these myths and tales differ from Plains Indians to Woodlands Indians to Pueblo Indians and to Coastal California Indians?

2. Based on the variety of readings in this volume, please speculate on the place that dreams and visions hold in Native American religious traditions. How do dreams and visions, and their meaning to the individual and to the community, compare across tribal groups?

3. Based on your reading of the fictional and non-fictional literature in this volume, please discuss the ways by which religious rituals and other traditional ceremonies serve to reconnect Native peoples to their ancestral past? What is it about these traditions that by maintaining them Native peoples experience healing and wholeness in their lives?

4. After reflecting upon the ways that men and women are portrayed in both the fictional and non-fictional literature in this volume, please identify and discuss, the kinds of roles that men and women appear to play (or have played) in Native tribal communities? Which, if any, of these roles have remained largely unchanged?

5. An uneasy tension seems to exist between those Native Americans, on the one hand, who view the embrace of Christianity as a betrayal of traditional Native beliefs and practices, and those, on the other, who hold that believing in Christ is not a betrayal but rather a fulfillment of Native spiritual aspirations. A question one might ask from the related readings in this volume is how do Native Indians reconcile their traditional beliefs and religious practices with their personal commitment to Christ? In this context, what then might be meant by the phrase "life long dialogue with self" as offered in the chapter by Rev. Laverne Jacobs?

1. Coyote Steals the Sun and Moon

[Zuni]

Coyote is a bad hunter who never kills anything. Once he watched Eagle hunting rabbits, catching one after another—more rabbits than he could eat. Coyote thought, "I'll team up with Eagle so I can have enough meat." Coyote is always up to something.

"Friend," Coyote said to Eagle, "we should hunt together. Two can catch more than one."

"Why not?" Eagle said, and so they began to hunt in partnership. Eagle caught many rabbits, but all Coyote caught was some little bugs.

At this time the world was still dark; the sun and moon had not yet been put in the sky. "Friend," Coyote said to Eagle, "no wonder I can't catch anything; I can't see. Do you know where we can get some light?"

"You're right, friend, there should be some light," Eagle said. "I think there's a little toward the west. Let's try and find it."

And so they went looking for the sun and moon. They came to a big river, which Eagle flew over. Coyote swam, and swallowed so much water that he almost drowned. He crawled out with his fur full of mud, and Eagle asked, "Why don't you fly like me?"

"You have wings, I just have hair," Coyote said. "I can't fly without feathers."

At last they came to a pueblo, where the Kachinas happened to be dancing. The people invited Eagle and Coyote to sit down and have something to eat while they watched the sacred dances. Seeing the power of the Kachinas, Eagle said, "I believe these are the people who have light."

Coyote, who had been looking all around, pointed out two boxes, one large and one small, that the people opened whenever they wanted light. To produce a lot of light, they opened the lid of the big box, which contained the sun. For less light they opened the small box, which held the moon.

Coyote nudged Eagle. "Friend, did you see that? They have all the light we need in the big box. Let's steal it."

"You always want to steal and rob. I say we should just borrow it."

"They won't lend it to us."

"You may be right," said Eagle. "Let's wait till they finish dancing and then steal it."

After a while the Kachinas went home to sleep, and Eagle scooped up the large box and flew off. Coyote ran along trying to keep up, panting, his tongue hanging out. Soon he yelled up to Eagle, "Ho, friend, let me carry the box a little way."

"No, no," said Eagle, "you never do anything right."

He flew on, and Coyote ran after him. After a while Coyote shouted again: "Friend, you're my chief, and it's not right for you to carry the box; people will call me lazy. Let me have it."

"No, no, you always mess everything up." And Eagle flew on and Coyote ran along.

So it went for a stretch, and then Coyote started again. "Ho, friend, it isn't right for you to do this. What will people think of you and me?"

"I don't care what people think. I'm going to carry this box."

Again Eagle flew on and again Coyote ran after him. Finally Coyote begged for the fourth time: "Let me carry it. You're the chief, and I'm just Coyote. Let me carry it."

Eagle couldn't stand any more pestering. Also, Coyote had asked him four times, and if someone asks four times, you better give him what he wants. Eagle said, "Since you won't let up on me, go ahead and carry the box for a while. But promise not to open it."

"Oh, sure, oh yes, I promise." They went on as before, but now Coyote had the box. Soon Eagle was far ahead, and Coyote lagged behind a hill where Eagle couldn't see him. "I wonder what the light looks like, inside there," he said to himself. "Why shouldn't I take a peek? Probably there's something extra in the box, something good that Eagle wants to keep to himself."

And Coyote opened the lid. Now, not only was the sun inside, but the moon also. Eagle had put them both together, thinking that it would be easier to carry one box than two.

As soon as Coyote opened the lid, the moon escaped, flying high into the sky. At once all the plants shriveled up and turned brown. Just as quickly, all the leaves fell off the trees, and it was winter. Trying to catch the moon and put it back in the box, Coyote ran in pursuit as it skipped away from him. Meanwhile the sun flew out and rose into the sky. It drifted far away, and the peaches, squashes, and melons shriveled up with cold.

Eagle turned and flew back to see what had delayed Coyote, "You fool! Look what you've done!" he said. "You let the sun and moon escape, and now it's cold." Indeed, it began to snow, and Coyote shivered. "Now your teeth are chattering," Eagle said, "and it's your fault that cold has come into the world."

It's true. If it weren't for Coyote's curiosity and mischief making, we wouldn't have winter; we could enjoy summer all the time.

—Based on a story reported by Ruth Benedict in 1935.

2. Coyote, Iktome, and the Rock

[White River Sioux]

Coyote was walking with his friend Iktome. Along their path stood Iya, the rock. This was not just any rock; it was special. It had those spidery lines of green moss all over it, the kind that tell a story. Iya had power.

Coyote said: "Why, this is a nice-looking rock. I think it has power." Coyote took off the thick blanket he was wearing and put it on the rock. "Here, Iya, take this as a present. Take this blanket, friend rock, to keep you from freezing. You must feel cold."

"Wow, a giveaway!" said Iktome. "You sure are in a giving mood today, friend."

"Ah, it's nothing. I'm always giving things away. Iya looks real nice in my blanket."

"His blanket, now," said Iktome.

The two friends went on. Pretty soon a cold rain started. The rain turned to hail. The hail turned to slush. Coyote and Iktome took refuge in a cave, which was cold and wet. Iktome was all right; he had his thick buffalo robe. Coyote had only his shirt, and he was shivering. He was freezing. His teeth were chattering.

"*Kola*, friend of mine," Coyote said to Iktome, "go back and get me my fine blanket. I need it, and that rock has no use for it. He's been getting along without a blanket for ages. Hurry; I'm freezing!"

Iktome went back to Iya, saying: "Can I have that blanket back, please?"

The rock said: "No, I like it. What is given is given."

Iktome returned and told Coyote: "He won't give it back."

"That no-good, ungrateful rock!" said Coyote. "Has he paid for the blanket? Has he worked for it? I'll go get it myself."

"Friend," said Iktome, "Tunka, Iya, the rock—there's a lot of power there! Maybe you should let him keep it."

"Are you crazy? This is an expensive blanket of many colors and great thickness. I'll go talk to him."

Coyote went back and told Iya: "Hey, rock! What's the meaning of this? What do you need a blanket for? Let me have it back right now!"

"No," said the rock, "what is given is given."

"You're a bad rock! Don't you care that I'm freezing to death? That I'll catch a cold?"

Coyote jerked the blanket away from Iya and put it on. "So there; that's the end of it."

"By no means the end," said the rock.

Coyote went back to the cave. The rain and hail stopped and the sun came out again, so Coyote and Iktome sat before the cave, sunning themselves, eating pemmican, and fry-bread and *wojapi*, berry soup. After eating, they took out their pipes and had a smoke.

All of a sudden Iktome said: "What's that noise?"

"What noise? I don't hear anything."

"A crashing, a rumble far off."

"Yes, friend, I hear it now."

"Friend Coyote, it's getting stronger and nearer, like thunder or an earthquake."

"It is rather strong and loud. I wonder what it can be."

"I have a pretty good idea, friend," said Iktome.

Then they saw the great rock. It was Iya, rolling, thundering, crashing upon them.

"Friend, let's run for it!" cried Iktome; "Iya means to kill us!"

The two ran as fast as they could while the rock rolled after them, coming closer and closer.

"Friend, let's swim the river. The rock is so heavy, he sure can't swim!" cried Iktome. So they swam the river, but Iya, the great rock, also swam over the river as if he had been made of wood.

"Friend, into the timber, among the big trees," cried Coyote. "That big rock surely can't get through this thick forest." They ran among the trees, but the huge Iya came rolling along after them, shivering and splintering the big pines to pieces, left and right.

The two came out onto the flats. "Oh! Oh!" cried Iktome, Spider Man. "Friend Coyote, this is really not my quarrel. I just remembered, I have pressing business to attend to. So long!" Iktome rolled himself into a tiny ball and became a spider. He disappeared into a mousehole.

Coyote ran on and on, the big rock thundering close at his heels. Then Iya, the big rock, rolled right over Coyote, flattening him out altogether.

Iya took the blanket and rolled back to his own place, saying: "So there!"

A *wasichu* rancher riding along saw Coyote lying there all flattened out. "What a nice rug!" said the rancher, picking Coyote up, and he took the rug home.

The rancher put Coyote right in front of his fireplace. Whenever Coyote is killed, he can make himself come to life again, but it took him the whole night to puff himself up into his usual shape. In the morning the rancher's wife told her husband: "I just saw your rug running away."

Friends, hear this: always be generous in heart. If you have something to give, give it forever.

—*Told by Jenny Leading Cloud in White River, Rosebud*
Indian Reservation, South Dakota, 1967.
Recorded by Richard Erdoes.

3. Coyote and the Origin of Death

[Caddo]

In the beginning of this world, there was no such thing as death. Everybody continued to live until there were so many people that the earth had no room for any more. The chiefs held a council to determine what to do. One man rose and said he thought it would be a good plan to have the people die and be gone for a little while, and then return.

As soon as he sat down, Coyote jumped up and said he thought people ought to die forever. He pointed out that this little world is not large enough to hold all of the people, and that if the people who died came back to life, there would not be food enough for all.

All the other men objected. They said that they did not want their friends and relatives to die and be gone forever, for then they would grieve and worry and there would be no happiness in the world. Everyone except Coyote decided to have people die and be gone for a little while, and then come back to life again.

The medicine men built a large grass house facing the east. When they had completed it, they called the men of the tribe together and told them that people who died would be restored to life in the medicine house. The chief medicine man explained that they would sing a song calling the spirit of the dead to the grass house. When the spirit came, they would restore it to life. All the people were glad, because they were anxious for the dead to come and live with them again.

When the first man died, the medicine men assembled in the grass house and sang. In about ten days a whirlwind blew from the west and circled about the grass house. Coyote saw it, and as the whirlwind was about to enter the house, he closed the door. The spirit of the whirlwind, finding the door closed, whirled on by. In this way Coyote made death eternal, and from that time on, people grieved over their dead and were unhappy.

Now whenever anyone meets a whirlwind or hears the wind whistle, he says: "Someone is wandering about." Ever since Coyote closed the door, the spirits of the dead have wandered over the earth trying to find some place to go, until at last they discovered the road to the spirit land.

Coyote ran away and never came back, for when he saw what he had done, he was afraid. Ever after that, he has run from one place to another, always looking back first over one shoulder and then over the other to see if anyone is pursuing him. And ever since then he has been starving, for no one will give him anything to eat.

—*From a tale reported by George A. Dorsey in 1905.*

4. The Creation of Man (Second Version)

MORRIS EDWARD OPLER

In the beginning the dog was just like a Hactcin in appearance. This was because the Hactcin made everything. He was listless, however, and didn't do anything.

And Hactcin noticed this and spoke to him. He said, "Why don't you do something? Why don't you work?"

"I don't care to work. I'm too lazy. I'd better turn to the form of a dog I guess. Let my hands be round."

At first his hands were like ours, but he didn't use them and just stayed home so they became round.

When Hactcin made the dog in his present shape he took some of the yellow from the afterglow of the sunset and put it above each eye. And he took some of the white of the morning glow and put it on each paw. This was a sign that the dog would protect people.

And so today in the girl's ceremony, the girl has yellow ochre on her face and the boy who dances with her has white paint over his face.

Hactcin spoke to the dog and asked, "Where are you going to stay now?"

"Oh, you can make some people so I will have companions."

Hactcin asked, "What is the idea you have in mind? I never thought you would say a thing like that."

So the Hactcin lay down at a smooth place. He said to the dog, "Now draw a line around my feet and body. Trace my outline with your paw." So the Hactcin lay with his face down and his arms outstretched, and the dog drew his outline.

Then both got up. Hactcin said to the dog, "Go a little further on and do not look back yet."

The dog went on for a short distance.

"Now you can turn and look."

Dog looked back. "Someone is lying where you were, Grandfather," he said.

Hactcin said, "Face the other way and walk off again."

Dog did so.

"Now turn around."

"The Creation of Man", *The Myths and Tales of the Jicarilla Apache Indians*, by Morris Edward Opler, New York: American Folk-lore Society, 1938, in the series: Memoirs of the American Folklore Society, v. 31. Reprinted by permission of American Folklore Society.

The dog did so.

Someone was arising from the ground, bracing himself with his hands and knees.

"Grandfather," said Dog, "someone is on his hands and knees at the place where you were lying."

Hactcin said, "Turn and walk away again."

Dog did so. Then he was told to look once more. When he looked he saw a man sitting up.

"Grandfather, someone is sitting up!" he cried. There were surprise and happiness in his voice.

But Hactcin only said, "Turn once more and walk away."

He did so again.

"Turn around now and look," he was told.

He did so and cried out in astonishment and delight, "My grandfather, he is sitting up and moving around!"

Then Hactcin said, "Now come. We will go and see him."

They came to the man. He was sitting facing the east. Hactcin first faced him from the east. Then he went to the south, the west, and the north of him and then faced him again from the east. Then Hactcin went around to this man's back, and after motioning four times lifted him to his feet. Then he went around his body clockwise and returned in front of him at the east again.

Then Hactcin addressed the man. "You must watch me. I am going to take four steps, moving my right foot first. As I do it you must do it too."

Hactcin did walk this way and the man followed.

"Now," said Hactcin, "let's run," and with Hactcin leading, the two ran. They ran to the east and back again in a clockwise manner. That is why they run like that in the girl's puberty rite.[1] They came back to the starting place.

Then Hactcin shouted into the ear of the man four times, twice from the right side and twice from the left and asked, "Did you hear that?" Because of this the old woman shouts into the ear of the girl in the puberty rite four times from the right side, so that the girl will have good hearing always.

But the man could not yet speak. Hactcin stood before him. Four times he said to the man, "Talk, talk, talk, talk," and then the man spoke. "Laugh, laugh, laugh, laugh," he said, and the fourth time the man laughed. "Now shout, shout, shout, shout," Hactcin told him, and the fourth time it was said the man shouted.

"Now you are ready to live around here."

The dog was very happy. He jumped at the man and ran back and forth just as dogs do now when they are glad to see you.

The dog was very happy, but the man, with no one but the dog to talk to, soon grew lonesome.

He told Hactcin the cause of his sadness and Hactcin thought about it. Finally Hactcin resolved to make a woman for him. So he told the man to lie down on the ground, face downward with arms and legs extended. The man did so. Then Hactcin traced his outline on the ground and bade him rise. Then Hactcin had the man do exactly what he had had the dog do when he had been making the man. He had the man face the other way and walk to the east four times while the figure he had drawn successively rose to its knees, sat up, and moved. Then Hactcin lifted this figure in the same manner and taught it to speak, hear, laugh, shout, and walk and run. Then Hactcin was satisfied and sent Ancestral Man and Ancestral Woman off together.

These two people who had been created also came to Black Hactcin and asked, "What are we to eat? Where shall we live?"

He showed them all the roots and leaves and plants. "These are your foods," he told them.

They went to taste all that he pointed out. They tasted them all and found them good.

Then he took them out and showed them the animals. "Those who are cloven-footed will be your meat."

In those days the animals were very gentle, very mild. They all stayed around there.[2]

He told them, "When you kill the animal you must save the hide and use it for clothes." After that they did so.

"Where shall we put our heads?"

"Right on the earth. Stay anywhere you like to be. There is your place. There is your home."

That is why the Jicarilla Apache went from place to place. They would come to a desirable place and say, "This is pretty; let's stay here." Then they would go on to some other place later.

In those days the two people had no hair on their bodies or on their faces. The man had no moustache.

Hactcin told them the first day, "You must not let water touch your lips until I give you permission." He gave them tubes of reed and told them to use these. For three days they drank from the reeds as they were told.

The fourth day they grew impatient. It took too long to drink water that way, they thought. The man put his reed aside and lay down and drank from the stream. The front of his face touched the water and after that hair grew on his face. The woman had just stood there, however. Black Hactcin had told them what would happen if they disobeyed. The woman thought, "It would not look well for a woman to have hair on her face," so she did not do as her husband did.

Immediately the hair grew out on the man's face. The girl started to get angry because her husband looked so strange. In her rage she dashed some water under her armpits and around her pubic region. Hair grew at once in those places.

When the man saw this he thought, "I'd better do the same," and he splashed water on himself at those places too and hair grew there.

Hactcin came then and spoke to them. "Don't do that." He told the man, "Go up in the woods and find two branches which have been rubbed against each other by the wind and have become smooth. Rub your face with that."

To the woman he said, "Rub your face with abalone."

Now at the time of the girl's puberty rite when the girl acts as White-Shell Woman and the boy as Child-of-the-Water, they do this to themselves and then they do not get much body hair. It is not part of the ceremony. The young people do it by themselves.

A few generations passed. The animals, birds, and people increased, but they all lived in darkness. They had no sun as yet. The people were used to it, and because they were used to it they could see things. Still, one could not see objects clearly. But they did not have any hard times. All the animals were friendly. They had no enemies. If they wanted something to eat, it was present.

But Black Hactcin didn't think it was right. He sent for White Hactcin. They came together and talked of what they were going to do. They sent for a male eagle's white tail feather and a female eagle's spotted tail feather. And they sent for one tail feather of the blue jay too and for the yellow tail feather of the western tanager.

One mountain stretched upward. All around it lived the people. The Hactcin worked together. At the east side of the mountain, resting against it, they put the feather of the white male eagle. On the south side they put the blue feather, on the west the yellow feather, and on the north side the feather of the spotted female eaglet.[3]

The white feather sent a long beam of white light to the east. Because of the blue feather, everything looked blue to the south. To the west all looked yellow because of the yellow light of the feather. And on the north side the feather of the female eagle gave a flickering light, sometimes light and sometimes shadow.

The people kept gathering to the east and living there because of the greater light in that direction. On the blue side the light was not so clear. Just a few people liked that place and stayed over there. And for the same reason very few were living on the west and north sides.

Down in the underworld there were many brooks and streams. The people had all kinds of water.

Notes

1. For an account of the girl's puberty rite cf. p. 87.

2. In the Jicarilla myths the animals are represented as being extraordinarily tame in the beginning. For an account of how animals became wild see p. 215 and pp. 259–260.

3. The usual color-directional association, used whenever the materials or objects to which reference is made will permit is: east, black; south, blue; west, yellow; and north, glittering. Spotted or white is sometimes substituted for glittering and is associated with the north. The circuit is clockwise, beginning with the east. The association of east with white, as occurs in this passage, is unusual.

5. The Creation and Loss of the Sun and Moon

MORRIS EDWARD OPLER

Holy Boy was not satisfied. He thought there should be more light. By himself he started to make a sun. He tried hard in many ways. The first time he tried by himself. He used all kinds of specular iron ore and pollen. The result was not very satisfactory though. He used abalone too, but that didn't work any better. He tried turquoise and red beads and white beads, but without success. But he kept on. He tried over and over.

One time when he was at work the little whirlwind came. The little wind asked him, "What are you doing here all by yourself? You never go outside. I have not seen you for a long time."

Holy Boy said, "I have not been doing anything. I've stayed right here."

Wind said, "There must be some reason that you stay home."

Holy Boy said, "Yes, there is. I am making a sun. But it is not very bright."

Wind said to him, "There is a man who has a sun. Why don't you go to him?"

"Who is he?"

"Oh, it is White Hactcin. You go and ask him. But don't tell him who told you."[1]

So Holy Boy went to White Hactcin. He went into the home of White Hactcin.

"What do you want?" asked White Hactcin. "There must be some reason for your coming here. You never come to visit with us. What do you want, my grandson?"

Holy Boy said, "I came here to ask you for the sun."

White Hactcin said, "How do you know I have it? Who told you? No one could have seen that I have that sun."

White Hactcin sat there. He tried to think who could have seen it and reported it. Then he remembered that there was one who came often to his house. It was the wind.

"I believe it was Wind who told you I have the sun."

Holy Boy didn't mention Wind's name. He just continued to ask for the sun.

White Hactcin said then, "Yes, I have it." He picked up his bag and looked into it. He found it and he took it out. It was a very small sun and hard to see. It was just like the present sun, but it was no bigger than a pin head. He gave it to Holy Boy.

"This is for daylight," White Hactcin said.

"The Creation and Loss of the Sun and Moon", *Myths and Tales of the Jicarilla Apache Indians*, by Morris Edward Opler, New York: American Folk-lore Society, 1938, in the series: Memoirs of the American Folklore Society, v. 31. Reprinted by permission of American Folklore Society.

Wind had told Holy Boy when he had talked to him, "There is a moon too, but another person has it. Black Hactcin has it.[2] You can get the moon from him."

So now Holy Boy went over to Black Hactcin.

"What do you want, my grandson?"[3] asked Black Hactcin. "You never came to see me before. There must be some reason."

"Yes, I have come for the night light. I have come for the moon."

"How do you know I have it? Who told you I have it?"

Black Hactcin thought a while. "I believe that little wind told you," he said. "He's the only one who comes to see me often." So he looked in his bag and found it. He gave it to Holy Boy. It was a tiny one too.

Then he said, "You must go back and put it on a deerskin which has no holes.[4] First make a circle to represent the sun and one for the moon too. Paint them with pollen and other coloring matter.

Then put the sun that you have been given right in the center of the sun that you make with pollen. Make a painting of the moon in the same way with specular iron ore on the deerskin and put this moon that I have given you exactly in the center of it.[5] When you get ready perhaps White Hactcin and I will come over, and Red Boy will come too.[6] There will be four of us.[7]

"Make rays for each of your designs too. Let there be four black rays to the east, four blue rays to the south, four yellow rays to the west, and four glittering rays to the north. On each, within the first outer circle of pollen or specular iron ore, make a circle of red paint. Make this near the edge. This red one stands for the rainbow. Then bring downy eagle feathers and white tail feathers of the eagle and spotted feathers of the eagle so that we can sing over this sun and moon."

Then Holy Boy went back to his own home. He worked on the sun and moon as the Black Hactcin had told him. He sent for Red Boy, and Red Boy came over and assisted him. They painted what the Hactcin had told them on the buckskin. They were nearly finished when the two Hactcin came in.

They walked in and looked at the designs. They said, "Oh, it's pretty good!" They put pollen in their own mouths and the two boys did likewise. Then the Hactcin put some pollen on top of their own heads and the boys did it too. Then each threw some to the east, south, west, and north, then straight up in the air, and then on the sun and the moon both. Each one of the four did that. They sprinkled pollen on the sun and the moon four times after throwing it upward in the air.[8]

Then White Hactcin took the white feathers and the Black Hactcin took the spotted feathers. The downy feathers they gave to Holy Boy and Red Boy. One bead of a certain color was placed in each direction on the outer circle of each design: a red stone bead on the east side, turquoise on the south side, a white bead on the west side, and abalone on the north side.

The two drawings lay before them. Everything was ready. They asked each other who was going to start to sing and pray.

Then White Hactcin spoke to Holy Boy. "You are the one who started to make the sun. You had better start the singing too. You must know how."

"Yes, I started it. I can't deny that."

So Holy Boy sang songs. He sang a song to the pollen. Then he sang a specular iron ore song.

Now Red Boy sang, and he sang to the beads. And he sang a song to the red ochre too.

That is why they rub paint on the face of the girl and the boy the last morning of the puberty rite. They put the red paint on then. If the boy and girl would go out without having their faces painted with red paint it would be like going out without being under the care of these holy things. Then if you prayed the Hactcin would not hear you or help you, nor would anything else.

And the pollen is just like a summer offering. After they used the pollen and sang of it, all kinds of fruit of the summer were mentioned. That song gives long life too. They sang it for both the sun and the moon, that they would have long life.

Then White Hactcin sang in the same way. He sang the same songs. He sang to make the sun and the moon come to life.

As he sang the pictures began to move a little. They began to come to life.

Then Black Hactcin sang too. He sang to make them move.

Red Boy helped each of them sing; he joined in. He didn't sing alone himself though.

Now everything was ready. The sun and moon were ready to go. Then all went out, the four of them. White Hactcin had the sun in his hand. Black Hactcin had the moon in his hand. They stood in a single file facing the east. Holy Boy stood first, then White Hactcin, then Black Hactcin, and behind him Red Boy.

Holy Boy and Red Boy had pollen in their hands. Each threw some towards the north and then up and to the south. They were making a path, just the way the sun and moon were to go.

Then White Hactcin and Black Hactcin released the sun and moon, and the sun and moon went up that path. In the sky they came up from the north and moved toward the south.[9] It was a long time before they reached the sky. Then they could be seen faintly, just as at dawn. The light began to get stronger and stronger. The light began to show on the mountains.

The other people of the underworld didn't know what it was.

Then the sun came out and in the bright sunshine everything could be seen clearly. It was just as it is now in daytime.

There were all kinds of shamans around there among the people. These were men and women who claimed they had power from all sorts of things. They saw the sun going from the north to the south across the sky.

These shamans began to talk. One said, "I made the sun."

Another contradicted him and said, "No, I did it."

They got to quarrelling about it.

Hactcin told them not to talk like that for four days. "After four days say what you want to." That's what White Hactcin told them.

But the shamans didn't listen. They kept making claims like this and fighting. They talked all the more. One would say, "I think I'll make the sun stop overhead so that there will be no night. But no, I guess I'll let it go, because we need some time to rest too." And another would say, "I might get rid of the moon. We don't need any light at night."

But the sun arose the second day and was overhead at noon. The birds and animals were happy. The third day it was the same way; the sun rose as before.

And the fourth day came. The sun rose early. But the shamans, in spite of what the Hactcin had told them, continued to talk and kept it up till noon of the fourth day.

Then, at noon, there was an eclipse of the sun. It grew black. The sun went straight overhead, through a hole, and on to this earth. The moon followed and came to this earth too. That is why we have eclipses today.[10]

The rays of the sun came straight down through the little hole that connected the underworld with the earth above. The people could see the light faintly.

Notes

1. The use of the whirlwind as a messenger or spy for the supernaturals is an ever recurring theme in Jicarilla folk-lore and will be encountered many times in these pages.

2. The association of Black Hactcin with darkness and the things of the night is here continued by representing him the possessor of the "night light" or moon, thus contrasting him with White Hactcin, who owns the sun material.

3. The term grandson is honorific in this context, referring to relative age and not to kinship.

4. Unblemished buckskin was much prized by the Jicarilla for ceremonial purposes. It was required, for instance, in the rite conducted four days after the birth of a child (p. 44).

5. Pollen is often used to represent the light of the sun; specular iron ore the light of the moon.

6. Red Boy and Holy Boy do not appear in other Jicarilla stories. Holy Boy is mentioned in the Navaho origin legend also. See Matthews: *Navaho Legends*.

7. The Black Hactcin and White Hactcin were leaders of all the Hactcin. All the rest were just helpers. I think that Holy Boy and Red Boy were the children of Hactcin, but I am not sure (Informant).

8. This is one of the few references in Jicarilla mythology to offerings of pollen to upward and downward directions as well as to the cardinal points.

9. At first the sun and moon moved from north to south. For an account of the change to the present direction of movement see p. 22.

10. Another account (p. 160) attributes eclipses of the sun and moon to jealousy of their spouses.

6. The Emergence[1]

MORRIS EDWARD OPLER

The Hactcin said to the boastful shamans, "All right, you people say you have power. Now bring back the sun."

And so they lined up. On one side were all the shamans and on the other side were all the birds and animals. The shamans started to sing songs and make ceremonies. They showed all they knew. Some would sit singing and then disappear into the earth, leaving only their eyes sticking out. Then they would come back as before, but it couldn't bring back the sun. It was only to show that they had power. Some swallowed arrows, and the arrows would come out of their flesh at their stomachs. Some swallowed feathers. Some swallowed whole spruce trees and then spat them up. But they couldn't do anything about regaining the sun and moon.[2]

Then White Hactcin said, "All you people are doing pretty well, but I don't think you are bringing the sun back. Your time is up."

Then he turned to the insects and the birds and animals and said, "All right, now it is your turn."

The birds and animals spoke to each other politely, just as though they were brothers-in-law.[3]

Hactcin told them, "You must do something more than speak to each other in that polite way. Why don't you get up and do something with your own power and make the sun come back?"

The grasshopper was the first one to try. "That's not a difficult thing to do," he said. He put up his hand to the east, to the south, to the west, and to the north in turn and then put down bread which had been baked in ashes.

White Hactcin asked, "What is this?"

Grasshopper said, "That is bread."

"How do you make the bread?"

"Oh, with grain," he said.

"What is in it?"

"Wheat. It grows. It has roots and leaves and pollen and a stalk."[4]

"All right, I can use that," White Hactcin said.

Then the deer's turn came. He said, "Hactcin hasn't asked such a difficult thing." He put out his hand in the four directions. Then he put down some yucca fruit.

"The Emergence", *Myths and Tales of the Jicarilla Apache Indians*, by Morris Edward Opler, New York: American Folk-lore Society, 1938, in the series: Memoirs of the American Folklore Society, v. 31. Reprinted by permission of American Folklore Society.

White Hactcin asked, "What is it?"

"That is fruit. It is what I live on. It is a growing thing too. It has roots, stalk, leaves, blossoms, and pollen."

"I can use that too. It is wonderful," said Hactcin.

Then the bear stepped forth. He too put his hands out in the four directions. Then he put down a handful of choke-cherries. "This is what I live on," he said.

"What is it?" asked White Hactcin.

"It is a fruit too. It grows. It has root, stalk, leaves, blossom, and pollen."

"I can use it. It is good."

Then came Ground Hog. He too put out his right hand to the four directions. In his hand was a berry.

"What is it?"

"It is a fruit. It is what I live on. It has a root, stalk, flowers, and pollen."

"I can use it."

Then Chipmunk came out. He too put out his hand in the four directions. He put down a strawberry.

"What is it?"

"It is a fruit. It has roots, stem, blossom, and pollen. It is what I live on."

In the same way all the animals came forward in turn. Each put his hand to the four directions and each gave something which was his food to Hactcin. The birds and insects came too. The birds brought all kinds of seeds.

The last one to come was Turkey. He went to the east, strutting. Black corn lay there as if spilled. He did the same to the south, and blue corn lay there. He strutted to the west, and yellow corn lay there. And then he went to the north, and all kinds of vegetables and fruit lay there.

Hactcin asked him, "What is all this?"

"This is what I live on. They have roots, stems, pollen, and the corn has tassels on top. It has dew on it too."

"That is very good. I think I am going to use you. You can help us make it grow," he said to the turkey.

Then White Hactcin sent for Thunder of four colors from the directions. And these thunders brought clouds of four colors. The rain fell from these clouds. Then Hactcin sent for Rainbow to make it beautiful while they planted these things on the mountain.

Then those four, White Hactcin, Black Hactcin, Holy Boy, and Red Boy, brought sand. It was sand of four colors. They brought pollen from all kinds of trees and from the fruits. They leveled off a place so they could work with the sand. They smoothed down the place with eagle feathers.[5]

They had earth of four colors there too: black, blue, yellow, and glittering.

First they laid the sand down evenly. Then they made four little mounds of earth with the dirt. In each one they put some seeds and fruits which the animals had given. And on top they put the needles and leaves of the trees that were to grow on the mountains. On the top of each one of the piles of earth they put a reed. On top of the reed was attached the downy feather of an eagle and the downy feather of a turkey. The mounds of earth were in a row extending from east to west. The first one was the one of black earth, next the one of blue earth, then the one of yellow earth, and last the one of glittering earth.

Before the mountain started to grow, the Holy Ones took a black clay bowl and filled it with water. They did this because water was needed to make the mountain grow. How could it grow that tall without water? When they did this there was still no single tall mountain there. But they put the clay bowl of water there and then added all the things that the animals gave, and the mountain began to grow. That is why the black clay bowl, full of medicine, is used in the bear dance.[6] And when the old people wanted holy water after that, they always got it from the mountain tops.

All the birds of the mountain and the mountain animals were there helping to make these mounds of earth grow. They all prayed. Then the two Hactcin and Holy Boy and Red Boy started to sing. They sang and sang and after a while all the fruit began to grow in these piles of earth.

The turkey was gobbling and strutting. When the mountain expanded he always did this. But they did not know how many times the mountain grew, for they had no sun and could not count.[7] Now we watch the sun and see the days pass, and in this way learn to count.

Every time the mountain grew there was a noise as though something was squeezed, a squeaking noise. All the four mounds of earth, as they grew, merged and became one mountain.

When the dirt had all grown together into one mountain, the two Hactcin and Holy Boy and Red Boy picked out twelve shamans who had performed many things when the people were showing off their power before. These were the ones who had been able to cut themselves and to swallow arrows. These people had ceremonies from different sources, from animals, from fire, from Turkey, from frogs and others things. They each had a shamanistic ceremony and they were shamans. They could not be left out. They had power and they had to help too. All with power were helping to make the mountain grow. Each animal and bird was contributing his power.

The four Holy Ones painted these twelve men and made them appear like the Tsanati of today.[8] They dressed them up with spruce branches and yucca leaves, using the narrow-leafed yucca and the broad-leafed yucca too. They wove the yucca and made a short skirt of it for the men to wear. They stuck spruce branches in around their waists. They tied yucca at the wrist and lower part of the arm and spruce at the upper arm. Six represented the summer and six the winter season. Therefore six were painted blue all over and six white all over. Yucca was tied to their ankles and to a place above the knee, and spruce branches were stuck in these circles of yucca. The faces, hands, and feet were painted. A line of black ran outward and down from each eye. They wore buckskin moccasins. One white eagle feather was tied in the hair of each, on top. In their hands were branches of spruce and blades of yucca. They held four kernels of blue corn in each hand.

Then the four Holy Ones made six clowns.[9] They were painted white all over except for four black stripes, one across the face, one across the chest, one across the upper leg, and one across the lower leg. The stripes went around the whole body. Each arm also had four black stripes. On their wrists they wore a band of narrow yucca and one around the neck. They wore loin cloths of deerskin, and they wore moccasins. Yucca bands were put around their ankles. Rattles of deer hoof were tied to the yucca at the ankle, two to each foot. The hair was gathered up and brought to a point on each side. These "horns" were painted white with four black stripes. They stuck out like horns. And at the top of each one was one eagle feather.

In the right hand they carried the broad blades of yucca. This was called their whip. It had a downy eagle feather at the very end. With this the clown protects the holy places against any woman whose menstrual period has come. If a woman is in that condition the feather points to her and the clown chases her away with it. This whip is used against sickness too.

In the left hand they carried a branch of spruce. These people are powerful. If you have touched the bone or marrow of a man or dog, though you did not realize it, and then later put your hand to your mouth, it makes you sick. You can't digest food. You vomit all the time. Then these clowns are the people who can cure you.

All those who were present helped. They all worked to make the mountain grow. It was getting large. The people wanted to travel on it. The mountain had much fruit on it now. There were cotton-wood and aspen trees on it and streams of water flowed from it too. It was very rich in everything. Yucca fruit and all other fruits were growing on it by this time, all kinds of berries and cherries.

The turkey, more than anything else, was the one who made the mountain grow. When he gobbled and strutted it would begin to rise.

It was very dark and they couldn't see well. They had the feathers by which they obtained some light, but they could not see all over.

Two girls went up on the mountain when no one was watching them. A little later the mountain stopped growing and would rise no more.

Then the Holy Ones[10] said, "Something must have happened up there."

They sent the whirlwind to find out about it. The wind went up there. He saw tracks.

They all continued with their songs and prayers, but the mountain would no longer move.

Whirlwind sent a message to the two Hactcin telling them to go up and fix the damage. Turkey was responsible for all growing things and so he first went up and saw what the two girls had done. He came back and told the two Hactcin. The Hactcin requested that the people remain where they were.

The two Hactcin went up with Holy Boy and Red Boy. They saw all that the girls had done. They saw how the reeds and many other plants were damaged. The girls had been chasing each other and wrestling and trampling on the holy plants. They had even used the holy mountain as a toilet. So the Holy Ones cleaned up everything and fixed it up. The girls were no longer there. They had gone down the mountain again.

The Holy Ones came down to the people again after performing a ceremony there. They asked the people who had been on top of the mountain, and they found out which girls had done it.

"Why did you go up there?" they asked these girls.

They blamed each other. One said, "She wanted me to go up." The other said, "No, she told me to go." They said they had intended to go only a little way but that they had seen berries and fruit ahead, and so had gone from one plant or tree to another until they had climbed to the top.

Now all the people came together once more and sang, and the mountain began to grow again. It grew just a little higher. It grew four times and then it wouldn't rise any more.

The four Holy Ones went up the mountain again. They saw that the top of the mountain was still a little way from the sky and from the hole through which they could see to the other earth. So they all held a council to decide what they would do next.

They sent up Fly and Spider. The spider put his web all around, and the fly and the spider went up on it. That is why, in February or March, when the first warm weather starts and the first flies appear, they come on the sunbeams, which stand for the spider's web.[11] You will see the sun's ray come through the window and the fly will come in on it, right into the house.

Those two went up where the sun was. They took four rays of the sun, each of a different color, and pulled on them as if they were ropes. They pulled them down to the mountain top. The ropes came down, black, blue, yellow, and glittering, one on each corner of the opening. From these rays of the sun the four Holy Ones made a ladder. Out of the same material they made twelve steps and placed them across.

When Spider first came up on this earth, there was only one mountain, and that was to the east. Flint Mountain was its name. It is still there, west of Abiquiu.

The first animals to be sent up after Spider came down and announced that water was plentiful there, were two wild ducks.[12] These are the ones they hunt now in October. They were sent up because it was thought that they could get along well in the water. But as soon as they came up they flew over to this mountain and stayed there until the water was sent away. When everyone was up on the earth, they came back and joined the others.

Now the fly and the spider went upward again on that ladder. They saw a great deal of water up there. They could see no ground at all. The spider made a cylinder of web which protected them and they went up to the top through this. Spider then wove four webs on top of the earth of four different colors and stretching in four directions so that the four Holy Ones could ascend.

The four came up. Black Hactcin stood on the black web to the east, and the others took their places too. They talked of what to do, for the sun was past the middle of the sky already.

Then they said, "Let us make four hoops of the different colors, one black, one blue, one yellow, and one glittering.[13]

They did so and threw the black one to the east, the blue one to the south, the yellow one to the west, and the glittering one to the north. Every time they threw one, the water rolled back and grew less where they were standing. By the time they threw the fourth one, there was land where they stood. The water had receded from the land and had made the oceans as they are now.

But everything was still muddy. So they sent for the four Big Winds of the different colors and for the little winds too. The winds blew and made it all dry. But the winds couldn't dry off certain places where the springs and rivers were.

When the wind was hurling the water back and exposing the land, it lifted the water high in the sky and held it there. Over by the oceans the water is still held there by the wind.

White Hactcin said to the wind, "Hold the water there and when it is needed we will let you know and you must blow and bring the rain."

Hactcin talked to the thunder, "You must lead," he said, "so people will hear and know the rain is coming and get ready. They will prepare buckets to fill and be ready to receive the rain."

Then he spoke to the sun saying, "You must shine on the lakes and rivers so that the steam will arise and turn to water and give rain. But Wind, you will always carry the water in the air; you are responsible for it. If the heat does not pick up the water but leaves it around on the earth in the same way all the time, the water will become dirty and unfit for use. But by changing it in this manner it will be made pure and good for the people."

High in the air there are four winds: the black wind from the east makes the water warm, the blue wind from the south makes it cool and fresh, the yellow wind from the west freezes the water and turns it to snow, and the guttering wind from the north turns it to ice and hail.[14] These four people are always there handing around the moisture of the air. When it is handed to the wind of the north, it turns to ice. Then, when it is handed back to Black Wind of the east, he warms it and it turns to water again. That is why we have the moisture of the air in all these forms.

And some people who also control water live in the mountains. These are the people who were directed by the Hactcin to stay in the mountains and take care of them and of all within them.[15]

When the people first came up on earth there were no mountains. But when the monsters began to grow, the mountains too began to rise, for Hactcin made them to be barriers so that the monsters could not get to the people easily.

And Hactcin stationed people in those mountains then, saying, "This mountain will be your home."

These people allow the water of the mountains to flow out, and thus there are springs.

We say that the fly is the messenger of the sun. It carries the news of the coming of the sun. And the spider has long ropes, we say. In ceremonies he helps people, and when he helps it is just as if a rope were lowered to one who has fallen in a deep place.

The four Holy Ones said to Fly and Spider, "We need your help still. Make a web and extend it to the sky," they said to Spider, "and then you two bring the sun down."

The Hactcin sang and sang so the sun and moon could be gotten down, for the sun and moon had not asked permission when they went up as they did. It was the fault of the sun and moon that the people had such a hard time and had to come up on this earth.

Spider did as he was told, and he and Fly brought the sun and moon down. Then all held council and they decided that they would change Sun to a person, a living person, because he had disobeyed. They were afraid that if they didn't do this the sun would go up again to some other place, and they had had a difficult time regaining the sun. They decided to do the same to Moon too. Before this Sun and Moon were alive, but they were not people.

So the four Holy Ones talked it over and said, "Of the sun we will make another people." And they made the sun into a Taos Indian boy. And out of the moon they made a Jicarilla Apache girl.[16]

"Let them marry," said the four Holy Ones, "and then the Jicarilla Apache and the Taos Indians will be good friends and will not fight over little things."

And so these two helped each other after this. They helped each other shine and give light.

Now they sent the sun and the moon back to the north again after they had become living persons. So they went back to the north. Then the sun started to go to the south. The moon followed. They went like this for one full day.

But then they thought about it.

"I don't believe it's right," Sun said, "for one side of the earth has light when we go this way and one has not."[17]

The Holy Ones thought about it. Then they changed it and had the sun and moon go from east to west. And the Milky Way that you see stretching from north to south across the sky is the first path of the sun and moon.

At first the sun and moon went together, at the same time.

"That's not right," they thought. "We will hold back the moon. Let the sun go first and then the moon can go at night."

The moon was flat and round. It followed the sun, coming later. When the sun set in the west, it could be seen. The moon is a girl and was having her menstrual period just at that time. She was tipped up so that only the rim could be seen. That is what we call the new moon when it occurs now. So it is that our women have a period after a new moon, and that is why the girl's puberty ceremony is always held at the new moon. And the new moon is used now for keeping track of the seasons.

The sun just kept going all the time.

When everything was ready in this upper world the Holy Ones went down below to the place where the people were waiting.

The people had a great deal of food on that mountain. They had much to eat while they were traveling. But they had not yet started upward. They were still below, in the underworld.

Then the four Holy Ones sent up the crows, the four crows of the different colors. "You must go up there and see how everything is getting along."

The crows came up. Some of the fish and water animals had died when the water was thrown back by the Holy Ones. The crows began to eat these dead bodies.

The other people were expecting them back. They wondered why the crows did not return. So finally they sent up White Weasel.

White Weasel went up and saw what the crows were doing. He returned and told the people, "No wonder they don't come back. They are busy eating."

So they sent Badger up then. Badger stepped into some place that was still muddy. He thought it must be muddy like that all over, so he went back and told them, "Oh, it's still very muddy." Because he stepped in the mud he has black on his paws now.

Then they sent up Beaver. When he got up there he tried to dam up the water. He stayed up there working and making dams.

Then Black Weasel was sent. Black Weasel came to Beaver and said, "What are you doing? The people are waiting for you."

"Oh, I'd better dam up this water so that the water will be ready when the people come up."

The rivers that are left us here today are the ones he dammed up.

Beaver knew that the people were on the journey to this earth and would be very tired. So he built a sweat house there where the people could come and get rested.

When Weasel came up he saw it. He asked, "What are you doing here? The people are waiting for you."

"I'm making a dam for the people, so they will have water. When the people come they will already have water for drinking and to bathe in."

"And what are you building?"

"That is my house. I call it *keltca*."[18]

"Is this for the people?"

"No, it is my home. But whenever the bodies of the people are doubled up they will use it. When they are tired they will use it too. After a long sickness when they are run down they will use it. When they come up I will explain to them how to use it. I'll explain to them what they should do. They should build a fire outside and put rocks in it. When these rocks are well heated they must throw them into the sweat house. The doorway must be closed by my own skin, by beaver skin, for when I go into my house I never wear my skin but take it off and hang it at the door. So let the people do likewise when they take a sweat bath. The door must always face to the east. The people must roll the hot rocks in with sticks and pile them all on the north side. Then they must throw water on the rocks and steam will arise. When it begins to cool down, more water must be thrown on the rocks. And the songs that are sung should be about Little Night. They must sing these, for they go into that small dark place which gives them the sweat bath and the cleansing.

"Two or four may go in and all can sing in there. And they should sing for long life too and sing of the sun and moon. Women may go in but not with the men.

"The sweat house shall be made of bent pieces of wood with brush and dirt over these. And it must be made by the water's edge so that all can go into the water and wash after the sweat bath.

"The men must not use the same sweat house that the women use. If they do so they will become blind, and the women will become blind too if they go into the one the men have used.

"The sweat house, after use, is to be left standing, and it may be used again."

Then from below the Holy Ones sent the birds up first, because they have wings to fly. They came up in a flock.

Hactcin told the animals and people. "Now get ready. We must go up in the sky."

At this time the girls were big with children.[19] This was the result of the things they had used on themselves in the absence of the men, when the women and the men had separated. They were already in late pregnancy when they started.

Now they all began traveling on the mountain going toward the top. The Hactcin made sure that everything was right and holy before they let the people start. There was no sun and so one cannot say that the people took four days to reach the vault of the underworld. But they traveled four times until they were tired and then stopped each time. The top of the mountain where they stopped last was twelve ladder steps from the earth hole. That was the distance between the mountain top and the earth hole. They had four ladders. The black ladder to the east was the one the men climbed up on. The blue ladder to the south was for the girls and women. The yellow ladder to the west was used by the young boys. The north ladder of a glittering color was used by all the little children.

First they prayed before the ladders. Holy Boy was the real leader of the ascent. It was due to him that the people were coming on this earth. So he prayed for the ladders and for the Hactcin, the clowns, and Tsanati.

Then the clowns came up first, for they had the whips of yucca with which to chase sickness away. At that time it was not known whether there was sickness on earth. They thought that perhaps the water animals which had died had some sickness. So the clowns came up and made everything wholesome for the people. They made the path that the people could follow.

White Hactcin was the next to come up. Holy Boy first dressed him up. He put a downy eagle feather on top of his head. He dressed him up with spruce. White Hactcin held a big whip made of yucca. A downy feather was at its end. In his left hand he held spruce branches.

The clowns uttered a certain laugh when they came up, so that all the sickness would be frightened, and the Hactcin made a different noise for the same reason. Black Hactcin ascended immediately after White Hactcin did. He had black specular iron ore and pollen all over his face. White Hactcin had pollen all over his face, and on the right side the seven stars of the Big Dipper were painted with specular iron ore. A sun of specular iron ore was designed on the middle of the forehead. On the left cheek was the moon, designed with specular iron ore. The bodies of both Hactcin were covered with white clay. They wore skirts of woven yucca like those of the Tsanati. At the arm and leg joints they wore yucca bands tied, and spruce branches were fastened on these.

Next Red Boy ascended. He, like the Hactcin, went up the ladder of the east. Then the twelve Tsanati came up. Then Holy Boy came up. After him came Turkey. All these came up the ladder to the east.

Now all these were up on this earth, and they prepared everything so that no harm should befall the people.

Now it was the turn of the people. Ancestral Man was the first of the people to ascend. Ancestral Woman followed and was the first woman to emerge. Both walked up with age sticks in their hands.[20] They were dressed as White-Shell Woman and Child-of-the-Water dress for the girl's puberty ceremony now. The other people followed. The men were to the east, the women to the west, and the children to the north and south.[21]

After the people the animals came.

The people emerged from a hole in a mountain. At that time this was the only mountain on the earth, besides Flint Mountain to the east. The other mountains grew up later, at the time of the monsters. Some say that the emergence mountain lies north of Durango, Colorado. Others say it is near Alamosa, Colorado. It was called Big Mountain.[22]

Sky is our father, Earth is our mother. They are husband and wife and they watch over us and take care of us. The earth gives us our food; all the fruits and plants come from the earth. Sky gives us the rain, and when we need water we pray to him. The earth is our mother.[23] We came from her. When we came up on this earth, it was just like a child being born from its mother. The place of emergence is the womb of the earths.[24]

The animals came up, the elk, the deer, and all the others. But they were not wild animals. They were gentle and tame then. The animals came up any ladder which was nearest. After a while the ladders were all worn through, so many had passed over them.

There were two old people, an old man and a very old woman who were far behind the animals. These two couldn't see well; their sight was dim. Those two silly girls who had interfered with the growth of the mountain before were far behind too. They had been chasing each other and playing, and the people didn't know it.

When the two old people came to the ladders, the ladders were worn out and they couldn't get up. They stood there and called, "Come and get us. Take us too." But there was no ladder nor any way to get them up. The old people tried to get the others to help them.

Finally they became angry. "All right," they said, "we shall stay here. But you must come back some day." They meant that the people must return to the underworld when they die.

Night came. The people on top tried to sleep. But they couldn't sleep the first night. They couldn't sleep the second nor the third. They wondered why. They wondered whether it was because something had been left behind.

Then they discovered that they had no lice in their hair. There were three kinds, black ones, grey ones, and the small ones, the nits. So they sent down to the old people for these. The two old people threw some up. The people divided the lice among themselves. The fourth night they all slept soundly.

The people looked down through the hole, for they couldn't find those two silly girls among those on top. The light of the sun went through the hole and hit the tip of the mountain, illuminating it. There, in the light, sat those two foolish girls sewing shallow tray baskets.

They called to these two girls, but they wouldn't come up. They wouldn't obey.

Then Holy Boy made two butterflies out of the flowers. He made the kind that always go in pairs, the yellow ones.

The sun had power now. Holy Boy sent word to Sun. "You must help us and send a beam for the butterflies." The sun did so and the butterflies went right in on that beam.[25]

The two silly girls caught sight of the butterflies.

"Let's catch them and make designs. We have always made mountain designs on our baskets. Now we'd better make a butterfly design," they said. "That is more beautiful."[26]

So they started to chase the butterflies. The ray of the sun came down and provided a ladder. The butterflies kept just out of reach above them. So they began to ascend the ladder, trying to get those butterflies. Before they knew it they were on top.

Notes

1. For abbreviated accounts of the emergence see Goddard, p. 193; Mooney, p. 197; Russell, p. 254.

2. The attribution of the loss of the sun and moon to the boasts of shamans (those who obtain supernatural power through a personal encounter with some animal or natural force) and

the ridicule heaped on the ceremonies and legerdemain in which the shamans subsequently engaged in order to retrieve the loss, are indicative of the subordinate place shamanism plays in Jicarilla religion. Shamanistic ceremonies are used for emergencies and minor crises. For important occasions and for times when planning and preparation are possible, "long life ceremonies," traditional rites, which have their genesis and rationalization in the myths and not in any personal experience of an individual, are invoked instead.

3. A number of Jicarilla affinities must be addressed by a special third person form, called "polite form" because of the restraint and circumspection which are supposed to accompany it. By taking pains to be more formal and dignified, the birds and animals hoped to avoid the excesses of the thoughtless shamans.

4. The grasshopper is considered the guardian of wheat. See pp. 177–178 for further development of this theme.

5. Sand on which ground drawings are to be traced is leveled off with eagle feathers today.

6. For a description of the bear dance see pp. 27–44.

7. Another version: Some say that the mountain grew twelve times; that it grew eight times and then the foolish girls stopped it. Then the Hactcin fixed it, and it grew four more times (Inf.).

8. The marked tendency of the Jicarilla to discourage shamanism in favor of the "long life ceremonies" finds unmistakable expression here. To become effective in this rite of the growing emergence mountain, shamans have to be transformed into a dance group which functions in the traditional or "long life" ceremonies today. The word Tsanati refers to ritual gesticulation. Since a literal translation would be awkward, the native term will be retained in these pages.

9. The literal translation of the term for the Jicarilla clown is "striped excrement." Their ability to cure stomach ailments is connected with scatological practices which will be presently described (p. 184). The clowns of the emergence were decorated with four black stripes. Clowns which function in war-path ceremonies are designed with six black stripes.

10. The Holy Ones are White Hactcin, Black Hactcin, Red Boy, and Holy Boy. Actually the informant mentioned these four names each time, but to avoid repetition this convention of referring to them collectively will be followed.

11. The Jicarilla will not kill spiders for this reason. The nexus in Jicarilla ideology between the spider's web and the sunbeam is made explicit in the birth rite, where a cord of unblemished buckskin, called in the rite "spider's rope," is stretched from the umbilicus of the child towards the sun.

12. For the origin of the water found on the earth at the time of the emergence see p. 267.

13. The device of rolling back waters by the tossing of colored hoops occurs in more than one place in Jicarilla mythology. See p. 106.

14. Like other natural forces, Wind is often personified. The Jicarilla's conception is of an animate universe which understands and responds to his needs.

15. The belief that people or supernaturals have been stationed within mountains for one purpose or another is a common theme. See also p. 112.

16. Apache cosmology is not consistent concerning the sex of the moon. When the moon is thought of in connection with the woman's menstrual cycle it is given female attributes. But Moon is also associated with Water, and Water becomes the father of one of the Culture Heroes. In an important ceremonial race Moon is represented as a male (p. 81) as is the case in the origin myth of the Hactcin ceremony (p. 141).

17. The earth is said to have the form of a woman whose feet point toward the east and whose head lies to the west.

18. This word means "beaver pelt" and is quite similar to the word for sweat-house, *kiltca*. The informant is employing a bit of folk etymology to hint that the word for sweat-house originally came from "beaver pelt." Since there is a difference of tone as well as outline between these two words, this is extremely unlikely.

19. For the explanation of these pregnancies see p. 266. The account of the misbehavior of the girls in the underworld is as often told as a part of the origin legend also.

20. The age stick, or the staff which an old person uses for support, is here mentioned as a symbol of the long life that man shall have on earth. It is constantly named in Jicarilla ritual songs.

21. At the time of the emergence, the man who came out last had his hair parted, not in the middle, but on the side. The line of the parting was painted red. If you know this emergence story well, you can wear your hair that way. Both men and women did this (Inf.).

22. For identification of the emergence mountain as the San Juan of Colorado see pp. 163–164.

23. Taos is at the heart of the earth. Our own country used to be the Cimarron region (Inf.).

24. That the emergence tale is a myth of gestation is patent enough. It is seldom, however, that the native draws the parallel so conclusively.

25. Butterflies and the rays of the sun are connected with love charms in Jicarilla theory and are therefore well designed to lure the girls to the upper earth. One way to gain the favor of a member of the opposite sex is to flash a beam of light in his direction by means of a shiny object. The butterfly, symbol of the fluttering and inconstancy of women, is encised or painted on flutes which young men play to attract swethearts.

26. A woven basket, one of the ceremonial gifts of the bear dance, is decorated with designs of mountains and butterflies to commemorate this.

7. Creation and the Origin of Corn

FRANK HAMILTON CUSHING

I once heard a Zuñi priest say: "Five things alone are necessary to the sustenance and comfort of the 'dark ones' [Indians] among the children of earth."

"The sun, who is the Father of all.

"The earth, who is the Mother of men.

"The water, who is the Grandfather.

"The fire, who is the Grandmother.

"Our brothers and sisters the Corn, and seeds of growing things."

This Indian philosopher explained himself somewhat after the following fashion:

"Who among men and the creatures could live without the Sun-father?, for his light brings day, warms and gladdens the Earth-mother with rain which flows forth in the water we drink and that causes the flesh of the Earth-mother to yield abundantly seeds, while these—are they not cooked by the brand of fire which warms us in winter?"

That he reasoned well, may be the better understood if we follow for a while the teachings which instructed his logic. These relate that:

First, there was sublime darkness, which vanished not until came the "Ancient Father of the Sun," revealing universal waters. These were, save him, all that were.

The Sun-father thought to change the face of the waters and cause life to replace their desolation.

He rubbed the surface of his flesh, thus drawing forth *yep'-na*.[1]

The *yep'-na* he rolled into two balls. From his high and "ancient place among the spaces," (*Te'-thlä-shi-na-kwin*) he cast forth one of these balls and it fell upon the surface of the waters. There, as a drop of deer suet on hot broth, so this ball melted and spread far and wide like scum over the great waters, ever growing, until it sank into them.

Then the Sun-father cast forth the other ball, and it fell, spreading out and growing even larger than had the first, and dispelling so much of the waters that it rested upon the first. In time, the first became a great being—our Mother, the Earth; and the second became another great being—our Father, the Sky. Thus was divided the universal fluid into the "embracing waters of the World" below, and the "embracing waters of the Sky" above. Behold! this is why the Sky-father is blue as the ocean which is the home of the Earth-mother, blue even his flesh, as seem the far-away mountains—though they be the flesh of the Earth-mother.

Now while the Sky-father and the Earth-mother were together, the Earth-mother conceived in her ample wombs—which were the four great underworlds or caves—the first of men and creatures. Then the two entered into council that they might provide for the birth of their children.

"How shall it be?" said the one to the other. "How, when born forth, shall our children subsist, and who shall guide them?"

"Behold!" said the Sky-father. He spread his hand high and abroad with the hollow palm downward. Yellow grains like corn he stuck into all the lines and wrinkles of his palm and fingers. "Thus," said he, "shall I, as it were, hold my hand ever above thee and thy children, and the yellow grains shall represent so many shining points which shall guide and light these, our children, when the Sun-father is not nigh."

Gaze on the sky at night-time! Is it not the palm of the Great Father, and are the stars not in many lines of his hand yet to be seen?

"Ah yes!" said the Earth-mother, "yet my tiny children may not wander over my lap and bosom without guidance, even in the light of the Sun-father; therefore, behold!"

She took a great terraced bowl into which she poured water; upon the water she spat, and whipping it rapidly with her fingers it was soon beaten into foam as froths the soap-weed, and the foam rose high up around the rim of the bowl. The Earth-mother blew the foam. Flake after flake broke off, and bursting, cast spray downward into the bowl.

"See," said she, "this bowl is, as it were, the world, the rim its farthest limits, and the foam-bounden terraces round about, my features, which they shall call mountains whereby they shall name countries and be guided from place to place, and whence white clouds shall rise, float away, and, bursting, shed spray, that my children may drink of the water of life, and from my substance add unto the flesh of their being. Thou has said thou wilt watch over them when the Sun-father is absent, but thou art the cold being; I am the warm. Therefore, at night, when thou watchest, my children shall nestle in my bosom and find there warmth, strength and length of life from one day light to another."

Is not the bowl the emblem of the Earth, our mother?, for from it we draw both food and drink, as a babe draws nourishment from the breast of its mother, and round, as is the rim of a bowl, so is the horizon, terraced with mountains, whence rise the clouds. Is not woman the warm, man the cold being? For while woman sits shivering as she cooks by the fire in the house-room, man goes forth little heeding the storms of winter, to hunt the feed and gather pine-faggots.

Yet alas! Men and the creatures remained bounden in the lowermost womb of the Earth-mother, for she and the Sky-father feared to deliver them as a mother fears for the fate of her first offspring.

Then the Ancient Sun pitied the children of Earth. That they might speedily see his light, he cast a glance upon a foam cap floating abroad on the great waters. Forthwith the foam cap became instilled with life, and bore twin children, brothers one to the other, older and younger, for one was born before the other. To these he gave the *k'ia'-al-lan*, or "water-shield," that on it they might fly over the waters as the clouds—from which it was spun and woven—float over the ocean; that they might blind with its mists the sight of the enemy as the clouds darken the earth with rain-drops. He gave them for their bow, the rainbow, that with it they might clear men's trails of enemies, as the rain-bow clears away the storm-shadows; and for their arrows gave he them the thunder-bolts, that they might rive open the mountains, as the lightning cleaves asunder the pine trees; and then he sent them abroad to deliver, guide and protect the children of earth and the Sky-father. With their bow they lifted from his embraces the Sky-father from the bosom of the Earth-mother, "for," said they, "if he remain near, his cold will cause men to be stunted and stooped with shivering and to grovel in the earth," as stunted trees in the mountains delve under the snow to hide from the cold of the Sky-father. With their thunder-bolts they broke open the mountain which gave entrance to the cave-wombs of the Earth-mother, and upon their water-shields they descended into the lowermost of the caves, where dwelt the children of earth—men and all creatures.

Alas! It was dark as had been the world before the coming of the Sun, and the brothers found men and the beings sadly bewailing their lot. When one moved it was but to jostle another, whose complaints wearied the ears of yet others; hence the brothers called a council of the priest-chiefs—even ere the coming forth of men such lived—and they made a ladder of tall canes which they placed against the roof of the cavern. Up this rushed the children of earth. Some, climbing out before of their own wills, found deliverance from the caves above and, wandering away, became the ancestors of nations unknown to us; but our fathers followed in the footsteps of the older and younger brothers. Does not the cane grow jointed to-day, showing thus the notches which men traversed to day-light?

In the second cave all was still dark, but like starlight through cloud rifts, through the cleft above showed the twilight. After a time the people murmured again, until the two delivered them into the third world where they found light like that of early dawn. Again they grew discontented, again were guided upward, this time into the open light of the Sun—which was the light of this world. But some remained behind, not escaping until afterward; and these were the fathers of the Western nations whom our ancients knew not.

Then indeed for a time the people complained bitterly, for it was then that they *first* saw the light of the Sun-father, which, in its brilliancy, smote them so that they fell grasping their eye-balls and moaning. But when they became used to the light they looked around in joy and wonderment; yet they saw that the earth seemed but small, for everywhere rolled about the great misty waters.

The two brothers spread open the limbs of the Earth-mother, and cleft the western mountains with their shafts of lightning and the waters flowed down and away from the bosom of the Earth-mother, cutting great cañons and valleys which remain to this day. Thus was widened the land, yet the earth remained damp. Then they guided the people eastward.

Already before men came forth from the lower worlds with the priest-chiefs, there were many gods and strange beings. The gods gave to the priests many treasures and instructions, but the people knew not yet the meaning of either. Thus were first taught our ancients incantations, rituals and sacred talks (prayer), each band of them according to its usefulness. These bands were the "Priesthood"—*Shi'-wa-na-kwe*; the "Hunter-band"—*Sa'-ni-a-k'ia-kwe*; the "Knife-band"—*A'tchi-a-k'ia-kwe* or Warrior, and the *Ne'-we-kwe*, or Band of Wise

Medicine Men. The leaders of each band thus came to have wonderful knowledge and power—even as that of the gods! They summoned a great council of their children—for they were called the 'Fathers of the People'—and asked them to choose such things as they would have for special ownership or use. Some chose the macaw, the eagle, or the turkey; others chose the deer, bear, or coyote; others the seeds of earth, or *a'-tâ-a*, the spring vine, tobacco, and the plants of medicine, the yellow-wood and many other things. Thus it came about that they and their brothers and sisters and their children, even unto the present day, were named after the things they chose in the days when all was new, and thus was divided our nation into many clans, or gentes (*A'-no-ti-we*) of brothers and sisters who may not marry one another but from one to the other. To some of the elders of these bands and clans was given some thing which should be, above all other things, precious. For instance, the clans of the Bear and Crane were given the *Mu'-et-ton-ne*, or medicine seed of hail and snow. For does not the bear go into his den, and appears not the crane when come storms of hail and snow?

When more than one clan possessed one of these magic medicines they formed a secret society—like the first four—for its keeping and use. Thus the Bear and Crane peoples became the "Holders of the Wand"—who bring the snow of winter and are potent to cure the diseases which come with them. In time they let into their secret council others, whom they had cured, that the precious secrets of their band might not be wasted. Thus it was that one after another were formed the rest of our medicine bands, who were and are called the finishers of men's trails, because, despite disease and evil, they guard and lengthen our lives; but in the "days of the new" there were only four bands.[2]

To the Eagle, Deer and Coyote peoples was given the *Nal'-e-ton*, or "Deer Medicine Seed," which the Hunter-band still guards; and to the Macaw, Sun and Frog peoples the *Kia'-et-ton*, or the "Medicine Seed of Water," which the priesthood and the Sacred Dance, or *Kâ'-kâ*, still hold—without the administration of which the world would dry up and even the insects of the mountains and hollows of earth grow thirsty and perish. Yet, not less precious was the gift to the "Seed-people," or *Ta'-a-kwe*. This was the *Tchu'-et-ton*, or the "Medicine Seed of Corn"—for from this came the parents of flesh and beauty, the solace of hunger, the emblems of birth, mortal life, death and immortality. To the Badger people was given the knowledge of Fire, for in the roots of all trees, great and little—which the badger best knows how to find—dwells the essence of fire.[3]

To all of these peoples it was told that they should wander for many generations toward the land whence the Sun brings the day-light (Eastward) until at last they would reach the "middle of the world," where their children should dwell forever over the heart of our Earth-mother until their days should be numbered and the light of Zuñi grow dark.

Toward this unknown country the "twin brothers of light" guided them. In those times a day meant a year, and a night another, so that four days and nights meant eight years. Many days the people wandered eastward, slaying game for their flesh-food, gathering seeds from grasses and weeds for their bread-food, and binding rushes about their loins for their clothing; they knew not until afterward, the flesh of the cotton and yucca-mothers.

The earth was still damp. Dig a hole in a hill-side, quickly it filled with water. Drop a seed on the highest table-land and it without waiting shot forth green sprouts. So moist, indeed, was the soil, that even foot-prints of men and all creatures might be traced whith-ersoever they tended. The beings and strange creatures increased with men, and spread over the world. Many monsters lived, by whose ferocity men perished.

Then said the twin brothers: "Men, our children, are poorer than the beasts, their ene-mies; for each creature has a special gift of strength or sagacity, while to men has been given only the power of guessing. Nor would we that our children be web-footed like the beings that live over the waters and damp places."

Therefore, they sent all men and harmless beings to a place of security; then laid their water shield on the ground. Upon it they placed four thunder-bolts, one pointed north, another west, another south, and the other eastward. When all was ready they let fly the thunder-bolts. Instantly the world was covered with lurid fire and shaken with rolling thun-ders, as is a forest to-day burned and blasted where the lightning has fallen. Thus as the clay of vessels is burned to rock, and the mud of the hearth crackled and reddened by fire, so the earth was mottled and crackled and hardened where now we see mountains and masses of rock. Many of the great monsters and prey-beings were changed in a twinkling to enduring rock or shriveled into twisted idols which the hunter and priest-warrior know best how to prize. Behold, their forms along every mountain side and ravine, and in the far western val-leys and plains, still endure the tracks of the fathers of men and beings, the children of earth. Yet some of the beings of prey were spared, that the world might not become over-filled with life, and starvation follow, and that men might breathe of their spirits and be inspired with the hearts of warriors and hunters.

Often the people rested from their wanderings, building great houses of stone which may even now be seen, until the Conch of the Gods sounded, which lashed the ocean to fury and beat the earth to trembling.[4] Then the people started up, and gathering the few things they could, again commenced their wanderings; yet often those who slept or lingered were buried beneath their own walls, where yet their bones may sometimes be found.

Marvelous both of good and evil were the works of the ancients. Alas! There came forth with others, those impregnated with the seed of sorcery. Their evil works caused discord among men, and, through fear and anger, men were divided from one another. Born before our ancients, had been other men, and these our fathers sometimes overtook and looked not peacefully upon them, but challenged them—though were they not their older brothers? It thus happened when our ancients came to their fourth resting place on their eastward jour-ney, that which they named *Shi-po-lo-lon-K'ai-a*, or "The Place of Misty Waters," there already dwelt a clan of people called the *A'-ta-a*, or Seed People, and the seed clan of our ancients challenged them to know by what right they assumed the name and attributes of their own clan. "Behold," said these stranger-beings, "we have power with the gods above yours, yet can we not exert it without your aid. Try, therefore, your own power first, then we will show you ours." At last, after much wrangling, the Seed clan agreed to this, and set apart eight days for prayer and sacred labors. First they worked together cutting sticks, to which they bound the plumes of summer birds which fly in the clouds or sail over the waters. "Therefore," thought our fathers, "why should not their plumes waft our beseechings to the waters and clouds?" These plumes, with prayers and offerings, they planted in the valleys, and there, also, they placed their *Tchu'-e-ton-ne*. Lo!, for eight days and nights it rained and there were thick mists; and the waters from the mountains poured down bringing new soil and spreading it over the valleys where the plumed sticks had been planted. "See!" said the fathers of the seed clan, "water and new earth bring we by our supplications."

"It is well," replied the strangers, "yet *life* ye did not bring. Behold!" and they too set apart eight days, during which they danced and sang a beautiful dance and prayer song, and at the end of that time they took the people of the seed clan to the valleys. Behold, indeed! Where the plumes had been planted and the *tchu'-e-ton* placed grew seven corn-plants, their tassels waving in the wind, their stalks laden with ripened grain. "These," said the strangers, "are the severed flesh of seven maidens, our own sisters and children. The eldest sister's is the yellow corn; the next, the blue; the next, the red; the next, the white; the next, the speckled; the next, the black, and the last and youngest is the sweet-corn, for see! even ripe, she is soft like the young of the others. The first is of the North-land, yellow like the light of winter; the second is of the West, blue like the great world of waters; the third is of the South, red like the Land of Everlasting Summer; the fourth is of the East, white like the land whence the sun brings the daylight; the fifth is of the upper regions, many-colored as are the clouds of morning and evening, and the sixth is of the lower regions, black as are the caves whence came we, your older, and ye, our younger brothers." "Brothers indeed be we, each one to the other," said the people to the strangers, "and may we not journey together seeking the middle of the world?" "Aye, we may," replied the strangers, "and of the flesh of our maidens ye may eat, no more seeking the seeds of the grasses and of your water we may drink, no more wondering whither we shall find it; thus shall each help the other to life and contentment. Ye shall pray and cut prayer-plumes, we shall sing, and dance shall our maidens that all may be delighted and that it may be for the best. But beware! no mortal must approach the persons of our maidens."

Thenceforward, many of the *A'-ta-a* and the seed clan journeyed together, until at last the Sun, Macaw, and some other clans-people found the middle of the world; while others yet wandered in search of it, not for many generations to join their brothers, over they heart of the Earth-mother, which is *Shi-wi-na-kwin*, or the "Land of the Zuñis."

Day after day, season after season, year after year, the people of the seed clan and the *A'-ta-a*, who were named together the Corn-clan, or people, prepared, and their maidens danced the dance of the *thla-he-kwe*,[5] or "Beautiful Corn Wands," until their children grew weary and yearned for other amusements.

Sometimes the people saw over Thunder-mountain thick mists floating and lowering. At such times, near the Cave of the Rainbow, a beautiful halo would spring forth, amidst which the many-colored garments of the rainbow himself could be seen, and soft, sweet music, stranger than that of the whistling winds in a mountain of pines, floated fitfully down the valley. At last the priests and elders gathered in council and determined to send their two chief warriors (Priests of the Bow) to the cavern of the rainbow, that it might be determined what strange people made the sights and sounds. "Mayhap it will prove some new dancers, who will throw the light of their favor on our weary hearts and come to cheer us and delight our children." Thus said they to the warriors when they were departing.

No sooner had the warriors reached the cave-entrance than the mists enshrouded them and the music ceased. They entered and were received by a splendid group of beings, bearing long brightly-painted flutes, amongst whom the leader was Pai'-a-tu-ma, the father of the *Ne'-we* band, and the God of Dew.

"Enter, my children," said he, "and sit. We have commanded our dancers to cease and our players to draw breath from their flutes, that we might listen to your messages; for 'not for nothing does one stranger visit the house of another.'"

"True," replied the warriors. "Our fathers have sent us that we might greet you, and the light of your favor ask for our children. Day after day the maidens of the corn-people dance one dance which, from oft repeating, has grown undelightful, and our fathers thought you might come to vary this dance with your own, for that you knew one we were taught by your music, which we sometimes heard."

"Aha!" replied Pai'-a-tu-ma, "it is well! We will follow; but not in the day-time—in the night-time we will follow. My children," said he, turning to the flute-players, "show to the strangers our custom."

The drum sounded till it shook the cavern; the music shrieked and pealed in softly surging unison, as the wind does in a wooded cañon after the storm is distant, and the mists played over the medicine bowl around which the musicians were gathered, until the rainbow fluttered his bright garments among the painted flutes. Maidens filed out brandishing wands whence issued tiny clouds white as the down of eagles, and as the sounds died away between the songs the two warriors in silent wonder and admiration departed for their home.

When they returned to their fathers in Zuñi, they told what they had seen and heard. Forthwith the fathers (priest-chiefs and elders) prepared the dance of the corn-maidens. A great bower was placed in the court of the pueblo, whither went the mothers and priests of the Seed-clan. The priests of the Macaw, Sun and Water clans were there. A terrace of sacred meal was marked on the ground, an altar set up over its base, and along its middle were placed the *E'-ta-e* or Medicine Seeds of corn and water. Along the outer edges were planted the sticks of prayer, plumed with the feathers of summer birds, and down in front of the altar and terrace were set basket-bowls covered with sacred mantles made of the flesh of the Cotton-mother (Goddess of Cotton), whose down grows from the earth and floats in the skies (cotton and the clouds are one in the Zuñi mythology). By the side of each basket-bowl sat a mother of the clan, silent in prayer and meditation. To the right were the singers, to the left the corn maidens. Night was coming on. The dance began and a fire was built in front of the bower beyond where the maidens danced. More beautiful than all human maidens were those maidens of the corn, but as are human maidens, so were they, irresistibly beautiful.

As the night deepened, the sound of music and flutes was heard up the river, and then followed the players of the rainbow-cave with their sisters, led by the God of Dew. When the players entered and saw the maidens their music ceased and they were impassioned. And when their turn came for leading the dance, they played their softest strains over their medicine bowl—the terraced bowl of the world—whence arose the rainbow. The people were delighted, but the corn maidens were sad; for no sooner had the dancing ceased a little than the flute players sought their hands and persons. In vain the corn maidens pleaded they were immortal virgins and the mothers of men! The flute players continually renewed their suits 'till the next day, and into the night which followed, while the dance went on. At last the people grew weary. The guardian warrior-priests nodded, and no longer wakened them. Silently the corn maidens stole up between the basket-trays and the sleeping people. There, passing their hands over their persons they placed something under the mantles, vanishing instantly as do the spirits of the dying, leaving only their flesh behind. Still the people slept, and ere long even the flute-players and dancers ceased. When the sun came out the people awoke. Then every one cried to the others "Where are our maiden mothers, our daughters?" Yet not even the warriors knew; for only of the flesh of the maidens (corn) could be found a little in the trays under the mantles. Then the place was filled with moaning among the women and upbraidings among the men, each blaming every other loudly until the priests cried out to silence their wranglings, and called a council. Then said they:

"Alas, we have laden our hearts with guilt, and sad thoughts have we prepared to weigh down our minds. We must send to seek the maidens, that they desert us not. Who shall undertake the journey?"

"Send for the eagle," it was said. The two warrior-priests were commanded to go and seek him.

Be it known that while yet the earth was young her children, both men and the creatures, spoke as men alone now speak, any one with any other. This the aged among all nations agree in saying, and are not those who grow not foolish with great age the wisest of men? Their words we speak!

Therefore, when the two warriors climbed the mountain whereon the eagle dwelt, and found only his eaglets at home, the little birds were frightened and tried to hide themselves in the hole where the nest was built. But when the warriors came nearer they screamed: "Oh do not pull our feathers; wait 'till we are older and we will drop them for you."

"Hush," said the warriors, "we seek your father."

But just then the old eagle, with a frown on his eyebrow, rushed in and asked why the warriors were frightening his "pin-feathers."

"We came for you, our father. Listen. Our mothers, the beautiful corn maidens, have vanished, leaving no trace save of their flesh. We come to beseech that you shall seek them for us."

"Go before!" said the eagle, smoothing his feathers, which meant that he would follow. So the warriors returned.

Then the eagle launched forth into the sky, circling higher and higher up, until he was smaller than a thistle-down in a whirlwind. At last he flew lower, then into the bower of the dancers where the council awaited him.

"Ah, thou comest!" exclaimed the people.

"Yes," replied the eagle. "Neither a blue-bird nor a wood-rat can escape my eye," said he, snapping his beak, "unless they hide under rocks or bushes. Send for my younger brother; he flies nearer the ground than I do."

So the warriors went to seek the sparrow-hawk. They found him sitting on an ant hill, but when he saw them he would have flown away had they not called out that they had words for him and meant him no harm.

"What is it?" said he. "For if you have any snare-strings with you I'll be off."

"No, no! we wish you to go and hunt for our maidens—the corn maidens," said the warriors,—"your old brother, the eagle, cannot find them."

"Oh, that's it; well, go before—of course he can't find them! He climbs up to the clouds and thinks he can see under every tree and shadow as the Sun, who sees not with eyes, does."

The sparrow-hawk flew away to the north and the east and the west, looking behind every cliff and copsewood, but he found no trace of the maidens, and returned, declaring as he flew into the bower, "they can not be found. They are hiding more snugly than I ever knew a sparrow to hide," said he, ruffling his feathers and gripping the stick he settled on as though it were feathers and blood.

"Oh, alas! alas! our beautiful maidens!" cried the old women; "we shall never see them again!"

"Hold your feet with patience, there's old heavy nose out there; go and see if he can hunt for them. He knows well enough to find their flesh, however so little that may be," said an old priest, pointing to a crow who was scratching an ash-heap sidewise with his beak, trying to find something for a morning meal. So the warriors ran down and accosted him.

"O caw!" exclaimed the crow, probing a fresh place, "I am too hungry to go flying around for you stingy fellows. Here I've been ever since perching-time, trying to get a mouthful; but you pick your bones and bowls too clean, be sure for that!"

"Come in, then, grandfather, and we'll give you a smoke and something to eat," said the two warriors.

"Caw, haw!" said the old crow, ruffling up his collar and opening his mouth wide enough to swallow his own head. "Go before!" and he followed them into the dance-court.

"Come in, sit and smoke," said the chief priest, handing the crow a cigarette.

At once the old crow took the cigarette and drew such a big whiff into his throat that the smoke completely filled his feathers, and ever since then crows have been black all over, although before that time they had white shoulder-bands and very blue beaks, which made them look quite fine.

Then the crow suddenly espied an ear of corn under one of the mantles, for this was all the maidens had left; so he made for the corn and flew off with it, saying as he skipped over the houses, "I guess this is all you'll see of the maidens for many a day," and ever since then crows have been so fond of corn that they steal even that which is buried. But bye and bye the old crow came back, saying that he had a "sharp eye for the *flesh* of the maidens, but he could not find any trace of the maidens themselves."

Then the people were very sad with thought, when they suddenly heard Pai'-a-tu-ma joking[6] along the streets as though the whole pueblo were listening to him. "Call him," cried the priests to the warriors, and the warriors ran out to summon Pai'-a-tu-ma.

Pai'-a-tu-ma sat down on a heap of refuse, saying he was about to make a breakfast of it. The warriors greeted him.

"Why and wherefore do you two cowards come not after me?" inquired Pai'-a-tu-ma.

"We do come for you."

"No, you do not."

"Yes, we do."

"Well! I won't go with you," said he, forthwith following them to the dance-court.

"My little children," said he, to the gray-haired priests and mothers, "good evening;"—it was not yet mid-day—"you are all very happy, I see."

"Thou comest," said the chief priest.

"I do not," replied Pai'-a-tu-ma.

"Father," said the chief priest, "we are very sad and we have sought you that we might ask the light of your wisdom."

"Ah, quite as I had supposed; I am very glad to find you all so happy. Being thus you do not need my advice. What may I not do for you?"

"We would that you seek for the corn-maidens, our mothers, whom we have offended, and who have exchanged themselves for nothing in our gaze."

"Oh, *that's all,* is it? The corn maidens are not lost, and if they were I would not go to seek them, and if I went to seek for them I could not find them, and if I found them I would not bring them, but I would tell them you 'did not wish to see them' and leave them where they are not—in the Land of Everlasting Summer, which is not their home. Ha! you have no prayer-plumes here, I observe," said he, picking up one each of the yellow, blue and white kinds, and starting out with the remark—

"I come."

With rapid strides he set forth toward the south. When he came to the mouth of the "Cañon of the Woods," whence blows the wind of summer in spring-time, he planted the yellow-plumed stick. Then he knelt to watch the eagle down, and presently the down moved gently toward the north, as though some one were breathing on it. Then he went yet farther, and planted the blue stick. Again the eagle down moved. So he went on planting the sticks, until very far away he placed the last one. Now the eagle plume waved constantly toward the north.

"Aha!" said Pai'-a-tu-ma to himself, "It is the breath of the corn maidens, and thus shall it ever be, for when *they* breathe toward the northland, thither shall warmth, showers, fertility and health be wafted, and the summer birds shall chase the butterfly out of Summer-land and summer itself, with my own beads and treasures shall follow after." Then he journeyed on, no longer a dirty clown, but an aged, grand god, with a colored flute, flying softly and swiftly as the wind he sought for.

Soon he came to the home of the maidens, whom he greeted, bidding them, as he waved his flute over them, to follow him to the home of their children.

The maidens arose, and each taking a tray covered with embroidered cotton, followed him as he strode with folded arms, swiftly before them.

At last they reached the home of our fathers. Then Pai'-a-tu-ma gravely spoke to the council.

"Behold, I have returned with the lost maidens, yet may they not remain or come again, for you have not loved their beautiful custom—the source of your lives—and men would seek to change the blessings of their flesh itself into suffering humanity were they to remain amongst you.

"As a mother of her own blood and being gives life to her offspring, so have these given of their own flesh to you. Once more their flesh they give to you, as it were their children. From the beginning of the new Sun each year, ye shall treasure their gift, during the moon of the sacred fire, during the moon of the snow-broken boughs, during the moon of the great sand-driving winds, during the moon of the lesser sand-driving winds, ye shall treasure their flesh. Then, in the new soil which the winter winds and water have brought, ye shall bury their flesh as ye bury the flesh of the dead, and as die flesh of the dead decays so shall their flesh decay, and as from the flesh of the dead springs the other being (the soul), so from their flesh shall spring new being, like to the first, yet in eight-fold plenitude. Of this shall ye eat and be bereft of hunger. Behold these maidens, beautiful and perfect are they, and as this, their flesh, is derived from them, so shall it confer on those whom it feeds perfection of person and beauty, as of those whence it was derived." He lifted the tray from the head of the maiden nearest him. She smiled and was seen no more; yet when the people opened the tray it was filled with yellow seed-corn. And so Pai'-a-tu-ma lifted the trays, each in turn, from the heads of the other maidens, and, as he did so, each faded from view. In the second tray the people found blue corn; in the third, red; in the fourth, white; in the fifth, variegated; and in the sixth, black. These they saved, and in the springtime they carefully planted the seeds in separate places. The breaths of the corn maidens blew rain-clouds from their homes in Summer-land, and when the rains had passed away green corn plants grew everywhere the grains had been planted. And when the plants had grown tall and blossomed, they were laden with ears of corn, yellow, blue, red, white, speckled and black. Thus to this day grows the corn, always eight-fold more than is planted, and of six colors, which our women preserve separately during the moons of the sacred fire, snow-broken boughs, great sand-driving winds and lesser sand-driving winds.

It was Pai'-a-tu-ma who found the corn maidens and brought them back. He took the trays from their heads and gave them to the people; hence, when in winter, during the moon of the sacred fire, the priests gather to bless the seed-corn for the coming year, the chief-priest of the *Ne'-we-kwe* hands the trays of corn-seed into the estufa.

Ever since these days, the beautiful corn maidens have dwelt in the Land of Everlasting Summer. This we know. For does not their sweet-smelling breath come from that flowery country, bringing life to their children, the corn-plants? It is the south wind which we feel in spring-time.

Thus was born Tâ-a, or the "Seed of Seeds."

—*From "Zuñi Breadstuff," Millstone 9, no. 1 (1884): 1–3.*

Notes

1. Or the "substance of living flesh." This is exemplified as well as may be by the little cylinders of cuticle and fatty-matter that may be rubbed from the person after bathing. [F.H.C.]

2. It may be seen that the Zuñis have here their own way of accounting for their primitive social organization into *Gentes* and *Phratries*—organizations well nigh universal in the ancient world, as with the society of the early Greeks and Romans, and still prevalent amongst savage tribes of today. [F.H.C.]

3. In ancient times when desirous of making fire, and even today when kindling the sacred flame, the Zuñis produced and still produce, the first spark by drilling with a hard stick like an arrow-shaft into a dry piece of soft root. An arrow-shaft is now used by preference, as it is the emblem of lightning. [F.H.C.]

4. Doubtless this refers to the earthquake. Ruins may sometimes be found in the Southwest, buried like Pompeii beneath the ashes and lava of ancient eruptions, thus pointing either to a remote origin of the Pueblo or a recent cessation of volcanic action in New Mexico and Arizona. [F.H.C.]

5. Unexceptionably this is one of the most beautiful of the native ceremonials, and is one of the few sacred dances of the Zuñis in which women assume the leading part. It is still performed with untiring zeal, usually during each summer, although accompanied by exhausting fasts and abstinences from sleep. Curiously enough, it was observed and admirably, though too briefly described, by Coronado . . . nearly three hundred and fifty years ago.

   It was with this ceremonial that the delighted nation welcomed the water which my party brought in 1882 from the "Ocean of Sunrise." As I was then compelled to join the watch of the priests and elders, I had ample leisure during two sleepless days and nights to gather the above and following story from the song which celebrates the origin of the custom, but which both in length and poetic beauty far surpasses the limits and style of the present paper. [F.H.C.]

6. The *Ne'-we-kwe,* of whom the God of Dew, or Pai'-a-tu-ma, was the first Great Father, are a band of medicine priests belonging, as explained heretofore, to one of the most ancient organizations of the Zuñis. Their medical skill is supposed to be very great—in many cases— and their traditional wisdom is counted even greater. Yet they are clowns whose grotesque and quick-witted remarks amuse most public assemblies of the Pueblo holiday. One of their customs is to speak the opposite of their meaning; hence too, their assumptions of the clown's part at public ceremonials, when really their office and powers are to be reversed. Their grotesque costuming and face-painting are quite in keeping with their assumed characters, and would, were it possible, justify the belief that our own circus clowns were their lineal descendants or copyists. Often so like are human things, though geographically widely severed. [F.H.C.]

8. Red Sky's Scrolls and Origin Lore

SELWYN DEWDNEY

For the reader who is as dubious as I was when I first met James Red Sky Senior I offer this further preliminary account of his Midé credentials.

By Treaty nos. 131 and 132 signed in 1873, 55,000 square miles of territory were surrendered to the Canadian government by representatives of the Ojibway and Saulteaux-Ojibway occupying the Ontario section of the Winnipeg River watershed (bounded on the east by the heights of land into the Albany River system and the Lake Superior watershed), and the southeast corner of Manitoba east of the Winnipeg and Whitemouth Rivers and of a line running south from Whitemouth Lake to the 49th parallel.

The fifth signature on the list of native representatives was that of Powassan(g), pre-eminent among the Lake of the Woods leaders and Grand Shaman of the Midéwewin at Northwest Angle. Some, if not all, of Red Sky's scrolls were originally Powassan's, for Red Sky's mentor and uncle, Baldhead, learned his Midé lore at the feet of the great Northwest Angle Midé master. Further evidence of Red Sky's family standing among the Midé élite is the fact that it was Powassan, still living in 1895, who dreamed Red Sky's proper Ojibway name, Eshkway-keezhik (Last Sky). The name 'Red Sky' is the English translation of his father's personal name, Mushkwaykeezhik. Adopted by 'Baldhead' (Peshkwaykandip) as an English surname, the name Red Sky spread to the other brothers and today is one of the commonest surnames on the Shoal Lake Reserve. The person to whom these pages will refer as Red Sky, to distinguish himself from a younger James in the family connection, signs himself James Red Sky Senior.

The central concern of the Midé oral tradition was with origins: the creation of the world and of man, the origin of death, the introduction of the Midéwewin, and the ancestral origins of the Ojibway people. Instruction was of three sorts: a relatively simple, short term course of preparation for those to be initiated into the lower degrees, more complex information and requirements for those aiming at the higher degrees of initiation, and a long, gruelling apprenticeship which led—with or without actual initiations—to acquisition of the total Midé lore available and the summit of Midé status. Simple or complex, the instruction always included correct ritual procedures, some herbal and medical training, and a drilling in the origin traditions.

For each and all of these purposes a scroll could be devised as a mnemonic aid. On completion of an apprenticeship that extended over a period of many years Red Sky's uncle gave him all of his scrolls. Of the seven, four were mainly concerned with ritualistic details; three dealt with origins. The excerpts that follow are transcribed from tape-recordings made in 1969 of Red Sky's interpretations of his Creation and End scrolls, and of the first section of his Migration scroll. Supplementing these transcriptions are quotations from notes I had taken in previous years, from as early as 1960.

In anticipation of some confusion as the reader is confronted with varying interpretations by the same person of the same scroll, it should be explained that a Midé master was free to make selections from the total lore at his command, producing simple condensed accounts for one purpose or relating in detail one or more variations on the same theme, some of which, taken literally, contradict each other.

In this respect Red Sky was no exception. It would be arbitrary, even arrogant, for me to provide a running commentary, attempting to reconcile every contradiction, fill in all the gaps, or explain each obscurity in his interpretations, even if I could. It is time now for his voice to be heard.

Creation of the World (First Version)

When God first made this world he didn't think or work anything to make this world. He just said this and that, and it happened—just by the word of God. What he wanted [for] this world he took it. So he thought that nobody could live on this world, because nothing went right. There was too much ice. There was too much water. Nobody could live on this earth. Well, he said he'd try a second time. This [referring to the second unit in his Creation scroll] is the second world. And he tried and he knew he was going to make [accomplish] it. So after the second time there was still too much ice—too much ice and too much water. Nobody can live like that. It didn't take him one day or one week or one month. I was told that it took him probably 2000 years—maybe 4000 years.

Well, he was trying, but it didn't look very good. Nobody can live on this earth that way. Too much water, too much ice. He knew he was going to make it—make this world all right. So he tried it a third time. He tried it and he made it go. And he was convinced he was going to make it. The earth looked pretty good. Not so much water, not so much ice. So he tried it again. That was the third earth. After trying the third time he tried the fourth time.

When he tried it the fourth time everything went nice. The hills were green, the water was nice and the streams were running. The trees grew—the leaves on the trees—everything was beautiful. When he looked among the hills everything was very nice. Well, he thought, it was going to be perfect—perfect to live on. It looked very nice that anybody could live on it.

The fact that in all the surviving origin lore there is no counterpart to this account of the creation of the world might cast some doubt on its place in the Midé tradition were it not for a single hint from Kohl (1860, 150) whose informant, Loonfoot, interpreted eight footprints drawn on one of his birchbark records as 'the footsteps of the Great Otter, which soon after the creation of the world ran through the water and across the world. At the first movement it stepped on ice, at the second into a swamp, at the third into water, while at the fourth flowers sprang up.'

Creation of the World (Second Version)

On scanning Red Sky's Creation scroll (Figure 1) for hints of the first version one finds very little that relates to it. An earlier version that Red Sky dictated to me in 1967 offers a quite different perspective. During the earlier interviews, however, I had limited the interpretations to writing on a blueprint of his scrolls his comments on each figure.

Reading the scroll from left to right, the partially obscured Bear's head symbolizes 'God.' On another occasion Red Sky explained. 'The Bear is the strongest animal, so it came to represent God. A bear can do *any* thing.' The pictographic preface to the whole sequence means, 'God opens a way for you.' A 'tree' almost totally obscured by damage to the scroll comes next. 'When you enter the Midéwewin you have to pass through a big log which closes behind . . .'

Of the ten figures grouped around the left side of the first circle four are 'birds,' four are 'animals,' the dominant human figure is 'God,' and the lesser one 'the man who works for God.'

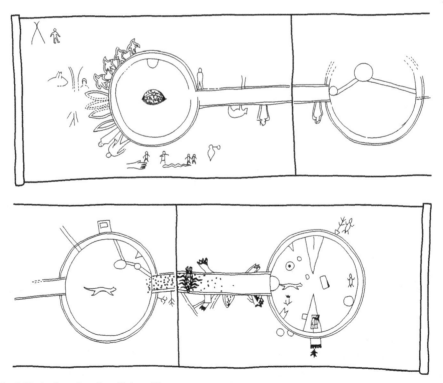

FIGURE 1   Red Sky's Creation Scroll (GAI-2)

The first circular unit was again identified as 'God's first attempt to create the world.' The object in the centre was explained as 'God gave the Megis—that's a shell—for body health.' Pointing to the small inward projection from the upper edge of the circle, 'He seen this point,' adding, 'in his first creation God put hills, rivers, water, etcetera.'

On the pathway leading to the second unit the Bear is again 'God,' and the three human figures are, from the left, 'the man that works for God' . . . 'the Oskahbewiss (assistant), the man who looks after everything,' and 'an elder, to show people the way.'

The second unit was labelled 'God's second attempt.' The first small circle on the interior path is 'where he stopped to look around'; at the second, 'God stopped there. It wasn't fit to live in.'

The third unit was 'God's third attempt.' The path to it was 'the right way.' Proceeding clockwise around the circle from the entering path, the double line projecting outwards

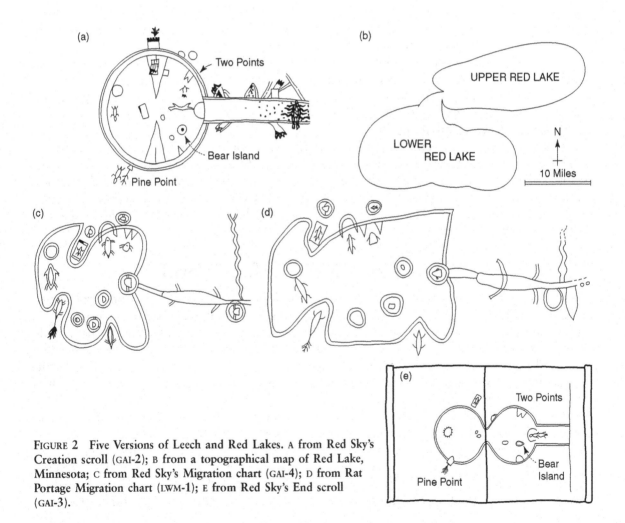

FIGURE 2   **Five Versions of Leech and Red Lakes. A from Red Sky's Creation scroll (GAI-2); B from a topographical map of Red Lake, Minnesota; C from Red Sky's Migration chart (GAI-4); D from Rat Portage Migration chart (LWM-1); E from Red Sky's End scroll (GAI-3).**

signifies 'He found out this was a river,' the rectangular form 'God saw that, thought it was a cloud [on the horizon], came close and saw it was a hill.' The interior detail showed pathways joining small circles that mark 'places where God stopped and looked around.' The animal near the centre is the Great Otter. 'God put the Otter there to bring life to the people.' The projecting tree just past the exit pathway is 'an oak tree,' and next to it is 'a pine.'

In this version, after God's disappointment with his first attempt is noted there is no further mention of failures. The fourth unit, however, is labelled 'God's last attempt to make the world: it was perfect.' In that unit the Otter, 'God's representative, the messenger,' appears again. Apparently in this version Red Sky's mention of a 'God' strangely unfamiliar with a world of his own making, really refers to the Otter seeking the people, to whom—as we shall see in other accounts—he was commissioned to bring the Midé message.

In the fourth unit (see Figure 2a), although it is labelled as the final successful creation, a transition has been made from theology to geography. Even the character of the pathway has changed. The zigzag lines on it indicated 'rapids,' the divergent lines just below indicate that the Otter 'went up that river and had to come back.' In an earlier explanation Red Sky told me 'There were no Indians there, he had to come back.'

'Then he made a portage and saw this long stretch of water. "If I stretch myself as long as this water then they will believe in me." So he made it.' The outward projections from the two ends of this passage were 'God's legs' and 'God's arms,' and a circular projection into the fourth unit was 'God's head.' The form superimposed over God's right arm was 'a reminder not to leave anything out.'

On his arrival at the end of the long stretch 'God looked around. He saw a great big lake.' Red Sky admitted, 'I don't know where that is,' but a moment later provided a substantial clue. The two triangular forms nearly meeting in the centre of the circle represent arms of land. 'At first there was no opening here, but God broke through. The water is still a bit muddy today.' Then he added, 'That's two big lakes in the States with a narrows between—*somewhere close.*'

Identity of 'God's Perfect World'

That was the first exciting inkling I had that the fourth unit of the Creation scroll represented an actual place. When I looked in my atlas—sure enough—there were two large lakes joined by a narrows in Minnesota, a mere fifty miles south of Lake of the Woods: Upper and Lower Red Lake. But I was puzzled by the places Red Sky named, features that had nothing to do with Red Lake: 'Two Points . . . Bear Island . . . and Pine Point.' On a hunch I examined Leech Lake, another 50 miles to the southeast (Figure 3). There they were, all three features!

Ever since my first good look at Red Sky's Migration scroll I had puzzled over a lake at the end of it (and of all other Migration scrolls I had found). This lake, and one from one of the others, shown in Figures 2c and d, although they fail to identify a Bear Island, clearly indicate the double point, and indicate Pine Point with the form of a tree (attached to the local manito). The highly formalized and decorative End scroll not only identified the two points, but marked Bear Island with the 'sacred dots' frequently used in Midé pictography to denote an especially reverenced feature. All through the latter half of the ninteenth century Leech Lake and Red Lake were the most active and prestigious centres in Minnesota, confirming the closeness of the Lake of the Woods tradition to the Midé mainstream. The fourth unit of Red Sky's Creation scroll and the figure in the End scroll are both *composites of the two centres.*

Red Sky explained that the End scroll was used only to be 'read' at the end of the Midé ceremonies when the public was admitted into the Midéwegun to share in the final Megis ritual. I suspect that the fourth unit of his Creation scroll was similarly separate, but eventually sewn to the sections containing the first three units, for reasons that will be examined in the next chapter.

There is further evidence of alterations to the original Creation scroll. In the upper and lower left corners are two 'pictographic footnotes' so faintly scratched on the bark that when Red Sky searched for them in vain under the light of a coal oil lamp I thought his memory had misled him. In the morning, however, with the bark flat on the table by the window the slanting rays of the rising sun threw the lines into clear, though delicate relief. In the

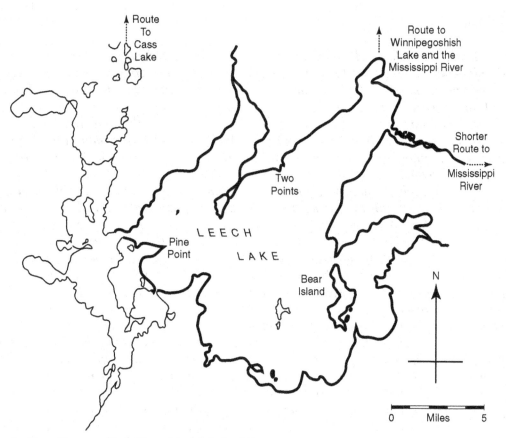

FIGURE 3   From Topographical Map of Leech Lake, Minnesota

upper corner a tiny human figure could be discerned, standing beside a conical wigwam. Below the first world was a sequence of figures relating to the creation of man. Both 'foot-notes' were interpreted in full detail, as recorded in the 1969 transcriptions that follow.

Creation of Man

So he thought he'd make a man. So he spat on the ground. And afterwards he picked the ground up, moistened it, and he held it in his hand. After he held it in his hand for a long time until it was warm, when he opened his hand there stood a man. And he laid his hand on it and breathed on it. So he laid it down on the ground. Then that man stood on the ground. Then he said . . . he spoke to him, and he spoke back to him. When the man spoke there was flames coming out of his mouth. And when he looked his eyes glistened. Lights came out of his eyes. Flames came out of his mouth. He says 'Well, that's not very good, because he'll be the same as I am if he breathes like that all the time—God's way.'

Here Red Sky is discussing the figure at the extreme right with the power (like God's) coming out of him.

'He would be able to do anything [God continued]: soften rocks, tear trees into shreds—pull them all out like hair. That wouldn't be very good if he was like that.' So he put his hand on him, to cut him down a little bit—there was too much high pressure in him of the godliness he had in him.

So he let him go wandering around—around the earth, through streams, forests, lakes, creeks—everything. All through that. 'Well,' he said to the man. 'I'm going to give you a name—Ogahbi'ohsahtung (Everlasting-walking-through-this-world)—that's your name.'

So, after a while wandering around, wandering around and around this beautiful world, he had pity on him being alone all the time, day and night all alone. So he put him to sleep. After he put him to sleep he got the liver out of him. I was told there are four layers to the liver. He took one layer of the liver out of him, took it out and he held it there in his hand while he was sleeping. And when he opened his hand there was a woman. Oh, a very nice woman. Her hair was right down to her knees. As she looked her eyes had a gleam—sparkled. And as she stood there her bosom—her teats—were sticking out far. And God thought by her teats a woman, a human being would rise there, from her teats.

And as she stood there, this beautiful woman, the man woke up. He was sur-prised to see her standing right there before him. She looked at him and he looked at her—looked all over. He thought she wasn't the same as he was. She was a lot different. After awhile they come together, started talking to each other and they got acquainted. It was [a long time] after that that they started sleeping together. They wandered around in the forest, the streams, creeks and lakes, and so they couldn't part from each other. After awhile God looked at them and he said 'I'm going to pour a little water on them so they won't forget everything, what I've done for them.' So he sprinkled a little water out of a little cloud that passed by. And that is how he baptized them.

After awhile Ogahbi'ohsahtung was working over on one side and she was working on that side. There came a great big snake right before her, says to her . . . 'Come here. I want to talk to you.'

'No,' she said, 'I'm not going to talk to you.'

'I want you to go over there and get Ogahbi'ohsahtung and go back in the woods there.'

'No,' she said, 'We were told not to do anything like that. Because God knows everything. God was there. He told us not to. There'll be a time when he'll tell us when we will get together.'

So after a long coaxing . . . trying to reach Ogahbi'ohsahtung . . . she was too anxious to get connections with him sexually. So he didn't want to do it. Well, when this snake coaxed her she didn't take too much coaxing because she already thought that. She was very anxious to get connections with him. So as soon as she was tempted . . . well, everything broke off, as if it were two bottles, one on top of the other, and one fell off. That's how anxious she was. Now this one fell off. She went over with him back in the bushes.

In the Genesis account, from which a large part of this tale was obviously borrowed, there is a prophecy that there would be enmity thereafter between the snake and the woman's descendants. In Red Sky's version this is given an ingenious twist. 'By bruising the heel' (here Red Sky is referring to a biblical phrase) 'the Snake caused the woman to have periods monthly.'

In the taped interview Red Sky went right on with a story to which there was no reference in any of his scrolls. In what follows the words 'family marks' refer to the identifying pictographs used as signatures in the treaties, engraved on personal possessions, and used in trail messages.

Origin of the Dodem (Totem) System

The world was full of people at that time already, after the creation of a man and a woman—full of people. So when God looked at them they were so wicked they didn't follow any of the ways that he wanted them to live. There was all kinds of wickedness, such as fornication, sexuality . . . all these things. They even went together with their sisters, aunts, and the men went together with their mothers. It was a very bad state.

So he wanted to punish them. So the thought of this great Thunderbird, and he told this Thunderbird to make up a great big storm. Because these people worked together they were all in one place. And when they got together these Thunderbirds came. High winds blew. Thunder, lightning, rain—every thing came down. So these people ran to get shelter all over the place. They couldn't find no shelter. Their places of abode couldn't hold the storm that came upon them.

Well, after awhile when everything had quietened they started to talk to each other. They couldn't understand each other when they talked together. They couldn't understand each other at all. One person said something, they didn't understand it.

So they all went—one family this way, one family another way. One family east, north, how far they went nobody knows. So when these families that went east started talking together they started to understand each other. The families that went south and north started to understand each other. So afterwards they made family marks, like Caribou [Red Sky's totem] and a Sturgeon, Moose, Elk, things like that. And all the birds of the air, their family marks.

One might dismiss Red Sky's accounts of man's temptation and fall, and of totemic origins as mere garbled versions of biblical lore that he himself inserted into the Midé tradition. To do this, however, would be to overlook the extent to which the Midéwewin from early times adapted a number of Christian concepts and biblical details for its own purposes. Kohl (1860), for instance, in a conversation he recorded, was astonished to hear Loonfoot refer to the Tower of Babel, the Flood, and even the Romans. Loonfoot's wife was a Crane, who claimed, Kohl was told, that the Crane's lineage reached back to the Flood and their name was recorded 'dans les livres des Romains.' Hearing this last reference Kohl smiled incredulously.

But Loonfoot protested: 'Non, non, Monsieur, sérieusement on a trouvé déjà à la destruction de la Tour de Babel tous les noms [totems] qui sont à présent parmi nous.'

The Ojibway word 'totem,' pronounced *dodem* by the southern Ojibway, has been adopted universally to refer to systems used by many preliterate cultures to prevent 'inbreeding' and incest, or more positively, to ensure a flow of fresh genetic strains from outside the gene pool of small isolated bands. Red Sky makes this point amply clear. In the absence of tribal organization the clan system provided close links with other bands, for two members of the same clan, even if they had no blood relationship, regarded each other as close relatives, regardless of how far apart their respective bands might wander.

My own first acquaintance with the strength and significance of totemic identity was a statement by the wife of the late James Horton on the Manitou Reserve near Emo, Ontario. She informed my wife and me that she could not eat sturgeon. Moreover, she knew whenever a sturgeon was caught in the Rainy River, because *she herself was a Sturgeon.*

The Manito Council (Two Versions)

When I asked Red Sky to interpret the birds and other figures shown around the first unit of his Creation scroll he gave me the following account, transcribed from the 1969 tape recording.

When this world was full of human beings it got so all the people were dying off— dying off like that and God didn't know what to do about it. So he thought he'd teach them some way to worship him. So later, when he got this all organized he said, 'I'll have them meeting at the centre of a . . . of a different continent across the water. That's where I'll have this meeting. So where I think God took it was in Palestine. And so when God got this organized he brought all these birds and animals—all the living creatures in the world—to this one place. So then they had a meeting.

This was one of his versions of the origin of the Manito Council. The second was an interpretation of the first unit of the Migration scroll (Figure 4), where five figures surround the circle.

'So God thought, "Well, I want these people to worship me. I don't know how to get them to worship me." So he called a meeting of all the birds—all the birds and all the creatures. And so they had a meeting to talk about it—somewhere across the Big Water, where this Manito was. So he said to this meeting, "Now who's going to take it? Who's going to take it across to the people?" Well, the Bear was there. He says, "I'll take it across to the people."'

The Bear's Mission

Now the Council's work was done and everything depended on the Bear. And, just as it took God three tries before his fourth successful effort to create a 'beautiful world,' so the Migration scroll records the Bear's four efforts to break through the barriers between himself and that same world (Figure 4).

So when he went out, this Everlasting Life that he was carrying was very heavy—very heavy. He could hardly walk. When he put his arms out he stuck his arms up to his elbows. Same with his hind feet; he stuck them right to his knees.

After walking a little ways he came to a wall. He couldn't go anywhere. He didn't know what to do. So he stuck his tongue out. Then his tongue went through as if

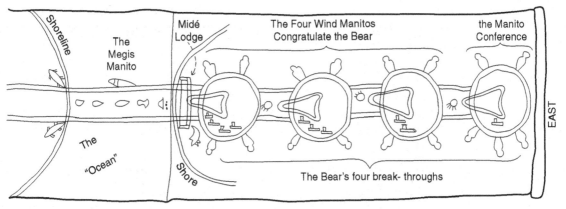

FIGURE 4   The Bear's Four Break-Throughs, from Red Sky's Migration Chart (GAI-4)

it were a bullet shot out of a rifle. It went right through to the other side. He went right through the little hole and then came out on the other side and took this Life—this Everlasting Life that he was carrying. After looking around he didn't see no earth—nothing. So he got out, he found another wall. He did the same thing— stuck his tongue out and it went right through as if it were a bullet shot out of a rifle. And in that hole he went through with this Pack he had—heavy Everlasting Life. And when these people saw this [here Red Sky pointed to the four manitos stationed around each of the introductory circles on the Migration scroll] the manito at the east, the manito at the south, manito at the west and manito at the north, they thanked him for the work he did.

Well, that wasn't the end. That was the second time. Well he started out . . . and he found another wall. That was the third time. And he did the same thing. He stuck out his tongue [Figure 5] and it went through as if shot out of a gun. Then he went through here. And when he got on the other side it happened the same thing. When he went through he did the same thing. That was the fourth time he did the same thing.

It is important, for later comparisons with other sources, to understand this passage, and its relation to the pictographs illustrated here. The four introductory units represent the Bear's four break-throughs. Stationed around each circle are the Wind manitos, the extra figure above the first circle representing God. The five together *also*, as I have mentioned, represented the Manito Council. The triangular abstraction overlapping the edge of each circle represents the Bear's head as it breaks through each barrier. Next we are allowed a glimpse of the whole Bear, just as he emerged after the fourth break-through.

After he was there—when he got out—he seen this little place [the small vertical rectangle]. He thought he'd go into this little place, what we call today Midéwegun [Midé lodge]. So towards the east there was a little door, and a little door to the west. After he got in he took eight steps. Then he took out a little tree and he planted it. He stuck the little tree into the middle of the Midéwegun. After a while, a Thunderbird came and landed on this tree.

'This is where I'm going to listen to the Indian whenever he calls upon God. When anything—some kind of sickness or some kind of bad luck happens—he'll have God. I'll listen to everything right from here.'

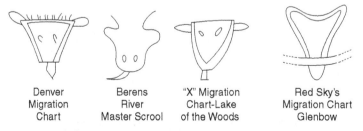

Denver	Berens	"X" Migration	Red Sky's
Migration	River	Chart-Lake	Migration Chart
Chart	Master Scrool	of the Woods	Glenbow

FIGURE 5   **Various Renderings of the Bear's Tongue, from Four Migration Charts**

This is what we see on this tree. There's a bird on the tree. And a little later there came a great big Rock. God said, 'This is the foundation of this Midéwegun. This is the foundation. I'll uphold this as long as the earth lasts. It won't fall down. Nobody will turn it over, can't take it down. If the Indian fights for it I'll still be here to protect it.'

This completes Red Sky's interpretations of the first part of the origin section of his Migration scroll. The Bear has successfully carried the Pack of Life through the first obstacles and has been strengthened for the task ahead by passing through the Midéwegun, that is, by himself undergoing initiation into the Midéwewin.

And after he came out [of the Midéwegun] he came down, he came to the shore of a Big Water. After a little while, while he was walking back and forth there, he didn't know what to do. So finally he heard someone talking to him.

'What have you got there?'

'Oh, I've got something I've got to take to the Indians, across this Big Water.'

'Well,' he said, 'I'm the one that can do it.' This is Megis, the Shell—seashell.

So they started unloading and reloading. They tell me it looked as if a white man was loading a great big ship. That's what it looked like when they transferred what he was carrying.

So he went out—the Megis—he came out of the water. He had followed the bottom of the ocean. And after a little while he came up. When he came up he looked around. He seen this great big hill. After he looked around there was a small narrows where he went through. On the right hand side he seen this great big hill—high . . . high. So he thought he'd go up and look around. So he found another manito there and he left word with him that wants help—that has sickness or disease or misfortune—is unlucky—he'll go to him. He'll fix him up.

Well, after a bit he came up, looked around. He didn't see nothing. No land anywhere—couldn't see no land. And he went down again and followed along the bottom of the ocean and came up again. Still he didn't see nothing—no land in sight nowhere. So, after awhile he went down again. He did the same thing—followed along the bottom of the ocean, came up again, went along there. So he'd come up again. Looking around, he seen land just as if it was a little string going along there. That was land.

There are three points to note here. It is now the Megis, not the Bear, who is carrying the message. Apparently, on his first emergence the Megis manito gave the Midé message to a local manito: that is, he set up a Midé lodge as he had done before he went down to the shore. Proceeding, he sighted land on his *fourth* emergence, just as the Bear broke through the fourth barrier, and God made four attempts to create the world.

'Well,' he said, 'I'm glad.' He was glad he found land. Well, he didn't go down this time. He just went along [on the surface] and he seen this river coming down into the ocean. Well, he thought he'd stop there and look around.

The Cutfoot Legend (First Version)

At this point, although there is no break in Red Sky's narrative, a new theme takes over whose significance will become clear only when we explore it in the next chapter as we become acquainted with other origin tales. Here the Megis goes ashore, and:

Well, he seen a little wigwam—a little tent. He seen a baby just standing—just holding himself up. He couldn't stand up—the only thing he could do by standing was hold himself up. That's how young this baby was—maybe one year. So he took this little baby, picked it up and went back across the ocean. And he took him there before this manito—this Midé manito. He told him he took this little baby, and there he was. He [the Midé manito] taught him everything about how to worship God through the Midéwewin. Taught him until he was a great big man.

So then these people who lost their baby were very sorrowful, crying day and night. They looked around the whole continent, crying—looked it over, trying to find their baby. So they went back to their tent while they were crying there. It took them quite a number of years. The old man was getting pretty grey, the lady was pretty grey, too. And they felt sorrowful.

They were sitting there sorrowful and a man stood before them.

'What's the crying about? What's all the crying about?'

'Oh,' they told him, 'We lost our little baby—a little baby boy.'

'Oh, don't think anything about it. I'm the little baby. I'm the one you lost.'

They went and hugged and kissed him. They were glad to see that little baby back again.

'Well,' he told them, 'I'm not staying here. I'm going back to where this Midéwewin came from.' So he left them there.

And when you dream about going to Midé [i.e., to be initiated] you want to sacrifice a few little things. This is the man who thinks about you when you're sick or have bad luck all the time. He looks upon you. He has mercy upon you. He pities you for having all the troubles. He comes to you in dreams, and that's where you [qualify to] enter the Midéwewin.

One point here may easily be missed: that even the loss of so valued a possession as a child would not be too high a price for the benefits of the Midé health-giving rites, so why not make some small sacrifices—that is, make worthwhile gifts to the Midé officials who will initiate you.

The Cutfoot Legend (Second Version)

In the upper left corner of the Creation scroll a small human figure stands beside a wigwam. This pictograph could remind us not only of the episode just described, but of the second version of a myth which we shall encounter again. For both versions have features in common that I believe reach back to an early period—perhaps the actual origin—of the Midéwewin.

There was a little boy and his father and mother. They were living close to the lakeshore. So he [the boy] was whittling away there. He was making a bow and arrow. So this man went to this little boy. And this little boy said to his Mother and Dad, 'Mother, there's a stranger here.'

'Is that so? Who is that talking to this little boy?'

He said, 'Will you get your bow and arrow ready today?'

'Oh yes, I'll have it ready today.'

So the father and mother came out and spread this cloth where they use a mat to eat on. Oh, they gave him something to eat and they noticed then that he wouldn't eat anything. He wouldn't take nothing at all that was set before him. And then, after they were through eating this man asked them, 'How far is the next village from here?'

'Oh, it'll take you quite a long time, because it's quite a long way. It'll take you two hands before sunset.' That's how they measured the time—about two hands before sunset.

'Could I have this little boy to take me a little ways before I get to the next village?'

'Oh yes. That'll be all right,' they tell him.

So he got the little boy and went out started walking. And it was pretty tough walking because there was no road—they travelled in the bush. After going a little ways—Oh boy! He got sweating. He got tired walking through the bush. After going a little more he asked if they could rest a bit.

'Oh yes. Yes, we'll rest a little bit.'

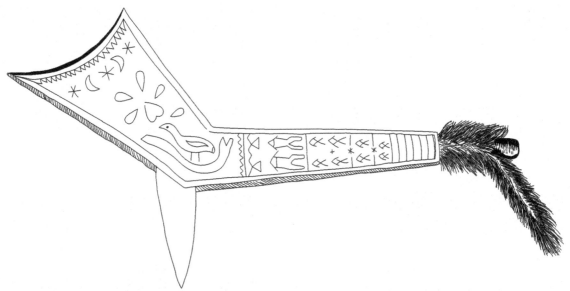

FIGURE 6   Dream Symbols Carved on Tomahawk, after Kohl

Then after they rested a little bit they started off again. After they started off he noticed he wasn't sweating at all. He was walking above the ground. He was walking in the air. Oh boy, he thought. He told this man, 'I think I'll stop here.'

'Wait a minute,' he said. And he started to teach him everything. Teach him about God, God's ways. Teach him about roots—herbal remedies. He taught him the remedy for whatever sickness he got. He told him about what he would take—what roots he would take.

So after this the little boy went home. Boy, was he glad!

This is the man that knew every *thing. Afterwards when he got to be a big man he was the head of everything [in charge of the whole ceremony]. He had a knowledge because he was taught the way God had fixed everything up [solved the problems of sickness and death by providing the Midéwewin].*

This is the last of Red Sky's more comprehensive interpretations and associated lore, with the exception of his comments on the main body of his Migration chart. These other comments and explanations, however, would lose much of their meaning without some familiarity with what has survived of the oral tradition from other sources.

9. Other Origin Tales and Scrolls

SELWYN DEWDNEY

Kohl's interest in the art of the villagers at La Pointe and his very human curiosity led him to insights into the Ojibway mystique that few other observers have matched. For example (1860, 296–7) there was the occasion when he noticed the engraved decoration on the wooden handle of a tomahawk (Figure 6) and asked its owner what the symbols signified. Surprisingly enough, in view of the many reports that significant dreams must be kept secret lest they lose their power, the man not only revealed that the pictographs represented the results of his boyhood dream quest during which he fasted for ten days, but interpreted their content, refusing only to reveal 'all the circumstances and course' of the dream. But he did reveal the intimacy that linked him with the powerful manito he had acquired in the dream as his lifetime personal guardian.

'I often think of this face, this eagle,' he said, 'and I not only think of it, but I speak to it in a loud voice.'

No better glimpse could be offered into the heart of the Ojibway survival system, inherited from ancestral life styles that were shared by many other Amerindian societies. Here, before examining the origin traditions that await our attention, it will be useful to take a further look into the sources of Ojibway identity and of Midé mythology.

The Manito World

All-pervasive in the oral tradition of the Midéwewin lie the concept of the manito world and the central role of the dream. Throughout this study of the sacred scrolls, and long before that in numerous interviews with Cree and Ojibway elders to learn what beliefs were associated with the rock paintings, it became more and more obvious to me that the word *manito* cannot be translated into English. Renderings such as 'spirit' or even 'god' reduce seriously the combination of substance, power and reality that the native word can express. For in the manito world, accessible only through the doorway of the dreams, were vested all the powers that determined whether the hunter and his family would survive or perish. To enter this world was to step *into*, not out of, the *real* world.

The dream, therefore, was man's most meaningful experience. A child's name might be dreamed up—literally—by a prestigious elder. And when the male child reached puberty he was sent into isolation, to build himself a tree nest, or find a secluded rock platform, where he fasted until he achieved the dream state that would reveal to him the manito who would be available for life to help him meet the crises of survival.

In a land where every winter brought close the threat of starvation a strong sharing code developed, a moral compulsion on the successful hunter to see that the weak, and even wandering strangers, were fed. So the manitos were conceived of as beings who might normally be indifferent to human welfare, but were vulnerable to the appeal of a human being who lay weak and helpless before them without food or water, exposed to the elements and alone.

Psychologically the boyhood dream quest prepared the youth for the stress of his future role as provider. Among the northern Algonkian-speakers the nature of the land and distribution of the food supply created a pattern of family groups subsisting on moose or caribou in isolated winter hunting territories, emerging after spring break-up to join other families in brief summer village gatherings around food concentrations: fish spawning grounds, berry picking areas, and—in the south—wild rice fields at harvest time. Even in summer there were animal epidemics and population cycles, forest fires and unseasonable weather that could threaten the food supply. But in the winter a spring that came too early, or too late, an unpredictable shift in caribou migrations, or prolonged blizzards—a dozen alternatives could bring disaster.

More than once in his lifetime the hunter as he ranged the frozen lakes and silent snow-laden forests would be stalked by the dreaded Windigo, grim allegory of winter starvation and the threat of cannibalism. Paradoxically, the more desperate the hunter's state the closer he would feel he was to earning the pity of the supernaturals. So he had the faith to muster his last resources for the final effort to survive; and his dreams—far from being impractical flights of imagination—gave him the self-confidence that was the most *practical* necessity of his life.

There was no limit to the manito concept. If in his boyhood dream the hunter had encountered and conversed with a mere stone or a cloud, that object became his manito guardian. Theoretically all supernatural beings were equal; in practice some were more, others less, powerful. The manitos, therefore, could be graded in terms of power and status. Very loosely, one might divide them into four sorts of supernatural beings.

At the lowest level there were the powers potential in the simplest of natural objects, whether organic or inorganic. At a much higher level were the manitos that Hallowell (1942, 7) refers to as the 'masters.' Writing about the Saulteaux-Ojibway of the Lake Winnipeg region he explains that 'in the case of animal and plant species there is in theory a "master" for each group, for bears as well as for birch trees.' The concept of a 'master' has always reminded me of the Platonic theory of reality, in which the 'doorness' of a door—the Idea out of which all doors emerge—is more real than any individual manifestation of the Idea. So, individual rabbits might come and go—live, die, and be eaten or rot—but the Great Rabbit was the source of all rabbits, and as long as he was respected in prescribed rituals he would continue to supply the temporary, edible manifestations according to man's need. Even among the Source Beings, as I prefer to call them, there were higher and lower ranks, partly determined by their importance as a food supply, partly reaching deep into traditional mysteries. Thus, though the Bear manito ranked high as a food animal, it ranked far higher than the Moose or Sturgeon manitos, as we shall see. As Hallowell puts it: 'in practice certain masters have assumed greater prominence than others, e.g. *mikinak*, the master of the great turtles . . . [of] the conjuring lodge [or Shaking Tent].'

Earlier (1942, 5) Hallowell contrasts the realities of the Saulteaux-Ojibway world with the Western concept of what is real, using as an example

> *a belief in the Thunder Birds who live in the South during the winter and spend spring and summer in the North. When you hear them they are pursuing snakes that live on the earth . . . They [the snakes] are* water monsters *[italics added] living in the lakes and swamps and some of the Indians have seen them . . . Since from our point of view thunder is a part of their physical environment and monster snakes are not, we might be inclined to make a distinction between them . . . I prefer to consider both the Thunder Birds and the monster snakes as part of the behavioral environment of these Indians and to ignore any such distinction. Both are 'real' in the sense that they have actual effects upon behavior.*

In the broader Ojibway context there was a tendency, never explicit, to distinguish between manitos referred to in the plural—as in Thunderbirds—and the same manito as a singular entity—as in *the* Thunderbird. In this sense *the* Thunderbird symbolizes all threats to man from the sky, especially lightning, and may be grouped with the Great Lynx (or Lion) Misshipeshu, associated with death by drowning, and the dreaded Windigo. Other manitos symbolizing the uncontrollable forces of nature are the four Wind manitos (East, South, West, and North) and the May-maygwessiwuk, mysterious denizens of shorewater rocks who can affect local weather on the open lakes.

Of the five great beings who might be referred to as the 'super-manitos'—Misshipeshu, the Thunderbird, the Sacred Bear, the Great Turtle and the Windigo—only the first three have a place in the Midéwewin; but some Midé practitioners were also skilled in the Shaking-tent rites (page 121). Here, too, there is great confusion; but at the deepest level, the most dangerous and therefore the most powerful of all the manitos were the Bear and the Lion, with roots reaching back into prehistory.

A confusing aspect of both Cree and Ojibway lore is the role of the shaman-trickster folk-hero, known to the southern Ojibway as Nanabozho, in the north as Wissakachauk. As the subject of hilarious and frequently earthy humour in hundreds of tales still circulating he was a very human figure, frequently misusing his supernatural powers to the point where he got himself into embarassing situations.

Ruth Landes (1968) accounts for the confusions and discrepancies that are typical of the Midé oral tradition by the Ojibway respect for *any* authoritative source of information about the supernatural. A Midé apprentice, she was told, was expected to memorize everything his instructor passed on to him, with uncritical zeal. Interruptions and questions were regarded as presumptuous and irrelevant, even dangerous, for to cross a shaman in any way was to invite destruction by sorcery. The shaman himself was equally uncritical of information he acquired from his colleagues in exchange for appropriate gifts. All such material, no matter how inconsistent or illogical it might seem, added to his status and manito power.

In any case Ojibway thinking was so allegorical, subtle and indirect that contradictions were not seen as such, but rather as hiding deeper levels of meaning that were the more powerful for being difficult to correlate with other information.

To minimize the confusion of origin accounts that follow I have grouped them into six categories: 1 *In the beginning*—creation of the world, of man and the animals; 2 *The origin of death*—and manito concern for the people; 3 *The Manito Council*—and appointment of an agent; 4 *The agent's breakthrough*—and initiation; 5 *The agent's mission*—and major stopping places; 6 *The visionary revelation*—Sun-boy and the Cutfoot legends.

In the Beginning

The widely current legend of how Nanabozho re-created the world after the flood let loose by Misshipeshu after the *fourth* of his helpers brought up a small scoop of mud is not included in the Midé tradition. It seems that there was far more interest in the creation of man than in that of the earth. One tale, other than Red Sky's account, was recorded by Howard (1965, 126) whose Bungi-Ojibway informant, Standing Chief, told him that the world was made by a spirit who took a piece of earth and kept blowing on it until it reached the earth's present size.

Standing Chief also related how the same spirit took a piece of clay and made a man by the same means, stopping when he felt that 'If you were larger it would be hard for you to make clothing for yourselves.' Another informant told Howard that Nanapus (Nanabozho) was the first man. The Bungi (Little) Ojibway were a branch of the more northerly migrations, probably from the northwest shore of Lake Superior, who moved out on the prairies in the early historical period, adopting the Plains culture of their Siouan and Cree neighbours, but maintaining many of the practices and beliefs—including variants of the Midéwewin—from their original bush milieu.

Hoffman (1883, 172) was told by his chief informant Sikassige at White Earth, Minnesota, that 'Dzhe Manitou' created two men and two women who had, at first, 'no power of thought or reason. He took them in his hands so that they should multiply; he paired them, and from this sprung the Indians.' The faculty of reason was added later. Landes (1968, 90) had another version, from Everwind. The great Spirit picked up some dirt, shut his hand over it, opened it, and there was a woman. He then gave the woman a man.

Hole in the Sky, however, offered Landes a very different story. In the beginning the Snake manito wrapped himself around the 'primal wigwam,' shading one side. Misshipeshu, the Underwater 'Lion,' got suspicious of the Snake's intentions and asked him why he was doing this. In reply the Snake grasped some dirt, opened his hand, and there was a black Indian. The lion knocked the dirt out of the Snake's hand, closed his own over some sand, and there stood an Indian 'shining like glass.' This referred to an early belief that originally men were protected from disease and death by a smooth, highly reflective coating like a fish's scales, that covered the whole body. According to Hole in the Sky the male was created first. In Everwind's second version the Great Spirit picked up some dirt and shut his hand on it till he felt something moving, opened it, and discovered a human being. So he placed him on the earth and told him to take four breaths. This created the lower air. Another four breaths created the earth and a final four produced the upper air.

Kohl (1860, 195) recorded that while Kitchi manito was walking along the beach surveying his creation, he 'noticed a being coming out of the water entirely covered with silver-glistening scales like a fish, but otherwise formed like a man.' The man appeared to be suffering deeply from loneliness, so Kitchi manito modelled some company for him 'nearly like what he had seen the man to be, and also covered her body with silver-glistening scales. Then he breathed life into her,' and set about arranging for the two to get together. The tale thereafter follows Genesis closely except for the finale. To punish the pair for their disobedience 'the silver scales with which the bodies had been covered fell off; only twenty of these scales remained on, but lost their brilliance, ten on the fingers and ten on the toes.'

Origin of Death

From Everwind's account too (Landes 1968, 92–3) it is clear that after losing the scales the human race became subject to disease and death.

Skinner picked up (1911, 157–9) a Bungi-Ojibway story that death had its origin in the jealousy of the Rattlesnake, who manoeuvred his closest friend the Natawa snake into a contest to see whose venom was the more powerful. Waylaying two youths—who were also very close to each other—each snake bit one. Death came into the world with that of the youth the Natawa snake had bitten.

Warren (1957, 43–4) reported an origin tale more central to the Midé tradition: how, 'when the earth was new, the An-ish-in-aub-ag congregated on the shores of a great salt water. From the bosom of the deep there suddenly appeared six beings in human form, who entered their wigwams.' One of them kept his eyes covered but finally had so strong an urge to look at the humans they were visiting that he looked at a man, who died instantly. The dangerous Manito was sent back; the other five remained, to become the original totemic clans of the Ojibway. But the damage had been done. The first man had died.

Whatever the origins of suffering and death, almost all the accounts relate that there was deep manito concern. Something must be done to alleviate human misery. Credit for this reaction, however, goes in different directions. In most accounts Nanabozho, the trickster-hero, plays a key role, but there is a surprising division of opinion as to whether his role was positive or negative. In one version, as we shall see, he was indirectly responsible for death. Regardless, the upshot of this concern was the calling of a Council by the 'Head' manito to work out a solution.

The Manito Council

Warren (1957), Hoffman (1891), and Densmore (1910) all agree that it was Nanabozho who was moved to compassion and persuaded the 'Great Spirit' to do something to help the people. But a northerly and earlier source, John Tanner (1830, 185), claimed that the Great Spirit whom he identified as Misshipeshu, the Great Underwater 'Lion,' agreed to give the Midéwewin to the people only as a peace-making gesture in his prolonged struggle with Nanabozho. For Red Sky, Nanabozho was 'the Devil.' His account and another recorded by Landes tell a very different story, whose style is far more in keeping with the traditional concept of the trickster. Nanabozho, these accounts state, was excluded from the Manito Council and determined to do something about it. In Red Sky's tale he tried to make a bargain with God, not to save the people but to share control of the world 'because I know [said Nanabozho] he can't run it by himself.' But 'God's helpers' were alerted, Nanabozho was intercepted on his way up to heaven to discuss his takeover with God, and after a brief tussle 'he came down faster than he went up,' Red Sky asserted, 'and right into this little pond—he fell right into this little pond there. Water splashed all over—he must have went pretty deep into this little pond.' So the tale accounts for the expansion of Lake Superior to its present size, and for the lake-splashed region around it. Nanabozho may still be seen on the hill where he crawled out of the water, to fall asleep as he sunned himself dry. Hence the 'Sleeping Giant' seen here as it may be viewed from the city of Thunder Bay.

In Everwind's account (Landes 1968, 92–3) Nanabozho, excluded from the Manito Council, wandered about until he encountered Great Black Rock, who had also been overlooked. Lured by Nanabozho's promise to compensate him for the gifts that would have been his as a Council member, Black Rock agreed to follow Nanabozho's suggestion. So he traversed the water, seeking an Ojibway settlement, submerging and surfacing in the same style as the Megis in Red Sky's main origin tale. Finally, on his *third* emergence, he reached an Ojibway village on a peninsula. There he met a child and followed Nanabozho's instructions to give the child one of his own 'gold and silver scales.' The child's own silvery coating then fell off—except the twenty scales on fingers and toes—and he became vulnerable to disease and death. Thereupon Nanabozho went running all over the country protesting the terrible thing Black Rock had done, a point in the story that invariably sent an Ojibway audience into spasms of laughter at the blatant hypocrisy involved.

Hoffman's informant, Ojibwa (1891, 172), spoke of 'ten Midé Manitous' having been summoned, but not so much to share in a decision as to offer their services in disseminating the prescribed antidote to disease and death—the Midéwewin. According to Sikassige, Dzhe Manitou called together four Midé manitos and four Wind manitos. Apparently the Sun manito was also present, for it was he who was directed to take the Midé message to the people. But this might merely have been an alternative name for the East manito (the sun rising in the east), for in Densmore's version (1910, 21) it was the East Wind who was given the task. Equally the Megis manito (also originating in the east and 'reflecting the rays of the sun') was the chosen Agent, as he became in Red Sky's version after the Bear had carried the Pack of Life to the edge of the 'great big water.'

The location of the Council meeting was conceived in either a vertical or a horizontal perspective, although the latter seems to disagree with the total concept. For though Red Sky's Bear is supposed to be travelling on the earth's surface the earthen walls he encounters seem to block off any sense of being on the surface until he breaks through the last one and 'there was the world—right there—a beautiful world,' as if he were seeing it for the first time. One periodically suspects Red Sky of trying to reconcile Christian and Midé mythology, which would account for his guess that the Council met in Palestine. Densmore's female informant Nawajibigokwe (1910, 21) located the Council site 'at the centre of the earth, not *under* the earth, but at some place far away' (italics added). It was almost as if there were evil connotations to the alternative concept, communicated to Landes and others, that the Council site was at the vertical centre of the earth, *beneath four earth layers.*

The introductory sections of all Origin, Migration, and Master scrolls make pictographic reference to the Manito Council, although some are abstracted or condensed to the point of atrophy. Of seven Origin scrolls reproduced on the following pages all show unmistakable similarities to the first three units of Red Sky's Creation scroll. Four of them show four bird forms, two human figures, and four indeterminate ones. The Bungi scroll adds two birds and two other unidentified forms, to make six of each. The Peterson scroll from Glenbow shows four manitos in human guise (perhaps the four Winds), then indicates eight other manitos by way of four bird tracks and four bear tracks entering the circle, although each set of tracks might represent the entry of only one manito—the Eagle (or Thunderbird) for example and the Bear. In every instance, as in the Creation scroll the first unit features the Megis, in the centre. All but the Logan and Larson scrolls show the Bear on the pathway leading away from the Council circle, but none symbolizes the Bear's break-through.

The Agent's Break-Through

As in Red Sky's interpretation, Landes was informed (1968, 99) that the Bear was the appointed messenger of the Council and carried with him a heavy load, with the one difference that he broke his way *upward* through four layers, using a pole (literally a 'cedar tree') instead of his tongue. Both versions convey that the Bear is, literally or metaphorically, in the dark until the world bursts into sight. The tree, moreover, comes into the Red Sky tale when the Bear plants it in the Midéwegun.

All other sources in the literature are silent as to the Bear's break-throughs in connection with the Manito Council, although not in another context which is irrelevant at this point. The priest's three hesitations followed by a fourth successful step into the Midéwegun during the ceremony probably symbolize the break-throughs but the probability is not directly documented. The fact that the four Wind manitos thank the Bear for each of his efforts certainly qualifies them pre-eminently for places on the Council.

Clear symbols of the four break-throughs appear in the introductory section of all but one of the Migration charts, in one case as a succession of rings overlaid by a Bear's head, in two others by four concentric rings to which a Bear's head with out-thrust tongue is attached, or in the New York and National Museum examples as four simple bars across the Bear's path (see Figure 1).

Hoffman's informant, Skwekomik (1891, 172–4), told him that the trickster-hero 'Minabozho' in a godlike role, 'while thoughtfully hovering over the centre of the earth'—a hint of the Council site—'. . . heard something laugh, and perceived a dark object appear upon the surface of the water to the west. He could not recognize its form, and while watching it closely it slowly

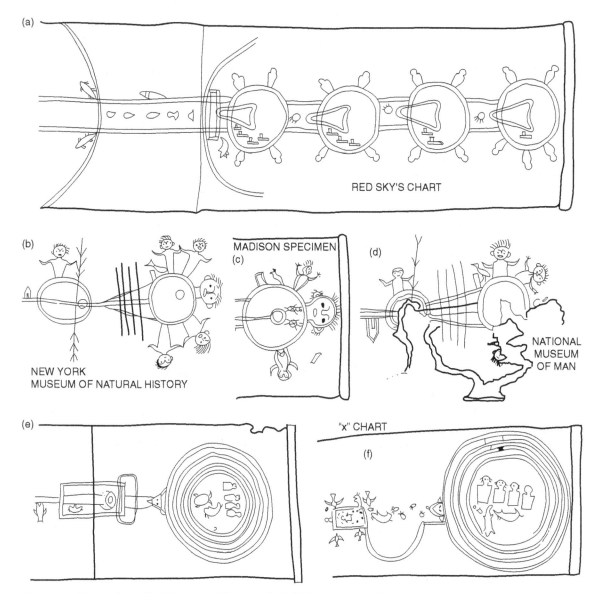

FIGURE 1   Details from Six Migration Charts. A Red Sky's chart (GAI-4); B a chart in the American Museum of Natural History (AMNH-1); C a chart in the State Historical Society of Wisconsin Museum (SHSW-1); D a chart in the National Museum of Man; E a chart in the Denver Art Museum (DAM-1); F 'x' chart (ax)

disappeared from view.' Although this object was repeatedly invited to come to the centre—an island—it disappeared and reappeared clockwise around the compass, returning to the western point before it swam in to meet Minabozho. Only then did the demi-god recognize the Otter, initiate him into the Midéwewin and appoint him as the special agent to carry the Midé message to the people.

There is no break-through, and the only hint of the Council is the Otter's emergence at each of the cardinal points of the compass, which suggests the presence of the four Wind manitos.

The Agent's Mission and Journey

In the account Hoffman got from Sikassige it is the Otter who is the official agent. We have already encountered Red Sky's story in which the Bear passes on his load to the Great Megis, who carries it under or over the 'ocean.' Hole in the Sky told Landes (1968, 108) in one version that on reaching the shore of this great body of water the Bear persuaded the 'Great Lion,' Misshipeshu, to subdue the waves so that he could carry his load across on the surface, while in a second version he simply walked along on the floor of the ocean. In this latter tale there is an encounter with the Megis, but no transfer of the load.

When we turn to the bark records there are some difficulties to sort out. The Migration charts trace the Agent's movements quite specifically. The Origin scrolls, on the other hand, although they seem to relate to the same theme, do so only vaguely.

Reading from left to right, the three large circular units that appear in all the Origin scrolls will be referred to as units I, II, and III. In every case Unit I is dominated by a representation of the Megis, and presided over by the Manito Council. The only interpretations available are the two versions obtained from Red Sky and those supplied to Skinner (1920) and Cadzow (1926) respectively by their informants. Of the two latter the account given to Skinner by Ogimauwinini (Chief Man) simply cannot be taken seriously, on two counts. In the first place we learn (Skinner, 1920, 318) that 'Ogimauwinini never opened the roll, excepting when he first received it, until he transferred it to the writer.' Secondly he interpreted the single-lodge side as referring to a fourth-degree initiation, and the three-unit side reproduced here (Figure 2) as showing 'the three upper degrees.' As we shall see in a later chapter this bears no relation to any authentic upper degree scroll. Skinner then adds, 'Unfortunately this side is not well known to Ogimauwinini, as his instructor died while at work here with him.' Cadzow's informant, Moose Bell, gives a far more convincing interpretation. Units I, II, and III (Figure 3) represent the first three degrees of initiation. The four otter-like forms below Unit I represent 'The sacred skin medicine bags of the cardinal points—east, south, west, north . . . ' The four bird forms are also identified: 'the bird of the east and summer . . . the thunderbird . . . the bird of the sun . . . the bird of winter.' (Cadzow, 1926, 126–7.) The central circle, surrounded by Megis shells, is 'the house in which the candidate is born into the fraternity'—in other words, initiated into the Midéwewin. The shells are interpreted in a rather ambiguous way as 'Nine magic shells . . . are given to the initiates for the purpose of making them fertile.' I suspect that the 'them' refers to the shells, not the candidates, for one man I interviewed—I believe it was Red Sky—told me that it was possible for the megis shells to *breed* more shells.

Of the paired human figures Moose Bell said they were 'The first man to be given the secrets of the medicine-lodge . . . and the first woman . . . ' The first bear keeps an eye on

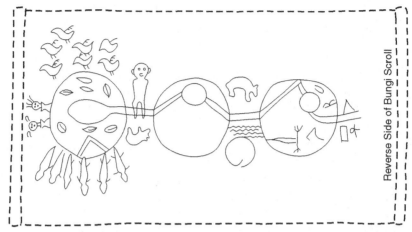

FIGURE 2   Three-Unit Side of Scroll Interpreted by Ogimauwinini (Sk-1a)

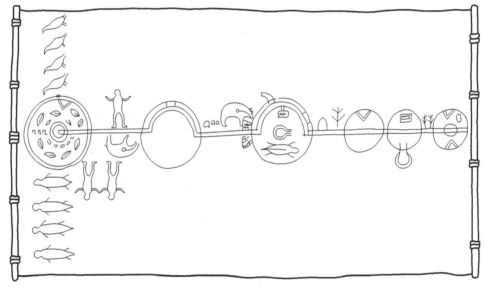

FIGURE 3   Three-Unit Side of Scroll Interpreted by Moose Bell (Ca-1a)

the candidates as they walk the path from one degree to the next, the second is 'the sacred white bear' who 'walks ahead four steps and makes three resting tents.' Here is a clear example of symbol conversion, the original 'tents'—judging by the conventions of many other scrolls—having been bear *tracks*.

The pictographic symbols on either side of the entrance to unit III represent 'rain,' the curved projection, 'a mountain [that] blocks the road' but disappears if the candidates have 'clean minds.' Within the central enclosure in unit III 'Various secret medicines . . . are given to the initiate . . . and the great lizard . . . creator of all water animals, becomes their friend.'

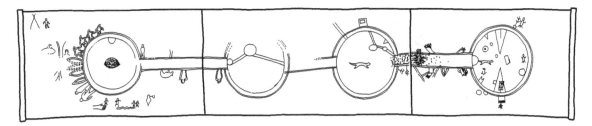

FIGURE 4   Red Sky's Creation Scroll (GAI-2)

This manito can be no other than the 'King of the Fishes . . . Great Lion . . . Underground Panther'—Misshipeshu, in prairie guise. Success in winning his patronage casts a shadow of suspicion over the powers conferred by the third degree, especially in view of the absence of any reference to promotion of the candidate's health.

   To find any features of Red Sky's (see Figure 4) and Moose Bell's interpretations of units II and III common to both would demand more ingenuity than I can muster, except for one item. In Red Sky's account 'God' sees what looks like a cloud on the horizon, goes closer and discovers it is a hill. In the Origin section of Red Sky's Migration chart the Megis encounters a hill, 'very high,' where he finds people and gives them the Midé message. In five of the seven Origin scrolls a projection recurs on the upper edge of unit III, suggesting an actual locality along the Agent's route. This shows up clearly in Moose Bell's Chart.

   I have already pointed out that the fourth unit of Red Sky's Creation scroll is a composite chart of Red Lake and Leech Lake, featuring two triangular projections from opposite sides that almost meet in the centre. Both Moose Bell's scroll and the one from Larson's collection (Figure 5) add three smaller circular units to the basic three. In both cases the third of these smaller units shows triangles in the same relationship as those in Red Sky's unit IV. There is no interpretation for the Larson scroll; and Moose Bell refers to the two triangles as places where the candidates 'rest in their tipis' while an unidentified manito 'talks to the Indians.' The Otter, too, who broke through to create the Red Lake narrows, has disappeared, and where we expect to find him in unit III—for all the specimens show

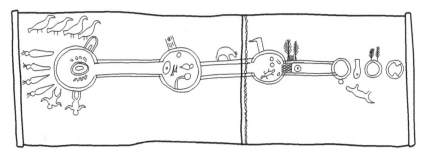

FIGURE 5   Origin scroll (la-1)

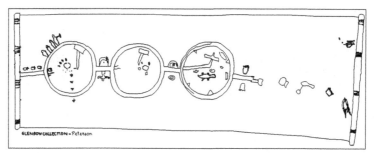

FIGURE 6   Origin Scroll (GAI-5)

a water creature that Red Sky identifies in his as the Otter—Moose Bell interprets him as 'the great lizard . . . creator of all the water animals!'

Before leaving these 'extended' Origin scrolls one further point needs making. Red Sky's copy seems to be older. Examining the bark, I strongly suspected that unit IV had been added by sewing on a new section to an original three-unit scroll. The Origin scrolls collected by Peterson (Figure 6), Larson and Cadzow were all—quite clearly—designed as they stand. If the sixth unit in the two latter scrolls is derived from Leech Lake, as seems likely, then a considerable lapse of time must be allowed for the original meaning to be metamorphosed into an entirely unrelated one. As for interpreting the Origin scrolls (see also Figure 7–9) in

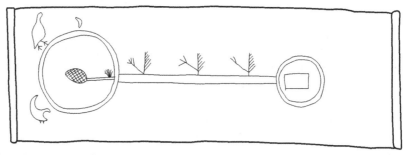

FIGURE 7   Condensed Origin Scroll (LM-2a)

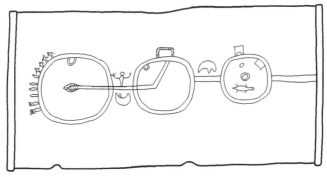

FIGURE 8   Origin Scroll (fi-1)

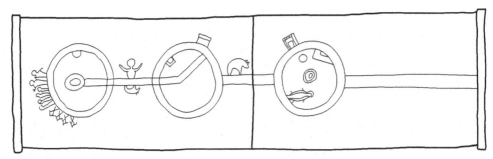

FIGURE 9   Origin Scroll (de-1)

toto as attenuated descriptions of the Agent's journeys a decision must be deferred until we examine the Migration scrolls in which the journeys are charted in great detail.

Returning to the literature, one reference in Landes (1968, 104) may have some bearing on the Megis featured in unit I. In this account the Bear, after crossing, or walking under, the first stretch of ocean, reaches a rocky island. In one version he climbs over the island, and finds himself 'stuck all over' with megis shells; in the other the island turns out to be the body of the Great Megis itself (Figure 10).

Variations
on the Megis Theme

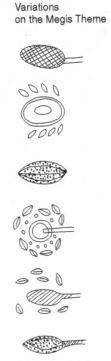

FIGURE 10   Six Versions of the Megis as Represented in the Origin scrolls

Warren (1957, 77–89) has some interesting things to say about the use of the Megis in a Midé ceremony he witnessed. 'One of the four We-kauns [Midé officials] . . . took from his medicine sack the Me-da-me-gis, a small white seashell, which is the chief emblem of the Me-da-we rite.' After some preliminaries he made this statement. 'While our forefathers were living on the great salt water toward the rising sun, the great Megis (sea-shell) showed itself above the surface of the great water, and the rays of the sun for a long period were reflected from its glossy back. It gave warmth and light to the An-ish-in-aub-ag (red race). All at once it sank into the deep, and for a time our ancestors were not blessed with its light.' The speech went on to relate that the Megis reappeared 'on the great river that drains the waters of the Great Lakes'; then disappeared, to show itself 'on the shores of the first great lake'; sank from sight again until it 'reflected the rays of the sun once more at Bow-e-ting' (Sault Ste Marie); and finally reappeared at La Pointe, or Shequamegon, near the west end of the south Superior shore.

Privately this Midé elder informed Warren that the Megis was merely a figure of speech for the Midé religion. Consulting the old men at Fond du Lac, Warren learned that among them the Otter was used 'in the same figurative manner' as the Megis, so that it was the Otter who appeared, first 'from the depths of the great salt water,' then at a succession of stopping places farther west. In yet another metaphor the Crane incorporates in its own person the migratory shifts, although the allegory does not refer directly to the Midé message; rather it seems to be a symbolic way of describing a migration. Tug-waug-aun-ay, head of the Crane phratry, in a speech to remind his audience of the leadership exercised by his totemic clan (Warren, 1957, 87) stated that 'the Great Spirit once made a bird, and he sent it from the skies to make its abode on the earth. The bird came and when it reached half-way down, among the clouds, it sent forth a loud and resounding cry, which was heard by all who resided on the earth, and even by the spirits who make their abode within its bosom.' The orator gestured toward the east as the direction from which the bird had flown. Circling the rapids at Sault Ste Marie it settled there, but eventually took to the air again to find its resting place at La Pointe.

Reagan's unpublished notes in the ethnology files at the National Museum of Man in Ottawa quote a Nett Lake informant as stating that 'The crane is the bird-god that lives in the heavens. He pays special attention to the supplications of men . . . the fire of his eyes will last forever . . . *his eye is the sun*' (italics added). The Megis, reflecting the sun, the Crane, and the Sun itself (Figure 11) are therefore interchangeable and allegorically

After Blessing   From Lac Seul

FIGURE 11   Two Versions of the Sun Manito

synonymous, and even the Council's Agent, who conveys the actual Midé message—whether Bear or Otter—shares in these figurative associations.

The Visionary Revelation

At this point in my studies I began to wonder if the Midéwewin was a device for re-enacting ritualistically the agent's original mission, at the same time re-creating, in the four lodges of the Master scrolls, not only the agent's original initiation, but the major stopping-places on the westward movements of the ancestral Ojibway. Yet there seemed to be a quite separate group of traditions that suggested a quite different origin for the Midéwewin.

This collection of origin lore makes no reference to saltwater shores, attributing the emergence of the Midé rites to a human agent who is directly taught the procedures by a delegate from the Manito Council. The go-between chosen by the Council is the East manito, equated by Landes's informants with the Sun manito, who, it will be recalled, is strongly associated with the Megis manito.

In the Densmore version (1910, 21–3) the East manito takes the form of a baby born to an elderly couple who lived on Madeline Island, but apparently on a shore that was isolated from the village of La Pointe. The baby grows up in close friendship with a cousin. Then, as the two are approaching manhood, the cousin dies. The young 'East-man' promises to restore his cousin to life. He instructs his parents in the construction of the Midéwegun, tells his father to sing and drum for four days, then disappears.

On the fourth morning 'they looked toward the east and saw the sky streaked with colours like those he [the East manito] had painted on their foreheads . . . A little before noon they heard a peculiar sound in the sky. It was from the east. Someone was calling *Wa, hi, hi, hi* . . . [they] saw four Indians walking toward them in the sky, giving this call. Each Indian had a living otter in his hand.' These were the four Wind manitos, who circled the body of the cousin four times, to bring him alive again.

Hole-in-the-Sky gave Landes a variant of this (1968, 110). An Indian couple living on 'Yellow Hammer Beach,' somewhere on the south shore of Lake Superior, had two children. As one of the two was dying his brother, the youthful Cutfoot, showed his parents the Midé healing technique which he had acquired in a vision. A second version, also supplied by Hole in the Sky, stated that the boy Cutfoot when only six or seven years old was summoned to visit the Megis manito. He disappeared for four years, came home for a year, then went away for another four. On his return his parents knew he had experienced a vision. When his elder brother fell sick they constructed a Midéwegun under Cutfoot's direction in which the young visionary conducted the rites that cured his brother.

Sikassige's version told to Hoffman (1893, 172–3) has some interesting variations. The Sun manito took the form of a little boy who was adopted by a couple who had a son of their own. Their natural son died, and the foster-child offered to restore him. After due preparations were made under his direction the family and friends gathered around the body in the Midéwegun. 'When they had all been sitting quietly for some time, they saw through the doorway the approach of a bear which gradually came towards the wigwam, entered it, and placed itself before the dead body and said hu, hu, hu, hu, when it passed towards the left side [clockwise] with a trembling motion, and as he did so, the body started quivering, and the quivering increased as the bear continued until he had passed around four times, when the body came to life again and stood up.'

Sikassige explained that the boy remained with his adopted parents until he had taught them the entire Midéwewin. Then he adds, although he had previously identified the boy as the Sun manito, that 'The little bear boy is the one who did this.'

Clearly, it was the vestiges of the Cutfoot legend that reached Red Sky without preserving the account of an actual curing. Farther from the Midé heartland Skinner (1911, 158–9) encountered a variant of the Cutfoot legend among the Bungi-Ojibway of Manitoba that had been both enriched and radically altered by merging with the Rattlesnake-Natawa lore of the prairies. Here again there were two young males—past puberty in this tale—who were deeply attached to each other. One died from the bite of the Natawa, and introduced death into the world.

The Natawa, after endowing the Rattlesnake with the warning device on his tail, set about making things right with the father of the deceased youth. Day after day the bereaved chief mourned by his son's grave. Then one day a huge snake appeared, who told him that he would be visited by a horned snake that would curl itself around the grave. The chief was then to lift the snake by its horns, three times. The prophecy materialized, the father obeyed instructions and the horned snake turned into a white-haired old man, with a 'fire-bag of life' made of Natawa skin.

'I have come to comfort and console you for the death of your son. The spirits of the earth, the wind, and the water have seen your sorrow,' (note the hint of a manito council) 'and I am sent to your race to show you the way of life which you will teach to your children, and which shall continue to the end of time. Now, therefore, light your pipe, and with your stem point to the sky, the abode of the Great Spirit, who shall give you life, to the abode of the spirits of the centre of the earth, whose will is to teach you the virtue of all herbs, and to the four winds who will protect you and give you power and success.'

The chief obeyed, then offered his pipe, whereupon three sharp taps of a drum were heard. The Natawa manito then sang a song, which began with the words, 'I come from the east where the long tent does rest . . .' He stayed with the bereaved chief for a full month, instructing him in all the Midé rites and lore. And the story concludes with the good news that after his mentor was gone the chief not only set up the Midéwewin, but in his old age another son was born, 'the very image of the one who died by the sting of the Natawa.'

It is noteworthy that this tale, unlike the others, places a sacred emphasis on the numeral *three*, rather than the usual four. This will be investigated further in a later chapter.

The common feature of all these tales is emphasis on the youth of the central figures. Although Red Sky's tradition had lost the healing role of the young visionary, his Creation scroll provides the only identified pictographic reference to the Cutfoot legend, the tiny figure beside a wigwam that is so faintly scratched into the top left corner of the bark.

Perhaps the most significant difference between the two traditions is the emphasis the one puts on the role of the manitos in disseminating the Midé 'gospel' while the other throws its weight on the human side. Now, as we turn to the Migration charts, the human role recedes.

References

Abbott, R.T. *American Seashells.* Toronto, 1954.

Boutwell, Rev W.T. 'School-craft's Exploring Tour of 1832.' *Minnesota Historical Society Collect'n.* F60IM66.

Beach, W.W. (ed.) *Indian Miscellany* (includes Walum Olum). Albany, 1877.

Blair, E.H. (ed., trans.) *Indian Tribes of the Upper Mississippi Valley and Region of the Great Lakes,* Vols. 1 and 2. Cleveland, 1912.

Blessing, F.K. 'Birchbark Mide scrolls from Minnesota.' *Minnesota Archaeologist* 29, no. 3 (1963).

Brassard, LEO. 'Grottes Intérêt Historique sur le Fjord Saguenay.' *Saguenaysia* (Revue de la Société historique de Saguenay), 3, nos. 3, 4 (1961).

Buffalo Child Long Lance, Chief 'When the Crees Moved West.' 34th Annual Archaeological Report. Appendix to *Report of the Minister of Education, Ontario.* Toronto, 1924.

Cadzow, D.A. 'Bark Records of the Bungi Midewin Society.' *Indian Notes and Monographs* 3. Museum of the American Indian, Hcyc Foundation. New York, 1926.

Coleman, Sister Bernard 'Decorative Designs of the Ojibwa of Northern Minnesota.' *The Catholic University of America Anthropological Series no. 12.* Washington, 1947.

Copway, George (Kahgega-Gahbowh) *Recollections of a Forest Life.* London, 1851a.

— *The Traditional History and Characteristic Sketches of the Ojibway Nation.* Boston, 1851b.

Cuocq, J.A. *Lexique de la Langue Algonquine.* Montreal, 1886.

Densmore, Frances *Chippewa Music.* US Bureau of American Ethnology, Bulletin 45. Washington, 1910.

— *Chippewa Customs.* US Bureau of American Ethnology, Bulletin 86: Washington, 1929.

Dewdney, Selwyn 'Ecological Notes on the Ojibway Shaman-Artist.' *artscanada,* 7, no. 4 (1970a).

— *Dating Rock Art in the Canadian Shield.* Art and Archaeology, Royal Ontario Museum Occasional Paper 24. Toronto, 1970b.

— and K.E. Kidd *Indian Rock Paintings of the Great Lakes.* Revised edition. Toronto, 1967.

Gelb, I.J. *A Study of Writing.* Chicago, 1952.

Hallowell, A. Irving 'Passing of the Midéwewin in the Lake Winnipeg Region.' *American Anthropology* 38 (1936), 32–51.

— *Conjuring in Saulteaux Society.* Philadelphia, 1942.

Hewitt, J.N.B. and W.H. Fenton 'Some Mnemonic Pictographs.' *Journal of the Washington Academy of Sciences* 35, no. 10 (1945).

Hickerson, Harold 'Notes on the Post-Contact Origin of the Midewewin.' *Ethnohistory* 9, no. 4 (1963).

— *The Southwestern Chippewa: an Ethnohistorical Study.* Memoir 92, American Anthropological Association. 1962.

Hoffman, W.J. *Midéwewin or Grand Medicine Society of the Ojibway.* 7th Report of the US Bureau of Ethnology to the Smithsonian Institution. Washington, 1891.

Howard, James H. *The Plains Ojibwa, or Bungi. Anthropological Papers,* no. I. South Dakota Museum, University of South Dakota. Vermilion, 1965.

Kinietz, Vernon *Indians of the Great Lakes.* Ann Arbor, 1940.

Kohl, J.G. *Kitchi Gami.* Trans. from the German. New English ed., with intro. London, 1860. Re-published, Minneapolis, 1957.

Kurath, G.P. 'The Christianization of Michigan Algonquians.' *Papers of the Michigan Academy of Arts, Science and Letters* 44, (1957).

Lafleur, L.T. 'On the Midé of the Ojibway.' *American Anthropology* (new series) 42, (1940).

Landes, Ruth *Ojibwa Sociology.* New York, 1937.

— *Ojibwa Religion of the Midéwewin.* Madison, 1968.

— *The Ojibwa Woman.* New York, 1971.

Moody, Harry 'Birchbark Biting.' *The Beaver* 287, (1957), 9–11.

Morris (S) Eau, Norval *Legends of My People, The Great Ojibway.* With introduction by S. Dewdney. Toronto, 1965.

Orr, R.B. 'Algonquin Clans and Sub-Tribes of Ontario.' 33rd Annual Archaeological Report. Appendix to *Report of the Minister of Education,* Ontario. Toronto, 1922.

Perrot, Nicholas see Blair, E.H.

Petersen, Karen *Howling Wolf.* Palo Alto, 1968.

Podolinsky-Webber, Alika Personal Communication (1959).

Radin, Paul 'Ojibwa Myths and Tales.' *Journal of American Folklore* 41 (1928).

— and A.B. Reagan 'Ojibwa of Southeast Ontario.' *American Anthropologist* (new series) 30 (1928).

Raudot, Antoine D. *Memoir Concerning the Different Indian Nations of N. America.* Letters 47 and 66. 1705-10.

Reagan, Albert B. Unpublished Field Notes in Collection of Boreal Woodlands Ethnology. National Museum of Man, Ottawa. 1912.

Rogers, E.S. *The Round Lake Ojibwa.* Royal Ontario Museum Occasional Paper 5, Toronto, 1962.

Schoolcraft, Henry R. *Oneota, or the Red Race of America.* New York, London, 1845.

— *Historical and Statistical Information Respecting the Indian Tribes of the United States.* Vol. vi, *Indian Pictography.* Philadelphia, 1851.

Skinner, Allison 'Medicine Ceremony.' *Indian Notes and Monographs.* Museum of the American Indian, Heye Foundation. New York, 1920.

— 'Notes on the Eastern Cree and Northern Saulteaux.' *Anthropological Papers* 9 (1911).

Stephens, H.B. *Jacques Cartier and his Four Voyages to Canada.* Montreal, 1890.

Tanner, John *A Narrative of the Captivity and Adventures of John Tanner.* Ed. Edwin James. Minneapolis, 1956.

Thwaites, R.G. (ed.) *The Jesuit Relations and Allied Documents (72 vols.).* Cleveland, 1896–1901. See ORR, R.B.

Warren, William *History of the Ojibways.* Collections of the Minnesota Historical Society, Vol. 5. St. Paul, 1885. Re-published, Minneapolis, 1957.

Winchell, N.H. *The Aborigines of Minnesota.* St. Paul, 1911.

Wintemberg, W.J. 'Was Hochelaga Destroyed or Abandoned?' *American Anthropologist* 29 (1927).

Wright, J.V. 'A Regional Examination of Ojibwa Culture History.' *Anthropologica* (new series) 7, no. 2 (1965).

— *The Ontario Iroquois Tradition.* National Museum of Canada, Anthrop. Series 75, Bulletin No. 210. Ottawa, 1966.

10. The Creation of the Ocean

(Kashaya Pomo; Told by Herman James, August 1957)

This is something from ancient times—I am going to tell about the creation.

Coyote was the smartest of all. He presided just like a heavenly being with his people. And he always used to tell them what to do, as if he were guarding the people. Because he was the smartest of all, he was the leader of his people. Coyote lived with a big group of people.

At that time there were no human beings; the animal people talked. They spoke a language like the Indian language we are speaking now. That's why they told this story in our fashion, in our language. We still speak the language that they spoke with. Having been given that, they told stories in our language about what Coyote did.

One time he went off into the wilderness. He must have gone a long way. The land was burning hot as he went. There was no water anywhere. Then he found a large opening, a level field. He was sick from thirst. He was really sick from thirst.

He still knew, he had everything in his head, just like Our Father knows; things were easy for him. We tell that he created the world like Our Father did.

Then sitting down, resting on his knees, he looked as far as his eyes could see. Having done so, he picked up a stick, and dug with it. He dug for water although there did not seem to be any anywhere in that dry land. It appeared as if there was no water there where he was.

It was burning hot there where he was sitting. In the old days they set fire to openings there in order to get food—those people had set fire to that opening in order to burn up the grasshoppers, in order to gather the grasshoppers.

Then, suddenly, it looked like there was a little water there where he was digging. He continued digging. Suddenly, water spouted up high, as if it were never to stop. Thereupon he ran away, not because he was afraid, but in order to see from a distance. He ran to the top of a small hill to watch from there. Then, where that land had been, it was filled completely with water.

Then, at first, he drank some of that water. Afterwards what we call the ocean started to taste salty. The ocean [literally bitter-water] became bitter with what we call ashes. Then he named it after it became a great body of water, saying, "This will be the ocean."

He watched it in the beginning. The water lay still just like a lake with no waves. It looked eerie lying there so still. Then, taking a stick, he said, "Do like this!" Making waves, moving the water up and down and making it splash, he said, "Make waves!" Then when he had walked up the hill a little way, the water surged up in high waves; the water was heaving and breaking way over the rocks.

Then he scratched a mark to set the limits to which the water could go—this is the ocean which we see, it rises no further. And after he prepared that, he fixed the limit to the tide. He again scratched a mark to determine how far the tide would go out.

Then he prepared something for the people—he made food in the ocean for people to gather. He knew that people were going to eat food when they became people-at first they were animals.

Then he made the food for people in the ocean and threw it down. "This will be this," he said, throwing it down in. First he threw down the biggest creature in the ocean. He named it calling out "whale." Thereupon he threw down a log.

Afterwards he threw down slightly smaller logs [for] what he called small seals and porpoises. "This will be a porpoise. This will be a seal," he said, throwing them down. And saying /tʰiwínsuʿsu/ he threw down a /hayhcʰa/. /hayhcʰa/ is what we call a dried manzanita bush—that he threw down. What I call a /tʰiwínsuʿsu/ [swordfish or shark?] has a horn. All kinds of fish he was naming and throwing down.

Then he also cast down edible foods to grow on the rocks, while naming them. First he threw down the abalone. Afterwards he said that mussels would grow, and goose barnacles—he was naming everything that people eat—bullhead to be fished with a line from the rocks. And he said edible seaweed would grow on the rocks. Limpets, small chitons, large chitons, sea anemones—he didn't miss making anything for people to eat.

Then he said that he was going to prepare people. But they say that the people lived in the woods—when he created us Indians, we didn't know about white people nor did we know anything about planting their food here in this land where we were created.

And then, it is said, after that the people lived in the wilderness, hunting deer, fishing—keeping alive by those means. The food that they ate was the best and healthiest of all; no one ever got sick but grew old and, when they reached the end of their lives, just died. At that time when they ate, they didn't have any food like the sweet food [now]. They didn't know about that. Only after a while, when the white people were present, only then did they eat food like that of the white people.

I am going to tell about this too before I stop. It turned out that Our Father was here, that Our Father had been born on this earth. That is what my grandmother used to tell me. It turned out that He had been a human being here on earth. Then he got ready and fixed all the people and subsequently, they say, departed again for the land above. The most skilled hunter, the one who could shoot an arrow the farthest and straightest, tied something onto one and shot it straight upwards, and [Our Father], by hanging onto that, departed for the world above, they say. That one that they used to talk about must have been Our Father. He stayed on earth with the people—at first he was born here, say the white people. It has turned out that we were right to pray to him. The elders in talking about it have brought forth that story; from it, we, having become people, knew righteousness—having told the story and having studied.

This is the end of my account of the start of the world in the old days and of the making of the ocean—that is what I have been telling about. This is finally the end.

11. The Creation of People and the Ocean

(Kashaya Pomo; Told by Herman James, August 1959)

There lived Junco, his mother, his father, and his children. They used to hunt deer.

One time they had been drawing decorative lines on their faces with something red and white—very flashy. Then they went to Coyote's place. "What is that you have painted yourself with that looks so good?" asked Coyote. The Junco brothers answered, "That's our marrow that we striped our faces with." "Is that so?" asked Coyote. "Yes," they replied, "If you broke your [bone] you could do it too."

Laying [a leg] on a rock—like this [demonstrated with a gesture]—[Coyote] picked up another rock and tested it. "Ouch!" he said jerking his foot back. For a long time he kept jerking his foot back while saying "Ouch!" After a while, saying, "Ouch, my leg!" he snapped it at the joint. He said he broke his leg in order to paint himself as [the Juncos had]. The Juncos laughed and ran far away so that he couldn't see them after he had been crippled.

Now he lay there unable to drag himself erect. No one helped him. He just lay there. After a while, from his leg, an odor wafted off to some birds. Those birds flew up to where he lay.

A vulture flew up first—then others arrived—to eat. He didn't make a move yet even though he was alive because he intended to pull their tail feathers out as they started to fly off. Various kinds of birds—condor, all birds—arrived and from everyone he pulled flight feathers.

After a while, having completely finished, suddenly Coyote became as well again as before, walking around with a good leg, cured. God did that—caused that to happen to him. In order that [Coyote] could prepare the world, [God] caused that to happen to him [Coyote].

At that time the sweathouse was built underground. Having gone down into a sweathouse, [Coyote] stuck those former flight feathers upright, making them be all the way around in a circle. "Let there be people!" he said four times. Suddenly, on the fourth time, Coyote heard people talking and laughing in that sweathouse. When he went down there to see the people he had created, amazingly there were people dwelling inside. It was full in the sweathouse.[1]

He gave them languages for different places and sent them off. That's why we talk in different ways—he created things that way. Giving [one group a certain] language, he sent them off [to one place]. Those speaking another language he sent elsewhere, saying that the

---

[1] The Kashaya are said to have been created from crow feathers and are therefore sometimes referred to as 'crow feathers.'

people can't all be together when they speak [differently] like that. We, too, having been given a language, stayed here at this place. We spoke the language that we are speaking now. Other people have different languages and we can't understand theirs even though we are of one flesh.

Suddenly [Coyote] was starving for food. He burned grasshoppers in a large opening. Then, having eaten them, he was desperately thirsty. He couldn't find water anywhere. Having walked up onto a hill, he stood there and looked over the opening that he had burned.

Then he went back to that place and started digging. He dug for a while. Having sharpened a stick, he dug with it. After a little while, when he got deeper, suddenly water spouted up. He couldn't remain standing there; the water was spouting up almost far enough to hit the sky. He ran off. Having run off, he ran along. The water filled all the land. When it did so, he scratched a mark and said, "Go only this far." That was the ocean where he made the mark. Afterwards, when everything was set, the ocean lay as if asleep.

Seeing it lying so still, Coyote said, "It looks eerie." Having walked down, holding a stick, he said, "Do like this," and made wavelike motions with his hand. "Do like this," he said. "Let it move," he said. When he had walked up a slope, suddenly the water surged, billowed, boiled over the rocks. Other [waves] followed one after another, never ever to cease. It's like that even today.

After that, when it had begun to look pleasing to him, he said he would make food for the people. "I will put various foods in the water for them to eat," he said. For mussels, he at first put in some things that didn't look like mussels—he put in a kind of mushroom. For abalone, he threw in a turtle. And for fish he threw in some things that looked like fish. Finally, saying "whale" he threw in a log. He made everything: seals, sea lions /tʰ iwínsʼuˑsʼu/—everything he made for people to look at and to eat.

Next he is going to fix the tide. Way to the west it kept being low tide with everything in plain sight—they, including the whale, were lying visible—all the big animals were lying around in plain sight. Saying that it looked eerie, he scratched a mark and ordered, "Ebb and flow as far as here." The mark he made there is what we see when the ocean flows closer in.

Now people ate the food that he had prepared, that he had made. Collecting it from the shore, they ate it. With that they stayed alive after having first been created on this earth. That's why the old people still eat that—those who know that food still eat it nowadays. That is what Our Father did. He made him [Coyote] do that. The one called God, the Creator, endures. This the end. The story of creation that our old people, my mother's mother and my father's father and my mother's people, told us is true. This is the end of this true account.

12. The Flood

(Kashaya Pomo; Told by Mrs. Essie Parrish, July 1958)

I am now going to tell about people turning into trees at the time of destruction. It was back here across [the canyon] at a mountain called Whale Crawling Up that what I am going to tell about occurred.

Long ago, when the world came to an end, it was destroyed by water. They say that there was a tidal wave, that the water rose up. When the water rose up, the people suffered.

The mountain named Whale Crawling Up was the only mountain that stood tall. Then, at that time, there were no other mountains visible anywhere. Everywhere the world stretched out flat—only that one big mountain stood out and appeared big to them. Then, when the water rose up, that was the only place they could go. When the water kept rising higher and higher, they went up there. Thinking they could stay alive there, they went up on the mountain.

When the water had all joined together, the rest of the people were all destroyed— everything was destroyed. Only the mountain peak—only the tip of the peak—was left. However, surprisingly they still did not stay alive—they turned into trees. That is what happened to them at the time of destruction. No one was supposed to survive because the destruction was caused by heaven; however, they became trees.

Then when all of the water drained away, everything that had been under the water was left, left here on the surface. When all of the water drained away, the land that had been flat, stretching into the distance, was, amazingly, land with big mountains standing, rivers flowing, plains sloping, and rocks projecting. And all those things like what they call scallops were left on the land. It happened that way. All of the water receded.

And then people existed there again. They told about it. They told what happened when the destruction came. I listened to that when I was still a child; they still talked about it. But I have never told this to my children. Our old people used to tell us about it, saying that was the way it was. That's the reason they said that mountain is taboo. People didn't go around that mountain, Whale Crawling Up, very often. They said the water rose up long ago when the world was destroyed. They told us that. This is all.[1]

---

[1] There are said to have been tall Douglas firs on the mountain in the past, which had been people, They burned off before the white man arrived. Herman James has heard a similar story in which the people turned into bushes, but were made into people again by Coyote. The flood inundated all mountains.

13. Doctoring

(Kashaya Pomo; Told by Mrs. Essie Parrish, September 1958)

I am going to tell about treating people, since you want to know these things about me. I have been a doctor and will be one for all my life on this earth—that's what I was created for. I was put here on earth to cure people.

When I was young I didn't know about it—whenever I dreamed things [had visions]—because that was the only way that I dreamed. I thought everyone was like that; I thought all children were that way. Those are the things that I used to tell about—things that I knew and saw.

The first person I cured was when I was more than twelve years old. At that time white doctors were hard to find; we were far away from any medicine doctor.

One time my younger sister fell sick. She was so extremely sick with sores in her mouth that they thought she would die. My great-uncle, the one who raised her, must have been making plans when I didn't know about it—I was playing around outside. Unexpectedly they summoned me from inside the house. I still remember that; that was towards four o'clock in the evening.

Then when he had called me into the house he said, "Couldn't you do something for your little sister? I say to you that you possess a prophet's body. You with your prophet's body could perhaps cure her. Couldn't you do something."

"I wonder what I should do now," I was thinking to myself because I was little and didn't know. But I said, "All right." That had been said to me. My power had told me, "If anyone ever asks anything of you, you should not say, 'No'; you are not for that purpose. You are one who fixes people. You are one who cures people." That's why I said, "All right."

After I had agreed, I prayed to heaven. My right hand I put on her head. When I had done so, a song that I didn't know came down into me. Amazingly that song came up out of me. But I didn't sing it out loud; it was singing down inside of me. "I wonder how I am going to cure her," I was thinking to myself. To my amazement she got well a few days afterward. That was the first person I cured.

At that time I still didn't know anything; I was green. I didn't know what I had done to cure her. After I had grown up and become a mature woman—at that time I was probably about, oh, about two years lacking of being twenty years old—my power told me this: "You are a doctor but you are still just a young woman. You will make a pole with designs. With that you will cure people. If, however, you don't do that, if you don't make that, you will die. If you don't make that, your eyes will become blind and your ears will grow deaf, and that's how you will be lying. This is your job on earth." I had been thinking about what I was going to do; surprisingly I had come to be like that. I know I am like that now.

Unexpectedly another person got sick. They say he was about to die with what the white people call 'double pneumonia.' He was lying almost gone. It was a long way to a [white] medicine doctor. His older sister had come for me. She said, "I have come to ask you a great favor. I want you to see him. See him! Even though I see that he is dying, I want you to look at him."

Then when I had gone there I laid my hand on him here and there. And I sucked him. Amazingly it cured him. While I am doctoring I get better and better. Like the white people learn, I learn. Every time I treat people I move upward [in skill].

After a long time—several years—it was probably twelve or thirteen years—I moved still higher. Then I noticed that I had something in my throat to suck pains out with. And my hand power, I found out about my hand power. That power is always near me. But other people can't see it; I alone can see it.

When I sit there alongside a person, I call on Our Father. That's my power—the one I call Our Father. Then it descends, my power comes down into me. And when that sick man is lying there, I usually see it [the power]. These things seem unbelievable but I, myself, I know, because it is in me. I know what I see. My power is like that. You may doubt it if you don't want to believe; you don't have to believe but it is my work.

Way inside of the sick person lying there, there is something. It is just like seeing through something—if you put tissue over something, you could see through it. That is just the way I see it inside. I see what happens there and can feel it with my hand—my middle finger is the one with the power.

When I work with the hand power it is just like when you cast for fish and the fish tug on your bait—it feels like it would with the fish pulling on your line. That's what it is like. The pain sitting somewhere inside the person feels like it is pulling your hand towards itself—you feels like someone—the disease—is pulling with a string. It is like what the white men call a "magnet." That's the way the disease in a person is—like a magnet.

And then it touches it. And when the power touches the pain, your breath is caught—it gets so that you can't breathe. But there is no fear. It is as if your chest were paralyzed—your breath is shut off. If you should breathe while holding that pain, the disease could hide itself. As the pain quiets your breathing, you can feel that pain there, with the result that your hand can take it out. However, if the breathing were not shut off I couldn't lift out the pain.

When I take it out you can't see it. You can't see it with your bare eyes, but I see it. Whenever I send it away, I see what the disease is. When the disease comes down into a person, which the white people talk about way differently; and we Indians too, we shamans, explain it way differently. That disease that comes down into a person is dirty; I suppose that is what the white people call 'germs' but we Indian doctors call it "dirty."

I am going to talk about my hand power some more. The palm of the hand has power. And the finger in the middle of the hand has power. That doesn't work just any time, only when I summon [power].

When there is a sick person somewhere to be found out, the hand power can find it out. Whenever someone thinks about it from somewhere, thinks toward me, there, on the tip of my middle finger, it acts as if shot—what the white people call "shock." If you touch something like electricity, you will know what the shock is like; that's how it acts there on the middle finger. When they think from some-where, it is then that the power finds out, that it gives a warning. That is when I know that someone wants me. And it always turns out to be true. That is my hand power.

There is still a lot more to that [subject of doctoring]. There is a doctoring power in my throat. Here, somewhere in the throat, the power sits. When that doctoring power first came down into me, I had already had some kind of growth there for about four years. It had affected me like diphtheria. I had almost died from its constricting [the throat] from the beginning, but I knew all along that it was becoming that [power].

But those that are staying with me didn't know; I had never told them about it. However, my power had told me saying, "That is because power has entered you there." When that happened [growth came], they called a white doctor to see me. The white doctor didn't rec-ognize it; he told me that it was probably diphtheria. But I knew what it was. When that thing had finished growing there, I recovered.

That felt like a tongue lying there and it first moved when I sang. I was probably that way for four years with that thing lying there. After it grew on me, my voice improved. It told me for what purpose it was developing. It told me, "Power is developing." Without that I couldn't suck out any diseases. Only when it had developed could I suck out pains.

Then it gave me this staff with designs and said, "This is your power. Those designs on there are symbols. Those are disease words." And it spoke further saying, "There are many rules to this: You can't treat a menstruating woman and you can't doctor in a house where someone is menstruating. [In those situations] the power will not be your friend; the power will not rise for you." It has turned out to be true.

When I first doctored with my throat, it was for a young woman. When I treated her and sucked the disease out, something like a bubble came up out of my throat; just as it would if you blew up a big balloon, that is how it came from my mouth. Everyone there saw it. It had become inflated quite a lot when it floated from my mouth. Everyone saw it. Like foaming soap bubbles would look, that is how it looked at the start.

Ever since that happened I have been sucking diseases out. The disease that I suck out works like a magnet inside too [as when using hand power]. On the place here where I said the power entered my throat, the disease acts as fast as electricity—it acts in a flash, like a magnet. And it shuts off the breath. When it does that, when it closes off the breath, like a magnet it comes along extremely slowly.

However, one doesn't notice how long he holds his breath. It's like being in what the white people call a "trance." While the disease is coming to me, I'm in a trance. It always speaks to me saying, "This is the way it is. It is such and such a kind of disease. This is why."

That disease flies and sticks to a certain place in the mouth. Our [shaman's] teeth have the power; there is something attached to our teeth. There is where the power is, on one certain tooth. There is where the disease sticks. Sometimes it flies under the tongue. When it sticks there it is extremely hard to release—it is, as I said, like a magnet. Then it dies there.

I spit out the dead disease.[1] Then I let it fall into my hand so that many people can see it. They always see the disease that I suck out. But that is not to be touched by anyone else—it is contagious. Whoever picks the disease up, into him it would enter. Whenever it sits in my hand, it sticks to it like a magnet. It won't fall off—even if you shake your hand it won't fall off. Even if you want to shake it loose it won't come loose.

You can put it in something like a piece of paper or a basket. If you are going to do that, you should sing for that purpose, you should call for that purpose. Some diseases sit for a while—sit for a few minutes—but others are fast. Some fast diseases stay just so many minutes after being put down and then disappear.

There is still much more [to tell about doctoring]. In those many years that I have been treating people, I have seen many different kinds of disease. I could tell everything. I am going to tell about this [the following] too.

Once my baby fell ill. Now, to my own children I can't do that; I feel weak. I like to get another doctor. I took my child to a white medical man. He had got so that he couldn't swallow his milk; he couldn't even move his tongue. I carried him to a white doctor. When I did so, he said [the baby] was going to die.

Then the father said, "Why don't you try it yourself? Even though you are a doctor you are just letting your child die." I said, "All right, I have been waiting for your OK; you're the one who will call. Even though it is my power, still if someone else calls, I will grasp [more] strength." Then he said to me, "Yes, do that."

Then I thought my child was as good as dead. I made power for the child. When I did so, my voice became stronger. "Oh, since I am like this [am a doctor], I can't let my child die; I must try," I thought to myself. Then as I looked at him, suddenly I saw that it was polio—in the throat.

Now giving that sucking treatment was just like when the white people (let's see now) take a chance operating. If one should suck a big disease out when [the patient] is really sick, he would die afterwards. Similarly too, when white people do an operation, when they operate on a really sick person, he might die afterwards. They say there are two chances [two choices—to operate or not].

---

[1] Essie Parrish added later that some other doctors spit the disease out with the germs still alive.

At first I tried with my hand power, in order to let [the disease] come up by itself from the child. When I tried with my hand power, suddenly the child spit it out by itself. He was retching, retching; I thought he was going to die. Suddenly he threw up.

It was as long as my thumb, like sinew. It looked like a long piece of what the white people call 'cottage cheese,' but like sinew, it couldn't be pulled apart. It looked like a tongue coming out of him that way. He spit out a mouthful. I picked it up. It felt like a magnet just as when I suck out a disease.

"Oh, this is a miracle," I said. "I'm going to show this to his father." The father was working at that time—it was daytime. Wrapping it up in paper, I stuck it on a certain place on the wall to show him when he arrived. But when he did, it turned out to have disappeared.

That is my way of doing things when doctoring—many of mine [my diseases] come up like that. Things turn out like that. This is the end. There are many things to talk about but this will be all.

14. Indians in Overalls

JAIME DE ANGULO

I went up north again the next summer. I found Jack Folsom and Lena at their place behind the little hill in the sagebrush. I noticed that Lena seemed apathetic, ill, Jack was as usual, with his quizzical smile, his quiet ways, his practical sense. "Say, Doc, I hear your friend Sukmit is around. There is a woman sick near town, you know, that place just before you reach town, Indians live there, well, there is a woman sick there, some doctor poisoned her, and they got your friend Sukmit to doctor her . . . and say, Doc, we are pretty near out of grub, you will be in town in two minutes with your car, today is Saturday and the stores will be open late, and will you bring back some grub, get some bacon, and bring some sweets for Lena, she loves sweets, I don't know what's the matter with that woman, Doc, something's wrong, she don't look well to me." "All right, Jack."

So I went to Alturas, did the shopping, and on the way back, it was dusk, I saw the familiar figure of Sukmit, a little way off the road, walking through the brush with long strides. I stopped the car, and honked and yelled. He paid no attention. I honked and yelled again. Surely he must hear me. I got out of the car and went up to him. He had heard me all right, and he was in a towering rage: "Goddam you, I am fixing for a doctoring! I have caught a new *damaagome* and I am training him, he is wild yet, he was following me like a dog, and here you come yelling your head off, you scared him away!" "I am sorry, Sukmit, I didn't know . . ." "You never know anything. You'll never learn anything, you'll never be an Indian, you'll always be a damfool white man!!" "All right, all right, you don't have to be so nasty about it," and I turned to go. He followed me: "Well, aren't you going to give me a ride? They are waiting for me, I have to doctor a sick woman." "What's the use if I scared your *damaagome?*" "Do you think I have only one *damaagome?* That's just a new one I am training."

So I took him to the place. There were a dozen or so Indians gathered around a campfire. There was a woman lying under a blanket on a bed of tules on the ground. Old Mary was there. She greeted me with her usual banter: "Here is the Indian white man. He is going to do the interpreting. No, maybe he'll do the doctoring. Ha-ha-ha, Indian white man." Most of the Indians already knew me. Greetings. "*Is kaakaadzi*, Man, you are alive, *is kaakaadzi*. Where have you been? Where is your wife, your son, *mi'mu amiteudzan, mi'mu belatsi?* Why didn't they come?"

Sukmit looked somber and abstracted. He went and looked at the sick woman silently; then he came back and knelt in front of the fire. Old Mary then got up and went a little way into the sagebrush and called the *damaagomes*.[1] Everybody became silent. Then Sukmit started one of his songs. Two or three people caught on, then others, then nearly everybody. Then he clapped his hands and the singing stopped abruptly. Now he is interpellating a poison, and old Mary, his mother, interprets (that is, repeats word for word, but more slowly, although Sukmit never got himself into a state of *bafouillage*, like Blind Hall and some others). And so on and so forth. In between interpellations of the poisons there was the usual relaxing and smoking by the audience and the usual gossip. But Sukmit never relaxed. He became more and more somber and abstracted. To me he seemed to be getting exhausted. After a while of this he got up and "sucked" the sick woman: he put his lips to different parts of her body and sucked with a strong hissing noise. Then he came back and knelt again in front of the fire, right next to me. He looked very sick. He asked for a container. Somebody passed him an empty can that had contained lard (a three-pound can), and he puked and puked and puked into it. I was right next to him. What he puked looked exactly like very dark blood, but the light was uncertain. He made a grimace and said to me: "Fuahh! . . . it looks like coffee." He was still retching. He poured the can into the fire.[2]

Most of the Indians then left. Old Mary looked very tired also. She said to me: "You take care of your Sukmit," and she disappeared. Sukmit was like a drunken man. I spread my blankets on the ground and dragged him in after me. For a long time he was crying like a child, and shaking all over. Finally he went to sleep.

In the morning he was quite all right. So also was the sick woman (she evidently had had a bad case of "funk"). She came to where we were having breakfast, and she gave Sukmit a string of beads for payment. She said: "It's not much but I am a poor woman." Sukmit took the string and threw it to his mother, and he said to the woman: "That's good. I am not doing it for payment." Then Sukmit pumped up his tires and he and old Mary started for Big Valley (which was their home), and I went back to Jack and Lena at their place in the sagebrush around the little hill.

Poor Lena was really sick. Jack would have liked to call in Blind Hall, but he was away somewhere down river. Then we heard that a bunch of Modocs was in town on their way to their home in Oregon, and with them was old Kate, a famous medicine-woman, and Jack decided to try her. She arrived in the afternoon, in a horse-wagon, with her son, a big strapping fellow (with whom I later studied the Modoc language). She was a little bit of an old old woman, so *racroquevillée* that she was almost bent double; she was nearly blind; still she insisted on "helping" (all the conversation had to be in English, since the Modocs didn't understand Pit River, and vice versa) with the cooking. She would totter around, extend a claw, peer, grab something and drop it in the skillet. Jessie (Jack's daughter by another wife—and a big, handsome woman Jessie was, somewhere around in her forties, graceful, dignified, a little bit haughty), who had come to help,[3] Jessie would sigh, turn her face aside to grimace, then calmly remove whatever *immondice* old Kate had dropped into the skillet.

Evening arrived. Old Kate had a sister who acted as her "interpreter," a much younger woman. Everything was ready; we were all inside the cabin; still old Kate was waiting for something; finally she said: "Dat white man going to stay?" "He is no white man!" said Jack. "He is Indian just like us." "What tribe?" she asked me. "Spanish," I answered. "Oh, dat's all right. Spanish good people." To her, too, Spanish meant Mexican.

Old Kate's procedure was slightly different from Blind Hall, Sukmit, or the other Pit River shamans I have associated with; but on the whole it followed the same lines—perhaps a little less loose, a trifle more conventionalized. For instance, her songs appeared to be directed less to an individual *damaagome* than to a generalized animal. Her sister would explain to me: "That's duck song . . . that's crane song . . . that's pelican song. . . ." The old woman's son had gone out. Doctoring didn't interest him. The Pit Rivers didn't know that kind of singing and were too self-conscious to try. Only the old woman's sister carried on the singing. Old Kate complained. Finally she turned to me: "Why you no sing? *Canta, canta!*" "All right, I'll try." The songs weren't difficult. They had more lilt than the Pit River ones. Anyhow, the important thing was to make a noise and be heard by the poisons.

Toward midnight or one o'clock (unlike the Pit River shamans, who never doctor for more than a couple of hours, Kate kept it up all night, right till dawn—although all the Pit Rivers had fallen asleep in various corners), Kate had a fit. She started to shake, foam at the mouth, and throw herself around. At first her sister tried to hold her down, but she wasn't strong enough. She called for help to the Pit Rivers; but for some reason no one moved. Then she yelled at me: "Hey, you Mexican, hold her, I'll call her son. . . ." He came in, a calm, big, powerful fellow. Yet, with the two of us sitting on her she managed once to free herself, that little bit of an old woman whom ordinarily you could have pushed over with your little finger! After a while she quieted down, and the singing started again, at intervals. But she was tired. Once she peered at the roof: "Is dat morning?" "No, Kate, it's the moon. There is a crack in the roof." She sighed.

Finally she started to extract the poison. She sucked and sucked. Then she straightened up, put her hand to her mouth, and grabbed something that was between her teeth. In the light of the lamp I saw distinctly what she did: she bit a piece of her own fingernail off. This she exhibited around as the poison. Then she called for a bowl of water; she drowned the poison in it and threw the water in a corner of the room.

In the morning the Modocs started to go. Jack Folsom wanted to give Kate some money, but she refused it, "I didn't do any good, Jack, you people don't sing, my poison no hear. Your woman going to die. Too bad." She said goodby to me. "You good man, Spanish, you help, you sing. Come see me my place Oregon." I said I would.

(I did go there, the next year, to study the Modoc language with her son. I had many talks with her. One day I was sitting on a log in the sun beside her; she was smoking her pipe; I said: "Kate, you remember that time at Jack Folsom's place when you doctored that woman. . . . You bit off your fingernail and said it was the poison. . . ." She gave me a sidelong look, pretty piercing in spite of her rheumy eyes; she grumbled: ". . . You know too much—sure dat's tomfoolery, good for people, make him believe—but my poison him no fool, him powerful, no nonsense, but he no hear dat time, son-of-a-bitch!" ". . . Kate, why did you become a doctor?" "Oh, long time ago, me young girl, go in woods look for berries, I no look for poison, poison find me." "Did he scare you?" "You bet he scare me!" "Does he still scare you when he comes?" She burst into her cackling laughter; "Hell NO! He don't scare me. I scare him now!!!")

Soon after the Modocs left, Lena's own father arrived from Hat Creek country. His name was Jack Wilson. He drove in in a horse-wagon, and with him was an "elder brother" (or cousin) of his, who must have been close to ninety or a hundred; Jack Folsom (who didn't know his own age by years) said of Bob-Chief, or Tom-Chief (like all Indians he had a variety of American names): "When I was a young fellow that old man had already buried three wives." He was still erect, but walked slowly; his skin was the color of chocolate; a few long white whiskers made him look like a walrus.

Jack Wilson was a "sort of doctor," according to Jack Folsom. He would doctor his own daughter, that night. Old Tom-Chief would interpret. Jack Wilson was a tall man, very silent. During the day Tom-Chief, who usually sat on a log, would totter into the sagebrush and make a sort of speech. "What is he doing?" I asked Jack. "Oh, he is telling old-time stories, what the people used to do long ago." "But there is nobody there. To whom is he talking?" Jack shrugged his shoulders: "To the sagebrush, I guess."

When evening came, old Tom-Chief went out and called the *damaagomes*. Three young Indians had arrived; but they were slightly drunk. They sang a *contre-temps* and laughed. Jack had to reprimand them. Old Tom was very deaf; he didn't hear what the doctor said; so everybody had to shout at him what the shaman had said so he could repeat it; the whole thing was a failure. After about an hour Jack Wilson gave up in despair. "No use! My poison don't hear. Mountain lion, wolf, too far away, don't hear!"

In the morning he said to me: "I lost all my children. This is the last one. I lose her too."

It was in the afternoon. Autumn and warm. The door of the cabin stood open. Away to the west I could see the hills of sagebrush, silent, and the mountains beyond. One of those days that do not move. There were half a dozen of us in the cabin, and the sick woman breathing heavily on her pile of blankets. I don't know how we all knew it, but we all felt that she was dying just then. At last, Jack Folsom broke down. He buried his face in his hands and started to cry. He cried like a little child, with convulsive sobs. Then that awful sound of the rattle. And even before that had died away Jessie began the wail. Oh, that weird, wild, atrocious thing that goes mounting like the shriek of a wounded beast, that infernal yell drawn away until it falls in a series of exhausted sobs. And again, and again. I was to hear that wail all night through the sagebrush until it drove me mad.

The old man, her father, was kneeling at her head. His face twitched uncontrollably. He closed her eyes, and laid a handkerchief over her face. Then he, too, broke down. He took the head of his child in his lap, he raised it to his breast, and he sobbed and sobbed.

All night long Jessie wandered through the brush, wailing, wailing. And all through the night Indians kept arriving. The men sat against the wall. The women went out into the night and wailed.

One Indian is dead.

Then Jack took his wife's body away to bury it in Hat Creek, her home. He said to me: "I'll be back here in about two weeks, and then we will burn her. Will you stay here for me, Doc?"

I was sort of puzzled about this business of burying first, and burning her after, but I didn't ask him any questions. I said I would stay until he got back. He said: "You sure you won't be scared?" "No, . . . why should I?" "Account of the woman who died." "But why?" "She might come and kill you by mistake." "Hell no!" I said.

The very night after they had left, Wild Bill arrived. He was a horse-breaker by trade and I had known him in the days of my venture in ranching. A delightful fellow, always full of fun and jokes, and a superb rider; in fact he was a crazy daredevil. We had always been friends.

I was surprised to see him. He had tied his horse to a post in the corral and came over to me. He said he had come for the funeral, and that the woman-who-had-died was his cousin. He said "sister."

"How can she be your sister, Bill?"

"Well, she is, Indian way."

"I don't see how."

"Oh, yes. Look: her *apun*, her grandfather on the mother side was the elder brother, what we call *apau*, to my sister, the younger than me, my *enun*."

"But Bill, that doesn't make her your sister!"

"Sure it does, Doc. . . . See, if a man is my wife's brother I call him *malis*, and my own brother, if he is older I call him *apau*, but if he is younger I call him *atun*. Just like my sister, *apis* or *enun*. But if he is my uncle, if he is my father's sister, then I call him . . . Oh, hell, Doc; you can't get it straight in English . . . But I tell you, this woman who died she is related to me, I know, because she always called this here Tom-Chief, *aqun*, and he also called me *aqun*, and that proves it."

Wild Bill said he would stay here and wait for Jack Folsom and the rest of the party to come back from the *atsuge* country. That evening he told me a lot about Coyote and the Coyote saga. The Coyote stories form a regular cycle, a saga. This is true of all of California; and it extends eastward even as far as the Pueblos of Arizona and New Mexico. Coyote has a double personality. He is at once the Creator, and the Fool. This antinomy is very important. Unless you understand it you will miss the Indian psychology completely—at least you will miss the significance of their literature (because I call their tales, their "old-time stories," literature).

The wise man and the buffoon: the two aspects of Coyote, Coyote Old Man. Note that I don't call them the good and the evil, because that conception of morality does not seem to play much part in the Pit River attitude to life. Their mores are not much concerned with good and evil. You have a definite attitude toward moral right and moral wrong. I don't think the Pit River has. At least, if he has, he does not try to coerce. I have heard Indians say: "That's not right what he is doing, that fellow . . ." "What d'you mean it's not right?" ". . . Well . . . you ain't supposed to do things that way . . . it never was done that way . . . there'll be trouble." "Then why don't you stop him?" "Stop him? How can I stop him? It's his way."

The Pit Rivers (except the younger ones who have gone to the Government School at Fort Bidwell) don't ever seem to get a very clear conception of what you mean by the term God. This is true even of those who speak American fluently, like Wild Bill. He said to me: "What is this thing that the white people call God? They are always talking about it. It's goddam this and goddam that, and in the name of the god, and the god made the world. Who is that god, Doc? They say that Coyote is the Indian God, but if I say to them that God is Coyote, they get mad at me. Why?"

"Listen, Bill, tell me . . . Do the Indians think, really think that Coyote made the world? I mean, do they really think so? Do you really think so?"

"Why of course I do. . . . Why not? . . . Anyway . . . that's what the old people always said . . . only they don't all tell the same story. Here is one way I heard it: it seems like there was nothing everywhere but a kind of fog. Fog and water mixed, they say, no land anywhere, and this here Silver Fox. . . ."

"You mean Coyote?"

"No, no, I mean Silver Fox. Coyote comes later. You'll see, but right now, somewhere in the fog, they say, Silver Fox was wandering and feeling lonely. *Tsikuellaaduwi maandza tsikualaasa.*[4] He was feeling lonely, the Silver Fox. I wish I would meet someone, he said to himself, the Silver Fox did. He was walking along in the fog. He met Coyote. 'I thought I was going to meet someone,' he said. The Coyote looked at him, but he didn't say anything. 'Where are you traveling?' says Fox. 'But where are YOU traveling? Why do you travel like that?' 'Because I am worried.'[5] I also am wandering,' said the Coyote, 'I also am worrying and traveling.' 'I thought I would meet someone, I thought I would meet someone. Let's you and I travel together. It's better for two people to be traveling together, that's what they always say. . . .'"

"Wait a minute, Bill. . . . Who said that?"

"The Fox said that. I don't know who he meant when he said: *that's what they always say.* It's funny, isn't it? How could he talk about *other* people since there had never been anybody before? I don't know . . . I wonder about that sometimes, myself. I have asked some of the old people and they say: That's what I have been wondering myself, but that's the way we have always heard it told. And then you hear the Paiutes tell it different! And our own people down the river, they also tell it a little bit different from us. Doc, maybe the whole thing just never happened. . . . And maybe it did happen but everybody tells it different. People often do that, you know. . . ."

"Well, go on with the story. You said that Fox had met Coyote. . . ."

"Oh, yah . . . Well, this Coyote he says: 'What are we going to do now?' 'What do you think?' says Fox. 'I don't know,' says Coyote. 'Well then,' says Fox, 'I'll tell you: LET'S MAKE THE WORLD.' 'And how are we going to do that?' 'WE WILL SING,' says the Fox.

"So, there they were singing up there in the sky. They were singing and stomping[6] and dancing around each other in a circle. Then the Fox he thought in his mind: CLUMP OF SOD, come!! That's the way he made it come: *by thinking.*[7] Pretty soon he had it in his hands. And he was singing, all the while he had it in his hands. They were both singing and stomping. All of a sudden the Fox threw that clump of sod, that *tsapettia,*[8] he threw it down into the clouds. 'Don't look down!' he said to the Coyote. 'Keep on singing! Shut your eyes, and keep them shut until I tell you.' So they kept on singing and stomping around each other in a circle for quite a while. Then the Fox said to the Coyote: 'Now, look down there. What do you see?' 'I see something . . . I see something . . . but I don't know what it is.' 'All right. Shut your eyes again!' Now they started singing and stomping again, and the Fox thought and wished: Stretch! Stretch! 'Now look down again. What do you see?' 'Oh! it's getting bigger!' 'Shut your eyes again and don't look down!' And they went on singing and stomping up there in the sky. 'Now look down again!' 'Oooh! Now it's big enough!' said the Coyote.

"That's the way they made the world, Doc. Then they both jumped down on it and they stretched it some more. Then they made mountains and valleys; they made trees and rocks and everything. It took them a long time to do all that!"

"Didn't they make people, too?"

"No. Not people. Not Indians.[9] The Indians came much later, after the world was spoiled by a crazy woman, Loon. But that's a long story. . . . I'll tell you some day."

"All right, Bill, but tell me just one thing now: there was a world now; then there were a lot of animals living on it, but there were no people then. . . ."

"Whad'you mean there were no people? Ain't animals people?"

"Yes, they are . . . but . . . "

"They are not Indians, but they are people, they are alive . . . Whad'you mean animal?"

"Well . . . how do you say 'animal' in Pit River?"

" . . . I dunno. . . ."

"But suppose you wanted to say it?"

"Well . . . I guess I would say something like *teeqaadewade toolol aakaadzi* (world-over, all living) . . . I guess that means animals, Doc."

"I don't see how, Bill. That means people, also. People are living, aren't they?"

"Sure they are! that's what I am telling you. Everything is living, even the rocks, even that bench you are sitting on. Somebody *made that bench for a purpose*, didn't he? Well then *it's alive*, isn't it? Everything is alive. That's what we Indians believe. White people think everything is dead. . . ."

"Listen, Bill. How do you say 'people'?"

"I don't know . . . just *is*, I guess."

"I thought that meant 'Indian.'"

"Say . . . Ain't we *people*?!"

"So are the whites!"

"Like hell they are!! We call them *inillaaduwi*, 'tramps,' nothing but tramps. They don't believe anything is alive. They are dead themselves. I don't call that 'people.' They are smart, but they don't know anything. . . . Say, it's getting late, Doc, I am getting sleepy. I guess I'll go out and sleep on top of the haystack. . . ."

"But you'll die of cold! It's already freezing, these nights."

"Naw, I won't. I am an Indian. I am used to it."

"But why don't you sleep here, inside?"

"WHAT?! Are you crazy? That woman might come and kill me."

"You mean Lena?"

"Shh! . . . Doc! For God's sake don't call her, don't call her name! Just say: the woman who died. That's bad enough. She is probably somewhere around, somewhere around here. They haven't burnt her things yet, you know, her baskets, her blankets, her clothes . . . all these things are calling her, are calling her shadow, her *de'lamdzi*."

"But why should she hurt you?"

"She don't want to hurt me."

"But you just said she might kill you. . . ."

"Well, she'll take my shadow away with her, and then I'll die."

"What for would she take your shadow away with her?"

"Oh, to keep from getting lonely on the road to the land of the dead people."

"Where is that?"

"I dunno. Nobody knows. Somewhere out west. They say there is a big lake there, no end to it, and the dead people live there on an island . . . I dunno . . . that's what I've heard."

"But, Bill, I still don't see why she should want to take you there. . . ."

"I just told you, Doc: to keep from getting lonely on the trip to the land of the dead. You would do the same thing yourself if you were going to a strange place. You would take along someone you knew and liked."

"Well then, she might take me, Bill. I know she liked me."

"Sure! That's why I tell you that you are a damn fool to sleep here!"

"Listen, Bill, tell me something else before you go . . . about the shadow, what do you call it, the *dalilamdzi*?"

"Naw, that means 'to make a shadow,' for instance *salilamdzi*, that means I am making a shadow, *kalilamdzi* it's you who are making a shadow. . . . No, Doc, I know what you are thinking about, that's the *de'lamdzi*, the shadow, that's not the same as *dalilamdzi*, that's the shadow . . . oh, hell, I dunno what's the difference, it kind of sounds the same, don't it? Lissen: I remember when I was a little boy I used to hear the old men when they woke in the morning, they used to sing:

dalilamdzi	*walilamdzi*	*de'lamdzi*	*seena seena*
(the dawn	is dawning	a shadow	I come home, I come home)

"So the *dalilamdzi*, that means the dawn, also! The old people they would hum like that when they woke up in the morning and they said: My shadow is liable to go wandering during the night and mebbe get lost and not find me again in the morning, that's why I sing to show him where I am! . . . Well, I think you are foolish to sleep here in this shack where she is liable to come back and take another look at her baskets that she made herself, and her stove, and everything, her shadow is, and it may ask your shadow to go along, and there will be no more Buckaroo Doc, and we will bury you and burn all your things, your saddle, and your book, and everything, and everybody will cry . . . well, good night, Doc!"

Wild Bill stayed there several days, waiting for Jack Folsom and the other people to come back from the Hat Creek country where they had buried "the woman who had died." He was an excellent raconteur and told me many old-time stories. There are tribes where the old-time stories and "myths" (as the anthropologists call them) are stereotyped, may even be cast in a rigid form and must be recited verbatim. But not so with the Pit Rivers! A poor story-teller gives you the barest outline, in short sentences (nearly all beginning with "and then . . ."), in a monotonous voice. But a good raconteur like Wild Bill or old Mary tells it with gestures, mimicry, imitation noises—a regular theatrical performance. If there are several people in the audience they grunt in approval after each telling passage. Instead of applauding by clapping as we do, they raise their chins and say: Hunh. . . .

Finally, one day about noon, Jack and all the relatives returned; five or six wagons full of them, and immediately everything was confusion and pandemonium in this quiet corner of the sagebrush behind the little hill. They started a big bonfire. There was a lot of argument going on. Some of the people were still wailing. A woman would come dragging things out of the house, maybe two or three baskets, maybe an armful of clothes, and throw them into the fire; then she would go out a little way into the sagebrush and wail. The men were mostly silent and preoccupied; some of them wailed in man fashion: a sort of deep grunt, Honh-ho-ho, honh-ho-ho. . . . They carried things swiftly out of the house, threw them into the fire, and went back for more. Some of them were arguing (they wouldn't have been Pit Rivers if there hadn't been some kind of argument going on!); there was a little man who kept coming to me and complaining that they ought to burn the house, also. That seemed to be a moot point because in the old days there were no individual houses. And besides, according to Wild Bill, it was Jack's house, as well as the woman's who had died. . . . But the little old man was all for destruction. At least they should throw the stove into the fire. "But it won't burn!" said Wild Bill. "Well, throw it into the creek, then," said the fundamentalist.

I was sitting in my little tent, trying to keep out of the way. All this had happened so fast, like a whirlwind out of the sagebrush, that I was dazed. But everybody kept coming into my tent either to prove to me or to themselves that they were right, or to ask me if this or that object were mine, before throwing it into the fire. My copy of *Moby-Dick* nearly went, and a horse's hackamore that belonged to me. Wild Bill stuck in my tent most of the time, sardonic as usual: "That's Indians for you! Just watch them, Doc. . . . Crazy goddam bunch. Always argue, always argue; argue all the time . . . I wish they would get through with that burning. I have three colts I am breaking, at Tuluukupi, I left them in the corrals, I guess them fellows will feed them . . . still, I ought to be getting back to them."

Jack Folsom himself didn't seem to be doing anything except going around, wailing, crying, grunting. He came into my tent and sat on my cot and sobbed like a little child. "She was very good, that woman, Doc. She never quarreled. I have had four, no, five, before her. We have been together a long time now. You know my daughter Jessie, well she raised her. Jessie has got grandchildren now."

"But, Jack, I thought Jessie was this woman's daughter. . . ."

"No, another woman's. I have had three women already, no, four. No, two only, according to Indian way. This woman I paid for her and she paid for me. That's according to Indian law. I gave Jack Wilson, you know . . . the old fellow who was singing that night, I gave him a white mare, she was awful fast, she had won several races for me, and her people gave me the right to fish on Hat Creek. . . . But you noticed that woman that's come in with them? She is ordering everything around, she is bossing everybody. . . ."

"Yes, I noticed her. Who is she?"

"She is younger sister of the woman who died, what we call *enun*, same as what you call "cousin." So, she has come to claim me."

"What do you mean, claim you?"

"It's this way, Doc: according to Indian law, *the dead people have got the say*; the relations of the dead person have got the right. If I had died, then my people, my relations, they are the ones who have the right to bring another man in my place. It don't matter he is an old man good for nothing. They say: We bought that woman, she belongs to us now; here's a man for her; she take him, or give us back our present; we gave you a horse for her; where is that horse? Now, this woman who died I married her according to Indian law. So, her people, her relations, they come here with this other woman, and they say to me: You lost one, here's another, you got no claim against us."

"Well, then, it's all right, isn't it?"

"No, it ain't all right, Doc. I don't want that woman. She is all right. She is young, I know. She is clean; she is a good worker . . . but she is bossy as hell! She'll boss me . . . I am too old to be bossed!"

Afterwards I took Jack down to my little ranch in the mountains south of Monterey. We had to go fifty miles by horse-stage, then fifteen miles more by trail over the ridges. When we were on top of the highest ridge the sun was dipping into the ocean, and we stopped to eat some sandwiches and make a little coffee. But before he ate, Jack chewed a piece and spat some to the east, and to the north, and to the south, and to the west. "See, Doc, I am doing that because I am in a new country. Them people you don't see, them coyotes and foxes and all kinds of *dinihowis* and *damaagomes* that live around here, they don't know me, because I am a stranger. They might hurt me. So I am telling them: I am all right, I don't mean no harm to you people, see, I am feeding you; and you people don't hurt me neither, because I am a stranger but I want to be friends with you. That's the way to do, Doc, that's the good way."

Night overtook us, and we went down the steep trail in the dark. Jack was stumbling. "Say, Doc, you sure picked you a darn steep country for your homestead." We reached the cabin at last, and I lit a fire in the hearth. There was an old rock mortar, of the kind the Indians use to pound acorns with a stone pestle. They still use them in Central California, but, for some reason which I don't understand, they don't use them any more in Pit River country. Indeed, the Pit River Indians are afraid to touch them. "Them things are dangerous, Doc, them things are full of power. You come across one lying on the ground, some place; and next day you'll find him mebbe a mile further away! He moved during the night!" Whether it was only the ones that were lying abandoned "some place," or whether it was *all* mortars, I never found out. Anyway, I never saw any in use among the Pit Rivers. And now, Jack was very much shocked because I had one of these mortars lying near the hearth! "You shouldn't do that, Doc! He is getting too hot there, near the fire . . . make him mad . . . he is liable to hurt you, bring you bad luck, maybe make your children sick. . . ."

But Jack did not stay very long at my little ranch. He was having bad dreams. "I been dreaming of blood, Doc. It's those people working against me, my wife's people, the one who died. They have got some powerful doctors on their side. I should have married that sister of hers when she came to claim me. That's Indian law. I can't get out of it!"

So I put him on the stage and he went back to Modoc and the joys of matrimony.

When I saw him the next summer he looked subdued. He greeted me with his usual warmth, but when I asked him how he was getting along with quondam sister-in-law, he said: "Oh, it's hell, Doc, just hell. I don't draw a free breath of my own."

I saw him again the next summer. He was radiant. "I got rid of her, Doc. I was camped at Davis Creek, and her brother he come and see me, and he says: Jack, I wouldn't stay with that woman, if I were you. She is too damn bossy! . . . Well, Doc, that's all I wanted to hear. He was her elder brother, so he had the say. So I called my own boy, Millard, you know him, and I said: I am going—when that woman comes back to the camp, don't tell her where I am gone—you don't know nothing about it, *sabe?*"

A few years later I found her married to Sukmit, of all people! But she had found her mate. They were yelling at each other, while old Mary smiled on complacently. Old Mary had earned her rest.

Notes

1. After the *damaagomes* have been called, no one is allowed to approach the meeting, whether Indian or white man. The reason is obvious: the sudden arrival of a stranger might scare away the *damaagomes* hovering in the air over the shaman's head.

2. The can looked about half full. Was it an intestinal hemorrhage of hysterical origin? Sukmit (unlike some of the shamans, Old Modoc Kate, for instance, of whom I will speak later) was incapable of *supercherie*. I can vouch for that. I knew him too well. When two boon companions get drunk together time and time again, the truth is bound to come out. I simply have no explanation for the stuff in that can except the one given above.

3. Lena had raised Jessie, but they must have been almost the same age, at most ten years' difference—so Jessie looked upon Lena as her mother.

4. When you tell old-time stories of long ago, every verb must begin with *tsik—*, which then is more or less blended with the pronominal prefix.

5. To be worried,—*inismallauw*—(conjugation II). When an Indian is worried, he goes wandering,—*inillaaduw*—. When he is "wandering" he goes around the mountains, cries, breaks pieces of wood, hurls stones. Some of his relatives may be watching him from afar, but they never come near.

6. Indian dancing is not like the European, by lifting the heels and balancing the body on the toes; on the contrary, one foot is raised *flat* from the ground while the other foot is pressed into the ground (by flexing the knee); then a very slight pause with one foot in the air; then the other foot is stamped flat into the ground while the first one is lifted. That is the fundamental idea; there are many variations; besides, the shoulders and head are made to synchronize or syncopate.

7. I am not romancing, nor translating loosely; *hay-dutsi-la* means literally "by thinking." The radical *hay*—means "thought"; *dutsi* is the verb "to be" used here as an auxiliary in participial form (i.e. "being");—*la* is the suffix representing the instrumental case (i.e. "by").

8. Those big clumps of coarse grass and sod which gradually rise above the level of the water on the marshes are called *tsappetia*.

9. The word for "people" is *is*. Nowadays it is applied especially to Indians, in contradistinction to the term applied to the whites: *enellaaduwi*.

15. Selections from *Black Elk Speaks*

[As told through John G. Neihardt (Flaming Rainbow)]

The Messiah

There was hunger among my people before I went away across the big water, because the Wasichus did not give us all the food they promised in the Black Hills treaty. They made that treaty themselves; our people did not want it and did not make it. Yet the Wasichus who made it had given us less than half as much as they promised. So the people were hungry before I went away.

But it was worse when I came back. My people looked pitiful. There was a big drouth, and the rivers and creeks seemed to be dying. Nothing would grow that the people had planted, and the Wasichus had been sending less cattle and other food than ever before. The Wasichus had slaughtered all the bison and shut us up in pens. It looked as though we might all starve to death. We could not eat lies, and there was nothing we could do.

And now the Wasichus had made another treaty to take away from us about half the land we had left. Our people did not want this treaty either, but Three Stars[1] came and made the treaty just the same, because the Wasichus wanted our land between the Smoky Earth and the Good River. So the flood of Wasichus, dirty with bad deeds, gnawed away half of the island that was left to us. When Three Stars came to kill us on the Rosebud, Crazy Horse whipped him and drove him back. But when he came this time without any soldiers, he whipped us and drove us back. We were penned up and could do nothing.

All the time I was away from home across the big water, my power was gone, and I was like a dead man moving around most of the time. I could hardly remember my vision, and when I did remember, it seemed like a dim dream.

Just after I came back, some people asked me to cure a sick person, and I was afraid the power would not come back to me; but it did. So I went on helping the sick, and there were many, for the measles had come among the people who were already weak because of hunger. There were more sick people that winter when the whooping cough came and killed little children who did not have enough to eat.

So it was. Our people were pitiful and in despair.

But early that summer when I came back from across the big water (1889) strange news had come from the west, and the people had been talking and talking about it. They were talking about it when I came home, and that was the first I had heard of it. This news came to the Oglalas first of all, and I heard that it came to us from the Shoshones and Blue Clouds (Arapahoes). Some believed it and some did not believe. It was hard to believe; and when I first heard of it, I thought it was only foolish talk that somebody had started somewhere. This news said that out yonder in the west at a place near where the great mountains (The Sierras) stand before you come to the big water, there was a sacred man among the Paiütes who had talked to the Great Spirit in a vision, and the Great Spirit had told him how to save the Indian peoples and make the Wasichus disappear and bring back all the bison and the people who were dead and how there would be a new earth. Before I came back, the people had got together to talk about this and they had sent three men, Good Thunder, Brave Bear and Yellow Breast, to see this sacred man with their own eyes and learn if the story about him was true. So these three men had made the long journey west, and in the fall after I came home, they returned to the Oglalas with wonderful things to tell.

There was a big meeting at the head of White Clay Creek, not far from Pine Ridge, when they came back, but I did not go over there to hear, because I did not yet believe. I thought maybe it was only the despair that made people believe, just as a man who is starving may dream of plenty of everything good to eat.

I did not go over to the meeting, but I heard all they had to tell. These three men all said the same thing, and they were good men. They said that they traveled far until they came to a great flat valley[2] near the last great mountains before the big water, and there they saw the Wanekia,[3] who was the son of the Great Spirit, and they talked to him. Wasichus called him Jack Wilson, but his name was Wovoka. He told them that there was another world coming, just like a cloud. It would come in a whirlwind out of the west and would crush out everything on this world, which was old and dying. In that other world there was plenty of meat, just like old times; and in that world all the dead Indians were alive, and all the bison that had ever been killed were roaming around again.

This sacred man gave some sacred red paint and two eagle feathers to Good Thunder. The people must put this paint on their faces and they must dance a ghost dance that the sacred man taught to Good Thunder, Yellow Breast, and Brave Bear. If they did this, they could get on this other world when it came, and the Wasichus would not be able to get on, and so they would disappear. When he gave the two eagle feathers to Good Thunder, the sacred man said: "Receive these eagle feathers and behold them, for my father will cause these to bring your people back to him."

This was all that was heard the whole winter.

When I heard this about the red paint and the eagle feathers and about bringing the people back to the Great Spirit, it made me think hard. I had had a great vision that was to bring the people back into the nation's hoop, and maybe this sacred man had had the same vision and it was going to come true, so that the people would get back on the red road. Maybe I was not meant to do this myself, but if I helped with the power that was given me, the tree might bloom again and the people prosper. This was in my mind all that winter, but I did not know what vision the sacred man out there had seen, and I wished I could talk to him and find out. This was sitting deeper in my mind every day, and it was a very bad winter, with much hunger and sickness.

My father died in the first part of the winter from the bad sickness that many people had. This made me very sad. Everything good seemed to be going away. My younger brother and sister had died before I came home, and now I was fatherless in this world. But I still had my mother. I was working in a store for the Wasichus so that I could get something for her to eat, and I just kept on working there and thinking about what Good Thunder, Yellow Breast, and Brave Bear had told; but I did not feel sure yet.

During that winter the people wanted to hear some more about this sacred man and the new world coming, so they sent more men out there to learn what they could. Good Thunder and Yellow Breast, with two others, went from Pine Ridge. Some went with them from other agencies, and two of these were Kicking Bear and Short Bull. News came back from these men as they traveled west, and it seemed that everywhere people belived all that we had heard, and more. Letters came back telling us this. I kept on working in the store and helping sick people with my power.

Then it was spring (1890), and I heard that these men had all come back from the west and that they said it was all true. I did not go to this meeting either, but I heard the gossip that was everywhere now, and people said it was really the son of the Great Spirit who was out there; that when he came to the Wasichus a long time ago, they had killed him; but he was coming to the Indians this time, and there would not be any Wasichus in the new world that would come like a cloud in a whirlwind and crush out the old earth that was dying. This they said would happen after one more winter, when the grasses were appearing (1891).

I heard many wonderful things about the Wanekia that these men had seen and heard, and they were good men. He could make animals talk, and once while they were with him he made a spirit vision, and they all saw it. They saw a big water, and beyond it was a beautiful green land where all the Indians that had ever lived and the bison and the other animals were all coming home together. Then the Wanekia, they said, made the vision go out, because it was not yet time for this to happen. After another winter it would happen, when the grasses were appearing.

And once, they said, the Wanekia held out his hat for them to look into; and when they did this, all but one saw there the whole world and all that was wonderful. But that one could see only the inside of the hat, they said.

Good Thunder himself told me that, with the power of the Wanekia, he had gone to a bison skin tepee; and there his son, who had been dead a long time, was living with his wife, and they had a long talk together.

This was not like my great vision, and I just went on working in the store. I was puzzled and did not know what to think.

Afterwhile I heard that north of Pine Ridge at the head of Cheyenne Creek, Kicking Bear had held the first ghost dance, and that people who danced had seen their dead relatives and talked to them. The next thing I heard was that they were dancing on Wounded Knee Creek just below Manderson.

I did not believe yet, but I wanted to find out things, because all this was sitting more and more strongly in my heart since my father died. Something seemed to tell me to go and see. For awhile I kept from going, but at last I could not any more. So I got on my horse and went to this ghost dance on Wounded Knee Creek below Manderson.

I was surprised, and could hardly believe what I saw; because so much of my vision seemed to be in it. The dancers, both women and men, were holding hands in a big circle, and in the center of the circle they had a tree painted red with most of its branches cut off and some dead leaves on it. This was exactly like the part of my vision where the holy tree was dying, and the circle of the men and women holding hands was like the sacred hoop that should have power to make the tree to bloom again. I saw too that the sacred articles the people had offered were scarlet, as in my vision, and all their faces were painted red. Also, they used the pipe and the eagle feathers. I sat there looking on and feeling sad. It all seemed to be from my great vision somehow and I had done nothing yet to make the tree to bloom.

Then all at once great happiness overcame me, and it all took hold of me right there. This was to remind me to get to work at once and help to bring my people back into the sacred hoop, that they might again walk the red road in a sacred manner pleasing to the Powers of the Universe that are One Power. I remembered how the spirits had taken me to the center of the earth and shown me the good things, and how my people should prosper. I remembered how the Six Grandfathers had told me that through their power I should make my people live and the holy tree should bloom. I believed my vision was coming true at last, and happiness overcame me.

When I went to the dance, I went only to see and to learn what the people believed; but now I was going to stay and use the power that had been given me. The dance was over for that day, but they would dance again next day, and I would dance with them.

Notes

1. General Crook headed the commission that arranged the treaty of 1889.

2. Mason Valley, Nevada.

3. "One Who Makes Live."

Visions of the Other World

So I dressed myself in a sacred manner, and before the dance began next morning I went among the people who were standing around the withered tree. Good Thunder, who was a relative of my father and later married my mother, put his arms around me and took me to the sacred tree that had not bloomed, and there he offered up a prayer for me. He said: "Father, Great Spirit, behold this boy! Your ways he shall see!" Then he began to cry.

I thought of my father and my brother and sister who had left us, and I could not keep the tears from running out of my eyes. I raised my face up to keep them back, but they came out just the same. I cried with my whole heart, and while I cried I thought of my people in despair. I thought of my vision, and how it was promised me that my people should have a place in this earth where they could be happy every day. I thought of them on the wrong road now, but maybe they could be brought back into the hoop again and to the good road.

Under the tree that never bloomed I stood and cried because it had withered away. With tears on my face I asked the Great Spirit to give it life and leaves and singing birds as in my vision.

Then there came a strong shivering all over my body, and I knew that the power was in me.

Good Thunder now took one of my arms, Kicking Bear the other, and we began to dance. The song we sang was like this:

> *"Who do you think he is that comes?*
> *It is one who seeks his mother!"*

It was what the dead would sing when entering the other world and looking for their relatives who had gone there before them.

As I danced, with Good Thunder and Kicking Bear holding my arms between them, I had the queer feeling that I knew and I seemed to be lifted clear off the ground. I did not have a vision all that first day. That night I thought about the other world and that the Wanekia himself was with my people there and maybe the holy tree of my vision was really blooming yonder right then, and that it was there my vision had already come true. From the center of the earth I had been shown all good and beautiful things in a great circle of peace, and maybe this land of my vision was where all my people were going, and there they would live and prosper where no Wasichus were or could ever be.

Before we started dancing next day, Kicking Bear offered a prayer, saying: "Father, Great Spirit, behold these people! They shall go forth to-day to see their relatives, and yonder they shall be happy, day after day, and their happiness will not end."

Then we began dancing, and most of the people wailed and cried as they danced, holding hands in a circle; but some of them laughed with happiness. Now and then some one would fall down like dead, and others would go staggering around and panting before they would fall. While they were lying there like dead they were having visions, and we kept on dancing and singing, and many were crying for the old way of living and that the old religion might be with them again.

After awhile I began to feel very queer. First, my legs seemed to be full of ants. I was dancing with my eyes closed, as the others did. Suddenly it seemed that I was swinging off the ground and not touching it any longer. The queer feeling came up from my legs and was in my heart now. It seemed I would glide forward like a swing, and then glide back again in longer and longer swoops. There was no fear with this, just a growing happiness.

I must have fallen down, but I felt as though I had fallen off a swing when it was going forward, and I was floating head first through the air. My arms were stretched out, and all I saw at first was a single eagle feather right in front of me. Then the feather was a spotted eagle dancing on ahead of me with his wings fluttering, and he was making the shrill whistle that is his. My body did not move at all, but I looked ahead and floated fast toward where I looked.

There was a ridge right in front of me, and I thought I was going to run into it, but I went right over it. On the other side of the ridge I could see a beautiful land where many, many people were camping in a great circle. I could see that they were happy and had plenty. Everywhere there were drying racks full of meat. The air was clear and beautiful with a living light that was everywhere. All around the circle, feeding on the green, green grass, were fat and happy horses; and animals of all kinds were scattered all over the green hills, and singing hunters were returning with their meat.

I floated over the tepees and began to come down feet first at the center of the hoop where I could see a beautiful tree all green and full of flowers. When I touched the ground, two men were coming toward me, and they wore holy shirts made and painted in a certain way. They came to me and said: "It is not yet time to see your father, who is happy. You have work to do. We will give you something that you shall carry back to your people, and with it they shall come to see their loved ones."

I knew it was the way their holy shirts were made that they wanted me to take back. They told me to return at once, and then I was out in the air again, floating fast as before. When I came right over the dancing place, the people were still dancing, but it seemed they were not making any sound. I had hoped to see the withered tree in bloom, but it was dead.

Then I fell back into my body, and as I did this I heard voices all around and above me, and I was sitting on the ground. Many were crowding around, asking me what vision I had seen. I told them just what I had seen, and what I brought back was the memory of the holy shirts the two men wore.

That evening some of us got together at Big Road's tepee and decided to use the ghost shirts I had seen. So the next day I made ghost shirts all day long and painted them in the sacred manner of my vision. As I made these shirts, I thought how in my vision everything was like old times and the tree was flowering, but when I came back the tree was dead. And I thought that if this world would do as the vision teaches, the tree could bloom here too.

I made the first shirt for Afraid-of-Hawk and the second for the son of Big Road.

In the evening I made a sacred stick like that I had seen in my first vision and painted it red with the sacred paint of the Wanekia. On the top of it I tied one eagle feather, and this I carried in the dance after that, wearing the holy shirt as I had seen it.

Because of my vision and the power they knew I had, I was asked to lead the dance next morning. We all stood in a straight line, facing the west, and I prayed: "Father, Great Spirit, behold me! The nation that I have is in despair. The new earth you promised you have shown me. Let my nation also behold it."

After the prayer we stood with our right hands raised to the west, and we all began to weep, and right there, as they wept, some of them fainted before the dance began.

As we were dancing I had the same queer feeling I had before, as though my feet were off the earth and swinging. Kicking Bear and Good Thunder were holding my arms. After-while it seemed they let go of me, and once more I floated head first, face down, with arms extended, and the spotted eagle was dancing there ahead of me again, and I could hear his shrill whistle and his scream.

I saw the ridge again, and as I neared it there was a deep, rumbling sound, and out of it there leaped a flame. But I glided right over it. There were six villages ahead of me in the beautiful land that was all clear and green in living light. Over these in turn I glided, coming down on the south side of the sixth village. And as I touched the ground, twelve men were coming towards me, and they said: "Our Father, the two-legged chief, you shall see!"

Then they led me to the center of the circle where once more I saw the holy tree all full of leaves and blooming.

But that was not all I saw. Against the tree there was a man standing with arms held wide in front of him. I looked hard at him, and I could not tell what people he came from. He was not a Wasichu and he was not an Indian. His hair was long and hanging loose, and on the left side of his head he wore an eagle feather. His body was strong and good to see, and it was painted red. I tried to recognize him, but I could not make him out. He was a very fine-looking man. While I was staring hard at him, his body began to change and became very beautiful with all colors of light, and around him there was light. He spoke like singing: "My life is such that all earthly beings and growing things belong to me. Your father, the Great Spirit, has said this. You too must say this."

Then he went out like a light in a wind.

The twelve men who were there spoke: "Behold them! Your nation's life shall be such!"

I saw again how beautiful the day was—the sky all blue and full of yellow light above the greening earth. And I saw that all the people were beautiful and young. There were no old ones there, nor children either—just people of about one age, and beautiful.

Then there were twelve women who stood in front of me and spoke: "Behold them! Their way of life you shall take back to earth." When they had spoken, I heard singing in the west, and I learned the song I heard.

Then one of the twelve men took two sticks, one painted white and one red, and, thrusting them in the ground, he said: "Take these! You shall depend upon them. Make haste!"

I started to walk, and it seemed as though a strong wind went under me and picked me up. I was in the air, with outstretched arms, and floating fast. There was a fearful dark river that I had to go over, and I was afraid. It rushed and roared and was full of angry foam. Then I looked down and saw many men and women who were trying to cross the dark and fearful river, but they could not. Weeping, they looked up to me and cried: "Help us!" But I could not stop gliding, for it was as though a great wind were under me.

Then I saw my earthly people again at the dancing place, and fell back into my body lying there. And I was sitting up, and people were crowding around me to ask what vision I had seen.

I told my vision through songs, and the older men explained them to the others. I sang a song, the words of which were those the Wanekia spoke under the flowering tree, and the air of it was that which I heard in the West after the twelve women had spoken. I sang it four times, and the fourth time all the people began to weep together because the Wasichus had taken the beautiful world away from us.

I thought and thought about this vision. The six villages seemed to represent the Six Grandfathers that I had seen long ago in the Flaming Rainbow Tepee, and I had gone to the sixth village, which was for the Sixth Grandfather, the Spirit of the Earth, because I was to stand for him in the world. I wondered if the Wanekia might be the red man of my great vision, who turned into a bison, and then into the four-rayed herb, the daybreak-star herb of understanding. I thought the twelve men and twelve women were for the moons of the year.

Bad Trouble Coming

While these things were happening, the summer (1890) was getting old. I did not then know all that was going on at other places, but some things I heard, and much more I heard later.

When Good Thunder and Kicking Bear came back in the spring from seeing the Wanekia, the Wasichus at Pine Ridge put them in prison awhile, and then let them go. This showed the Wasichus were afraid of something. In the Moon of Black Cherries (August) many people were dancing at No Water's Camp on Clay Creek, and the agent came and told them to stop dancing. They would not stop, and they said they would fight for their religion if they had to do it. The agent went away, and they kept on dancing. They called him Young-Man-Afraid-of-Lakotas.

Later, I heard that the Brules were dancing over east of us; and then I heard that Big Foot's people were dancing on the Good River reservation; also that Kicking Bear had gone to Sitting Bull's camp on Grand River, and that the people were dancing there too. Word came to us that the Indians were beginning to dance everywhere.

The people were hungry and in despair, and many believed in the good new world that was coming. The Wasichus gave us less than half the beef cattle they promised us in the treaty, and these cattle were very poor. For a while our people would not take the cattle, because there were so few of them and they were so poor. But afterwhile they had to take them or starve to death. So we got more lies than cattle, and we could not eat lies. When the agent told the people to quit dancing, their hearts were bad.

From the dancing on Wounded Knee I went over to the Brules, who were camping on Cut Meat Creek at this time, and I took with me six shirts like those I had seen the twelve men wearing in my vision, and six dresses like the twelve women wore. I gave these to the Brules and they made others for themselves.

We danced there, and another vision came to me. I saw a Flaming Rainbow, like the one I had seen in my first great vision. Below the rainbow was a tepee made of cloud. Over me there was a spotted eagle soaring, and he said to me: "Remember this." That was all I saw and heard.

I have thought much about this since, and I have thought that this was where I made my great mistake. I had had a very great vision, and I should have depended only upon that to guide me to the good. But I followed the lesser visions that had come to me while dancing on Wounded Knee Creek. The vision of the Flaming Rainbow was to warn me, maybe; and I did not understand. I did not depend upon the great vision as I should have done; I depended upon the two sticks that I had seen in the lesser vision. It is hard to follow one great vision in this world of darkness and of many changing shadows. Among those shadows men get lost.

When I came back from the Brules, the weather was getting cold. Many of the Brules came along when I came back, and joined the Oglalas in the dancing on Wounded Knee. We heard that there were soldiers at Pine Ridge and that others were coming all the time. Then one morning we heard that the soldiers were marching toward us, so we broke camp and moved west to Grass Creek. From there we went to White Clay and camped awhile and danced.

There came to us Fire Thunder, Red Wound and Young American Horse with a message from the soldiers that this matter of the ghost dance must be looked into, and that there should be rulings over it; and that they did not mean to take the dance away from us. But could we believe anything the Wasichus ever said to us? They spoke with forked tongues.

We moved in closer to Pine Ridge and camped. Many soldiers were there now, and what were they there for?

There was a big meeting with the agent, but I did not go to hear. He made a ruling that we could dance three days every moon, and the rest of the time we should go and make a living for ourselves somehow. He did not say how we could do that. But the people agreed to this.

The next day, while I was sitting in a tepee with Good Thunder, a policeman came to us and said: "I was not sent here, but I came for your good to tell you what I have heard—that they are going to arrest you two."

Good Thunder thought we ought to go to the Brules, who had a big camp on Wounded Knee below Manderson. So that evening we saddled and started. We came through Pepper Creek and White Horse Creek to Wounded Knee and followed it down to the Brule camp. They were glad to see us.

In the morning the crier went around and called a meeting. I spoke to the Brules, and this is what I said: "My relatives, there is a certain thing that we have done. From that certain sacred thing, we have had visions. In those visions we have seen, and also we have heard, that our relatives who have gone before us are in the Other World that has been revealed to us, and that we too shall go there. They are right now with the Wanekia. If the Wasichus want to fight us, let them do it. Have in your minds a strong desire, and take courage. We must depend upon the departed ones who are in the new world that is coming."

More Brules came there from Porcupine and Medicine Root creeks, and we all broke camp, moving down the Wounded Knee to Smoky Earth River (the White). There a Black Robe (Catholic Priest) came and tried to coax us to return. Our people told him that Wasichu promises were no good; that everything they had promised was a lie. Only a few Oglalas turned back with the Black Robe. He was a good man and he was badly wounded that winter in the butchering of Big Foot's band. He was a very good man, and not like the other Wasichus.[4]

From Smoky Earth River we moved to High Pockets' place southwest of the Top of the Badlands.[5] While we were there, American Horse and Fast Thunder came to us. They were both chiefs, and they came to bring us in to Pine Ridge. We had to obey. The Brules would not obey and tried to keep us from going. They struck us, and there was quite a struggle for a while; but we went anyway, because we had to go. Kicking Bear stayed with the Brules that time, but he came in to Pine Ridge a little later. A very few of the Brules went along with us.

We camped on White River, then on White Clay, then on Cheyenne Creek north of Pine Ridge. Most of the Oglalas were camping near there too.

It was about this time that bad news came to us from the north. We heard that some policemen from Standing Rock had gone to arrest Sitting Bull on Grand River, and that he would not let them take him; so there was a fight, and they killed him.

It was now near the end of the Moon of Popping Trees, and I was twenty-seven years old (December, 1890). We heard that Big Foot was coming down from the Badlands with nearly four hundred people. Some of these were from Sitting Bull's band. They had run away when Sitting Bull was killed, and joined Big Foot on Good River. There were only about a hundred warriors in this band, and all the others were women and children and some old men. They were all starving and freezing, and Big Foot was so sick that they had to bring him along in a pony drag.[6] They had all run away to hide in the Badlands, and they were coming in now because they were starving and freezing. When they crossed Smoky Earth River, they followed up Medicine Root Creek to its head. Soldiers were over there looking for them. The soldiers had everything and were not freezing and starving. Near Porcupine Butte the soldiers came up to the Big Foots, and they surrendered and went along with the soldiers to Wounded Knee Creek where the Brenan store is now.

It was in the evening when we heard that the Big Foots were camped over there with the soldiers, about fifteen miles by the old road from where we were. It was the next morning (December 29, 1890) that something terrible happened.

Notes

4. This was Father Craft.

5. Cuny Table, a high plateau in the midst of the Badlands.

6. He was very ill with pneumonia.

The Butchering at Wounded Knee

That evening before it happened, I went in to Pine Ridge and heard these things, and while I was there, soldiers started for where the Big Foots were. These made about five hundred soldiers that were there next morning. When I saw them starting I felt that something terrible was going to happen. That night I could hardly sleep at all. I walked around most of the night.

In the morning I went out after my horses, and while I was out I heard shooting off toward the east, and I knew from the sound that it must be wagon-guns (cannon) going off. The sounds went right through my body, and I felt that something terrible would happen.

When I reached camp with the horses, a man rode up to me and said: "Hey-hey-hey! The people that are coming are fired on! I know it!"

I saddled up my buckskin and put on my sacred shirt. It was one I had made to be worn by no one but myself. It had a spotted eagle outstretched on the back of it, and the daybreak star was on the left shoulder, because when facing south that shoulder is toward the east. Across the breast, from the left shoulder to the right hip, was the flaming rainbow, and there was another rainbow around the neck, like a necklace, with a star at the bottom. At each shoulder, elbow, and wrist was an eagle feather; and over the whole shirt were red streaks of lightning. You will see that this was from my great vision, and you will know how it protected me that day.

I painted my face all red, and in my hair I put one eagle feather for the One Above.

It did not take me long to get ready, for I could still hear the shooting over there.

I started out alone on the old road that ran across the hills to Wounded Knee. I had no gun. I carried only the sacred bow of the west that I had seen in my great vision. I had gone only a little way when a band of young men came galloping after me. The first two who came up were Loves War and Iron Wasichu. I asked what they were going to do, and they said they were just going to see where the shooting was. Then others were coming up, and some older men.

We rode fast, and there were about twenty of us now. The shooting was getting louder. A horseback from over there came galloping very fast toward us, and he said: "Hey-hey-hey! They have murdered them!" Then he whipped his horse and rode away faster toward Pine Ridge.

In a little while we had come to the top of the ridge where, looking to the east, you can see for the first time the monument and the burying ground on the little hill where the church is. That is where the terrible thing started. Just south of the burying ground on the little hill a deep dry gulch runs about east and west, very crooked, and it rises westward to nearly the top of the ridge where we were. It had no name, but the Wasichus sometimes call it Battle Creek now. We stopped on the ridge not far from the head of the dry gulch. Wagon guns were still going off over there on the little hill, and they were going off again where they hit along the gulch. There was much shooting down yonder, and there were many cries, and we could see cavalrymen scattered over the hills ahead of us. Cavalrymen were riding along the gulch and shooting into it, where the women and children were running away and trying to hide in the gullies and the stunted pines.

A little way ahead of us, just below the head of the dry gulch, there were some women and children who were huddled under a clay bank, and some cavalrymen were there pointing guns at them.

We stopped back behind the ridge, and I said to the others: "Take courage. These are our relatives. We will try to get them back." Then we all sang a song which went like this:

"A thunder being nation I am, I have said.
A thunder being nation I am, I have said.
You shall live.
You shall live.
You shall live.
You shall live."

Then I rode over the ridge and the others after me, and we were crying: "Take courage! It is time to fight!" The soldiers who were guarding our relatives shot at us and then ran away fast, and some more cavalrymen on the other side of the gulch did too. We got our relatives and sent them across the ridge to the northwest where they would be safe.

I had no gun, and when we were charging, I just held the sacred bow out in front of me with my right hand. The bullets did not hit us at all.

We found a little baby lying all alone near the head of the gulch. I could not pick her up just then, but I got her later and some of my people adopted her. I just wrapped her up tighter in a shawl that was around her and left her there. It was a safe place, and I had other work to do.

The soldiers had run eastward over the hills where there were some more soldiers, and they were off their horses and lying down. I told the others to stay back, and I charged upon them holding the sacred bow out toward them with my right hand. They all shot at me, and I could hear bullets all around me, but I ran my horse right close to them, and then swung around. Some soldiers across the gulch began shooting at me too, but I got back to the others and was not hurt at all.

By now many other Lakotas, who had heard the shooting, were coming up from Pine Ridge, and we all charged on the soldiers. They ran eastward toward where the trouble began. We followed down along the dry gulch, and what we saw was terrible. Dead and wounded women and children and little babies were scattered all along there where they had been trying to run away. The soldiers had followed along the gulch, as they ran, and murdered them in there. Sometimes they were in heaps because they had huddled together, and some were scattered all along. Sometimes bunches of them had been killed and torn to pieces where the wagon guns hit them. I saw a little baby trying to suck its mother, but she was bloody and dead.

There were two little boys at one place in this gulch. They had guns and they had been killing soldiers all by themselves. We could see the soldiers they had killed. The boys were all alone there, and they were not hurt. These were very brave little boys.

When we drove the soldiers back, they dug themselves in, and we were not enough people to drive them out from there. In the evening they marched off up Wounded Knee Creek, and then we saw all that they had done there.

Men and women and children were heaped and scattered all over the flat at the bottom of the little hill where the soldiers had their wagon-guns, and westward up the dry gulch all the way to the high ridge, the dead women and children and babies were scattered.

When I saw this I wished that I had died too, but I was not sorry for the women and children. It was better for them to be happy in the other world, and I wanted to be there too. But before I went there I wanted to have revenge. I thought there might be a day, and we should have revenge.

After the soldiers marched away, I heard from my friend, Dog Chief, how the trouble started, and he was right there by Yellow Bird when it happened. This is the way it was:

In the morning the soldiers began to take all the guns away from the Big Foots, who were camped in the flat below the little hill where the monument and burying ground are now. The people had stacked most of their guns, and even their knives, by the tepee where Big Foot was lying sick. Soldiers were on the little hill and all around, and there were soldiers across the dry gulch to the south and over east along Wounded Knee Creek too. The people were nearly surrounded, and the wagon-guns were pointing at them.

Some had not yet given up their guns, and so the soldiers were searching all the tepees, throwing things around and poking into everything. There was a man called Yellow Bird, and he and another man were standing in front of the tepee where Big Foot was lying sick. They had white sheets around and over them, with eyeholes to look through, and they had guns under these. An officer came to search them. He took the other man's gun, and then started to take Yellow Bird's. But Yellow Bird would not let go. He wrestled with the officer, and while they were wrestling, the gun went off and killed the officer. Wasichus and some others have said he meant to do this, but Dog Chief was standing right there, and he told me it was not so. As soon as the gun went off, Dog Chief told me, an officer shot and killed Big Foot who was lying sick inside the tepee.

Then suddenly nobody knew what was happening, except that the soldiers were all shooting and the wagon-guns began going off right in among the people.

Many were shot down right there. The women and children ran into the gulch and up west, dropping all the time, for the soldiers shot them as they ran. There were only about a hundred warriors and there were nearly five hundred soldiers. The warriors rushed to where they had piled their guns and knives. They fought soldiers with only their hands until they got their guns.

Dog Chief saw Yellow Bird run into a tepee with his gun, and from there he killed soldiers until the tepee caught fire. Then he died full of bullets.

It was a good winter day when all this happened. The sun was shining. But after the soldiers marched away from their dirty work, a heavy snow began to fall. The wind came up in the night. There was a big blizzard, and it grew very cold. The snow drifted deep in the crooked gulch, and it was one long grave of butchered women and children and babies, who had never done any harm and were only trying to run away.

The End of the Dream

After the soldiers marched away, Red Crow and I started back toward Pine Ridge together, and I took the little baby that I told you about. Red Crow had one too.

We were going back to Pine Ridge, because we thought there was peace back home; but it was not so. While we were gone, there was a fight around the Agency, and our people had all gone away. They had gone away so fast that they left all the tepees standing.

It was nearly dark when we passed north of Pine Ridge where the hospital is now, and some soldiers shot at us, but did not hit us. We rode into the camp, and it was all empty. We were very hungry because we had not eaten anything since early morning, so we peeped into the tepees until we saw where there was a pot with papa (dried meat) cooked in it. We sat down in there and began to eat. While we were doing this, the soldiers shot at the tepee, and a bullet struck right between Red Crow and me. It threw dust in the soup, but we kept right on eating until we had our fill. Then we took the babies and got on our horses and rode away. If that bullet had only killed me, then I could have died with papa in my mouth.

The people had fled down Clay Creek, and we followed their trail. It was dark now, and late in the night we came to where they were camped without any tepees. They were just sitting by little fires, and the snow was beginning to blow. We rode in among them and I heard my mother's voice. She was singing a death song for me, because she felt sure I had died over there. She was so glad to see me that she cried and cried.

Women who had milk fed the little babies that Red Crow and I brought with us.

I think nobody but the little children slept any that night. The snow blew and we had no tepees.

When it was getting light, a war party went out and I went along; but this time I took a gun with me. When I started out the day before to Wounded Knee, I took only my sacred bow, which was not made to shoot with; because I was a little in doubt about the Wanekia religion at that time, and I did not really want to kill anybody because of it.

But I did not feel like that any more. After what I had seen over there, I wanted revenge; I wanted to kill.

We crossed White Clay Creek and followed it up, keeping on the west side. Soon we could hear many guns going off. So we struck west, following a ridge to where the fight was. It was close to the Mission, and there are many bullets in the Mission yet.

From this ridge we could see that the Lakotas were on both sides of the creek and were shooting at soldiers who were coming down the creek. As we looked down, we saw a little ravine, and across this was a big hill. We crossed and rode up the hillside.

They were fighting right there, and a Lakota cried to me: "Black Elk, this is the kind of a day in which to do something great!" I answered: "How!"[7]

Then I got off my horse and rubbed earth on myself, to show the Powers that I was nothing without their help. Then I took my rifle, got on my horse and galloped up to the

106

top of the hill. Right below me the soldiers were shooting, and my people called out to me not to go down there; that there were some good shots among the soldiers and I should get killed for nothing.

But I remembered my great vision, the part where the geese of the north appeared. I depended upon their power. Stretching out my arms with my gun in the right hand, like a goose soaring when it flies low to turn in a change of weather, I made the sound the geese make—br-r-r-p, br-r-r-p, br-r-r-p; and, doing this, I charged. The soldiers saw, and began shooting fast at me. I kept right on with my buckskin running, shot in their faces when I was near, then swung wide and rode back up the hill.

All this time the bullets were buzzing around me and I was not touched. I was not even afraid. It was like being in a dream about shooting. But just as I had reached the very top of the hill, suddenly it was like waking up, and I was afraid. I dropped my arms and quit making the goose cry. Just as I did this, I felt something strike my belt as though some one had hit me there with the back of an ax. I nearly fell out of my saddle, but I managed to hold on, and rode over the hill.

An old man by the name of Protector was there, and he ran up and held me, for now I was falling off my horse. I will show you where the bullet struck me sidewise across the belly here (showing a long deep scar on the abdomen). My insides were coming out. Protector tore up a blanket in strips and bound it around me so that my insides would stay in. By now I was crazy to kill, and I said to Protector: "Help me on my horse! Let me go over there. It is a good day to die, so I will go over there!" But Protector said: "No, young nephew! You must not die to-day. That would be foolish. Your people need you. There may be a better day to die." He lifted me into my saddle and led my horse away down hill. Then I began to feel very sick.

By now it looked as though the soldiers would be wiped out, and the Lakotas were fighting harder; but I heard that, after I left, the black Wasichu soldiers came, and the Lakotas had to retreat.

There were many of our children in the Mission, and the sisters and priests were taking care of them. I heard there were sisters and priests right in the battle helping wounded people and praying.

There was a man by the name of Little Soldier who took charge of me and brought me to where our people were camped. While we were over at the Mission Fight, they had fled to the O-ona-gazhee[8] and were camped on top of it where the women and children would be safe from soldiers. Old Hollow Horn was there. He was a very powerful bear medicine man, and he came over to heal my wound. In three days I could walk, but I kept a piece of blanket tied around my belly.

It was now nearly the middle of the Moon of Frost in the Tepee (January). We heard that soldiers were on Smoky Earth River and were coming to attack us in the O-ona-gazhee. They were near Black Feather's place. So a party of about sixty of us started on the war-path to find them. My mother tried to keep me at home, because, although I could walk and ride a horse, my wound was not all healed yet. But I would not stay; for, after what I had seen at Wounded Knee, I wanted a chance to kill soldiers.

We rode down Grass Creek to Smoky Earth, and crossed, riding down stream. Soon from the top of a little hill we saw wagons and cavalry guarding them. The soldiers were making a corral of their wagons and getting ready to fight. We got off our horses and went behind some hills to a little knoll, where we crept up to look at the camp. Some soldiers were bringing harnessed horses down to a little creek to water, and I said to the others: "If you will stay here and shoot at the soldiers, I will charge over there and get some good horses." They knew of my power, so they did this, and I charged on my buckskin while the others kept shooting. I got seven of the horses; but when I started back with these, all the soldiers saw me and began shooting. They killed two of my horses, but I brought five back safe and was not hit. When I was out of range, I caught up a fine bald-faced bay and turned my buckskin loose. Then I drove the others back to our party.

By now more cavalry were coming up the river, a big bunch of them, and there was some hard fighting for a while, because there were not enough of us. We were fighting and retreating, and all at once I saw Red Willow on foot running. He called to me: "Cousin, my horse is killed!" So I caught up a soldier's horse that was dragging a rope and brought it to Red Willow while the soldiers were shooting fast at me. Just then, for a little while, I was a wanekia[9] myself. In this fight Long Bear and another man, whose name I have forgotten, were badly wounded; but we saved them and carried them along with us. The soldiers did not follow us far into the Badlands, and when it was night we rode back with our wounded to the O-ona-gazhee.

We wanted a much bigger war-party so that we could meet the soldiers and get revenge. But this was hard, because the people were not all of the same mind, and they were hungry and cold. We had a meeting there, and were all ready to go out with more warriors, when Afraid-of-His-Horses came over from Pine Ridge to make peace with Red Cloud, who was with us there.

Our party wanted to go out and fight anyway, but Red Cloud made a speech to us something like this: "Brothers, this is a very hard winter. The women and children are starving and freezing. If this were summer, I would say to keep on fighting to the end. But we cannot do this. We must think of the women and children and that it is very bad for them. So we must make peace, and I will see that nobody is hurt by the soldiers."

The people agreed to this, for it was true. So we broke camp next day and went down from the O-ona-gazhee to Pine Ridge, and many, many Lakotas were already there. Also, there were many, many soldiers. They stood in two lines with their guns held in front of them as we went through to where we camped.

And so it was all over.

I did not know then how much was ended. When I look back now from this high hill of my old age, I can still see the butchered women and children lying heaped and scattered all along the crooked gulch as plain as when I saw them with eyes still young. And I can see that something else died there in the bloody mud, and was buried in the blizzard. A people's dream died there. It was a beautiful dream.

And I, to whom so great a vision was given in my youth,—you see me now a pitiful old man who has done nothing, for the nation's hoop is broken and scattered. There is no center any longer, and the sacred tree is dead.

Notes

7. Signifying assent.
8. Sheltering place, an elevated plateau in the Badlands, with precipitous sides, and inaccessible save by one narrow neck of land easily defended.
9. A "make-live," savior.

16. Fall 1917—Spring 1918:
Manitou-geezis
Strong Spirit Sun

[Louise Erdrich]

There was nothing to say when Eli showed at my door. His hands were open and lifeless, hung at his sides. The hair flowed thick and loose down one cheek, as if he were in mourning. I saw his gun, tied across the pack on his shoulders, and a small bundle which he handed to me. When I opened the cloth I saw he'd brought me a stash of flour, lard, sugar, and I knew that he wanted to stay. I finally said to him, "You best sit down and have a plate of stew." So he came in, but he wouldn't eat. I suppose he could see for himself that the meat in the pot was only one poor gopher that should have hibernated while it could. He sat on the bed while I ate, but wouldn't look at me, or talk. I got weary of his shuttered face.

"I'm an old man who doesn't have much time left," I hinted.

He took a deep breath, let it out with sad force.

"Ah, the wind has come up!" I encouraged. But now he glared at me, annoyed that his advisor should fail to understand the serious nature of his problem. I understood well enough, however. I took my chair to the window for the fading light and looked at some catalogues and some letters from the land court that had come by mail. A system of post was still a new and different thing to Indians, and I was marked out by the Agent to receive words in envelopes. They were addressed to Mr. Nanapush, and I saved every one I got. I had a skin of them tied and stowed beneath my bed.

Fearing he had lost my interest, Eli mumbled some fierce words to the top of the table and locked his hands together. He knotted and unknotted his fingers until the knucklebones made irritating cracks.

"Spread that fire," is all I said, "the wood burns too hot and the sticks are snapping."

He wrung out his fingers, prodded the fire for a while, and fell back in his seat. Next I began to hear the sound of his clenched teeth grinding together, and finally he moaned between his lips.

"How much a man endures!"

"What man?" I said.

"This one!" He sank his face against his palms, and then, most impressive of all, let his head fall with a crash onto my table.

"Lucky my table is made of solid wood too."

"Uncle, have pity on your poor nephew!" he demanded angrily.

"My nephew already has sufficient pity on himself."

"You don't care for me either," he said in a bitter voice, pulling at the long messy flow of his locks. "None of them cares for me anymore."

I knew he was too full of vanity to remove a single hair.

"Some men would pull out a handful or two over what they've done," I told him, bending close. "Look at mine, so thin in spots there's almost nothing. I once shared your weakness—but for women, not little girls."

"She was no little girl!" He came to attention, stirred by the injustice of my judgment. "And besides, I was witched!"

"That's no good, " I counseled, shaking my head. "Fleur has known weak men before, and won't believe that excuse."

"All right," he countered, "but listen to this. *She* has done worse now. And I won't go back to her. She frightens me."

"At last." I continued to turn the dry, sharp pages of my papers. Between this unpromising winter, the pain in my hip that made me feel so poor I could not hunt, and the wholesale purchase of our allotment land by whites, the problems of Eli Kashpaw were of thin consequence, and yet he insisted on pelting me to death with grass.

"Look, fool," I said. "Open your eyes. Even your baby brother has a better grasp of what is going on. We're offered money in the agreements, cash for land. What will you do with the money?"

"Right now?" Eli asked in a belligerent, stalling way.

"Yes," I said, "what would you do with fifty dollars this moment?"

"I'd drink it up," he said in a pouting voice, daring my wrath even though I knew he rarely drank. I gave him no satisfaction, just kept the argument going.

"Like many," I said, "you'd wake with no place to put your foot down."

"I don't want to live around here anyway!" he yelled in rage.

I threw down the papers. "That's all you think about! You!"

Satisfied that he'd raised my temper, pretending he'd got my sympathy, Eli now busied himself with the cold stew. He gulped it all down as if it held tender beef, which we had not seen since the government issue. When he was done he leaned back and, without meaning to, his face registered the flat spoiled taste of the gopher meat. And with that, the first hint of pity for me. But I wanted none.

"I got a herd of this Indian beef corralled out in the woodpile and branded the government way," I told him. "I'm planning on holding a roundup."

He couldn't let himself laugh, so he punished me by staring blankly. He rolled a bit of tobacco and smoked to cut the edge of the grease.

He thought aloud after a while. "If Fleur was only in the church I could go there, get forgiveness by the priest, and then she would have to forget what happened."

He looked over at me, waiting with new hope for some reaction. But I was so disgusted at his foolish reasoning that I'd begun to wonder whether I would even help him. So many other things were on my mind. I had already given Father Damien testimony on this Anishinabe land, which was nibbled at the edges and surrounded by farmers waiting for it to go underneath the gavel of the auctioneer. There were so few of us who even understood the writing on the papers. Some signed their land away with thumbs and crosses. As a young man, I had made my reputation as a government interpreter, that is, until the Beauchamp Treaty signing, in which I said to Rift-In-A-Cloud, "Don't put your thumb in the ink." One of the officials understood and I lost my job. All of this could not have concerned Eli less. Now he put out the cigarette, grinding it onto the stove and saving the shred of tobacco. He kept looking hopeful, waiting for advice which he did not deserve.

"Lay your blankets down anywhere you want," I said to Eli. There was only the floor of beaten dirt, rock cold in the winter even by the stove. I expected that such constant discomfort would drive him home. He was disappointed, but knelt meekly and covered himself with the rough brown robe.

"My boy," I said into the dark after we were lying without sleep. "They'll eat much worse than gopher out there without a man to hunt. Margaret's no treaty Indian to get her rations in town."

Eli gave a harsh laugh. "Come winter, Fleur will chop a hole in the ice and fish the lake."

"Until then?"

"Until then, she's a good shot."

After six days I could not bear to hear any more from Eli. Each day of snow seemed endless, trapped with a sulking boy. Eli paced, muttered, slept, and also ate my cupboard completely bare, down to the last potato, and emptied the little bundle he brought, too, which would have lasted me the whole evil month. We went two days without anything but grease and crumbs of bread. On the seventh day I handed him his gun. He looked at it in surprise, but finally went north. I went out on my own, checking snares. I had caught some beardgrass, a clump of gray fur, a small carcass picked clean overnight by an owl, and a rabbit that was no good, full of worm. I went home and built the fire, drank some tea of dried nettles and considered that by the end of what looked to be a worse winter than I'd feared, I might be forced to boil my moccasins. That was one good thing at least. I hadn't taken to wearing tradestore boots of dyed leather. Those can kill you. After a while, I went and looked into the floursack, which I knew was already empty, and it was still empty. That's when I lay down.

In my fist I had a lump of charcoal, with which I blackened my face. I placed my otter bag upon my chest, my rattle near. I began to sing slowly, calling on my helpers, until the words came from my mouth but were not mine, until the rattle started, the song sang itself, and there, in the deep bright drifts, I saw the tracks of Eli's snowshoes clearly.

He was wandering, weak from his empty stomach, not thinking how the wind blew or calling on the clouds to cover the sky. He did not know what he hunted, what sign to look for or to follow. He let the snow dazzle him and almost dropped his gun. And then the song picked up and stopped him until he understood, from the deep snow and light hard crust, the high wind and rolling clouds, that everything around him was perfect for killing moose.

He had seen the tracks before, down near a frozen shallow slough. So he went there, knowing a moose is dull and has no imagination, although its hearing is particularly keen. He walked carefully around the rim of the depression. Now he was thinking. His vision had cleared and right away he saw the trail leading over the ice and back into the brush and overgrowth. Immediately, he stepped downwind and branched away, walked parallel and then looped back to find the animal's trail. He tracked like that, never right behind it, always careful of the wind, cautious on the harsh ground, gaining on his webbed shoes as the moose floundered and broke through the crust with every step until finally it came to a stand of young saplings, and fed.

Now the song gathered. I exerted myself. Eli's arms and legs were heavy, and without food he could not think. His mind was empty and I so feared that he would make a mistake. He knew that after the moose fed it would always turn downwind to rest. But the trees grew thicker, small and tightly clumped, and the shadows were a darker blue, lengthening.

Eli's coat, made by Margaret, was an old gray army blanket lined with the fur of rabbits. When he took it off and turned it inside out, so that only the soft pelts would brush the branches and not betray him as he neared, I was encouraged. He took his snowshoes off and left them in a tree. He stuffed his hat into his pocket, made his gun ready and then, pausing and sensitive for movement, for the rough shape, he slowly advanced.

Do not sour the meat, I reminded him now, *a strong heart moves slowly*. If he startled the moose so that adrenaline flowed into its blood, the meat would toughen, reveal the vinegar taste of fear.

Eli advanced with caution. The moose appeared. I held it in my vision just as it was, then, a hulking male, brown and unsuspicious in the late ordinary light of an afternoon. The scrub it stood within was difficult and dense all around, ready to deflect Eli's bullet.

But my song directed it to fly true.

The animal collapsed to its knees. Eli crashed from his hiding place, too soon, but the shot was good and the animal was dead. He used a tree limb to roll it on its back and then with his knife, cut the line down the middle. He was so cold he was almost in tears, and the warmth of the carcass dizzied him. To gain strength for the hard work ahead he carefully removed the liver, sliced off a bit. With a strip of cloth torn from the hem of his shirt, he wrapped that piece, sprinkled it with tobacco, and buried it under a handful of snow. Half of the rest, he ate. The other he saved for me.

He butchered carefully, but fast as possible, according to my instructions. One time in his youth, he had pierced the stomach of a deer with his knife, spreading its acids through the meat, and I'd hardly spoken to him all the rest of that day. He put his jacket right side out again, smeared it with tallow from a packet in his shirt, then quickly cut off warm slabs of meat and bound them to his body with sinew so that they would mold to fit him as they froze. He secured jagged ovals of haunch meat to his thighs, then fitted smaller rectangles down his legs, below the knees. He pressed to himself a new body, red and steaming, swung a roast to his back and knotted its ligaments around his chest. He bound a rack of ribs across his hat, jutting over his face, and tied them on beneath his chin. Last of all, he wrapped new muscles, wide and thick, around each forearm and past his elbows. What he could not pack, he covered with snow and branches, or hoisted laboriously into the boughs of an ash. He was too heavily laden to hide it all and the light was failing, so he fetched his snowshoes, then dragged the hide a distance away from the meat cache and left it for distraction. It was dusk then, and the walk was long.

There is a temptation, when it is terribly cold and the burden is heavy, to quicken pace to warm the blood. The body argues and steps fast, but the knowledge, informed by tales of hunters frozen with the flesh of their own bounty, resists. I know it well. Eli had become a thing of such cold by now, that, if he sweat, the film on his skin would freeze and draw from his blood all life, all warmth.

Without opening my eyes on the world around me, I took the drum from beneath my bed and beat out footsteps for Eli to hear and follow. Each time he speeded I slowed him. I strengthened the rhythm whenever he faltered beneath the weight he bore. In that way, he returned, and when I could hear the echo of his panting breath, I went outside to help him, still in my song.

He glowed, for the meat strapped to him had frozen a marbled blue. The blood from the moose was flour on his coat and on his face. His features were stiff, the strength in his limbs near exhausted. I freed him from the burden he held to his chest, and carried it home in my arms. He followed. I severed the rest from Eli's body and stashed it outside, in the lean-to. The meat stood on its own in pieces, a moose transformed into the mold of Eli, an armor that would fit no other.

He was stockstill, reluctant to move, his mouth dried open as I pulled him through the door. I took off his clothes, found the piece of saved liver under his arm, and ate it. Then I put a drop of water between his lips, wrapped him in a quilt and led him near the stove. I removed the kidneys and heart from Eli's pocket and cut them into smaller sections. My hands shook as I prepared the pieces with salt. My mouth watered as I put them in the fire and at the smell of meat roasting, I almost wept. I gave the first cut to Eli, who fell on it gratefully. As I put my share into my mouth, as I swallowed it, I felt myself grow solid in the chair. Lit by the burning stove, everything around me sharpened. Thoughts returned.

"You're my son," I said, moved by the scorched taste, "you're my relative."

17. Ceremony

Leslie Marmon Silko

Robert and Tayo stopped on the bridge and looked into the riverbed. It had been dry for a long time, and there were paths in the sand where the people walked. They were beginning to move. All along the sandy clay banks there were people, mostly men, stretched out, sleeping, some of them face down where they fell, and a few rolled over on their backs or on their sides, sleeping with their heads on their arms. The sun was getting hot and the flies were beginning to come out. They could see them buzzing around the face of a man under the bridge, smelling the sweetness of the wine or maybe the vomit down the front of the man's shirt. Robert shook his head. Tayo felt the choking in his throat; he blinked his eyes hard and didn't say anything. A man and woman came walking down the wash below them and looked up at them on the bridge. "Hey buddy!" the man yelled up. "You got a dollar you can loan us?" Robert looked at them and shook his head calmly, but Tayo started to sweat. He started reaching deep into his pockets for loose coins. The woman's hair was tangled in hairpins which had been pulled loose and hung around her head like ornaments. Her head weaved from side to side as she squinted and tried to focus on Tayo up above her. Her slip was torn and dragging the ground under her skirt; she had a dark bruise on her forehead. He found two quarters and tossed them into the man's outstretched hands, swaying above his head, and both the man and the woman dropped to their knees in the sand to find them. Robert walked away, but Tayo stood there, remembering the little bridge in a park in San Diego where all the soldiers took their dates the night before they shipped out to the South Pacific and stood throwing coins into the shallow pond. He had tossed the coins to them the way he had tossed them from the bridge in San Diego, in a gentle slow arc. Rocky wished out loud that night for a safe return from the war, but Tayo couldn't remember his wish. He watched them stumble and crawl up the loose clay of the steep riverbank. The man pulled the woman up the last few feet. The fly of his pants was unbuttoned and one of his shoes was flopping loose on his foot. They walked toward a bar south of the bridge, to wait for it to open.

They walked like survivors, with dull vacant eyes, their fists clutching the coins he'd thrown to them. They were Navajos, but he had seen Zunis and Lagunas and Hopis there too, walking alone or in twos and threes along the dusty Gallup streets. He didn't know how they got there in the first place, from the reservation to Gallup, but some must have had jobs for a while when they first came, and cheap rooms on the north side of the tracks, where they stayed until they got laid off or fired. Reservation people were the first ones to get laid off because white people in Gallup already knew they wouldn't ask any questions or get angry; they just walked away. They were educated only enough to know they wanted to leave the reservation; when they got to Gallup there weren't many jobs they could get. The men unloaded trucks in the warehouses near the tracks or piled lumber in the lumberyards or pushed wheelbarrows for construction; the women cleaned out motel rooms along Highway 66. The Gallup people knew they didn't have to pay good wages or put up with anything they didn't like, because there were plenty more Indians where these had come from.

It seemed to Tayo that they would go home, sooner or later, when they were hungry and dirty and broke; stand on 666 north of town and wait for someone driving to Keams Canyon or Lukachukai to stop, or borrow two dollars and ride the bus back to Laguna. But Gallup was a dangerous place, and by the time they realized what had happened to them, they must have believed it was too late to go home.

Robert was waiting for him on the hill. "Somebody you used to know?"

"Maybe," Tayo said. The sun was above them now, in a deep blue sky like good turquoise.

He looked back at the bridge, and he made a wish. The same wish Rocky made that night in San Diego: a safe return.

"What kind of medicine man lives in a place like that, in the foothills north of the Ceremonial Grounds?" Auntie wanted to know. Grandma told her, "Never mind. Old man Ku'oosh knows him, and he thinks this man Betonie might help him."

The Gallup Ceremonial had been an annual event for a long time. It was good for the tourist business coming through in the summertime on Highway 66. They liked to see Indians and Indian dances; they wanted a chance to buy Indian jewelry and Navajo rugs. Every year it was organized by the white men there, Turpen, Foutz, Kennedy, and the mayor. Dance groups from the Pueblos were paid to come; they got Plains hoop dancers, and flying-pole dancers from northern Mexico. They organized an all-Indian rodeo and horse races. And the people came, from all the reservations nearby, and some came from farther away; they brought their things to sell to the tourists, and they brought things to trade with each other: white deerhides, and feathers, and dried meat or piki bread. The tourists got to see what they wanted; from the grandstand at the Ceremonial grounds they watched the dancers perform, and they watched Indian cowboys ride bucking horses and Brahma bulls. There were wagon races, and the ladies' wood-chopping contest and fry-bread-making race. The Gallup merchants raised prices in motels and restaurants all Ceremonial week, and made a lot of money off the tourists. They sold great amounts of liquor to Indians, and in those years when liquor was illegal for Indians, they made a lot more money because they bootlegged it.

Old Betonie's place looked down on all of it; from the yellow sandrock foothills the whole town spread out below. The old man was tall and his chest was wide; at one time he had been heavier, but old age was consuming everything but the bones. He kept his hair tied back neatly with red yarn in a chongo knot, like the oldtimers wore. He was sitting on an old tin bucket turned upside down by the doorway to his hogan. When he stood up and extended his hand to Robert and Tayo, his motions were strong and unhesitating, as if they belonged to a younger man. He watched Tayo look around at the hogan and then back down at the Ceremonial grounds and city streets in the distance. He nodded his head at Tayo.

"People ask me why I live here," he said, in good English, "I tell them I want to keep track of the people. 'Why over here?' they ask me. 'Because this is where Gallup keeps Indians until Ceremonial time. Then they want to show us off to the tourists.'" He looked down at the riverbed winding through the north side of Gallup. "There," he said, pointing his chin at the bridge, "they sleep over there, in alleys between the bars." He turned and pointed to the city dump east of the Ceremonial grounds and rodeo chutes. "They keep us on the north side of the railroad tracks, next to the river and their dump. Where none of them want to live." He laughed. "They don't understand. We know these hills, and we are comfortable here." There was something about the way the old man said the word "comfortable." It had a different meaning—not the comfort of big houses or rich food or even clean streets, but the comfort of belonging with the land, and the peace of being with these hills. But the special meaning the old man had given to the English word was burned away by the glare of the sun on tin cans and broken glass, blinding reflections off the mirrors and chrome of the wrecked cars in the dump below. Tayo felt the old nausea rising up in his stomach, along with a vague feeling that he knew something which he could not remember. The sun was getting hot, and he thought about flies buzzing around their faces as they slept in the weeds along the arroyo. He turned back to Betonie. He didn't know how the medicine man could look down at it every day.

"You know, at one time when my great-grandfather was young, Navajos lived in all these hills." He pointed to the hills and ridges south of the tracks where the white people had built their houses. He nodded at the arroyo cut by the river. "They had little farms along the river. When the railroaders came and the white people began to build their town, the Navajos had to move." The old man laughed suddenly. He slapped his hands on his thighs. His laughter was easy, but Tayo could feel the tiny hairs along his spine spring up. This Betonie didn't talk the way Tayo expected a medicine man to talk. He didn't act like a medicine man at all.

"It strikes me funny," the medicine man said, shaking his head, "people wondering why I live so close to this filthy town. But see, this hogan was here first. Built long before the white people ever came. It is that town down there which is out of place. Not this old medicine man." He laughed again, and Tayo looked at Robert quickly to see what he thought of the old man; but Robert's face was calm, without any mistrust or alarm. When old Betonie had finished talking, Robert stepped over to Tayo and touched his shoulder gently. "I guess I'll go now," he said softly.

Tayo watched him walk down the path from the old man's place, and he could feel cold sweat between his fingers. His heart was pounding, and all he could think about was that if he started running right then, he could still catch up to Robert.

"Go ahead," old Betonie said, "you can go. Most of the Navajos feel the same way about me. You won't be the first one to run away."

Tayo turned to look for Robert, but he was gone. He stared at the dry yellow grass by the old man's feet. The sun's heat was draining his strength away; there was no place to go now except back to the hospital in Los Angeles. They didn't want him at Laguna the way he was.

All along there had been something familiar about the old man. Tayo turned around then to figure out what it was. He looked at his clothes: the old moccasins with splayed-out elkhide soles, the leather stained dark with mud and grease; the gray wool trousers were baggy and worn thin at the knees, and the old man's elbows made brown points through the sleeves of the blue cotton work shirt. He looked at his face. The cheekbones were like the wings of a hawk soaring away from his broad nose; he wore a drooping thick mustache; the hairs were steel gray. Then Tayo looked at his eyes. They were hazel like his own. The medicine man nodded. "My grandmother was a remarkable Mexican with green eyes," he said.

He bent down like the old man did when he passed through the low doorway. Currents of cool air streamed toward the door, and even before his eyes adjusted to the dimness of the room, he could smell its contents; a great variety of herb and root odors were almost hidden by the smell of mountain sage and something as ordinary as curry powder. Behind the smell of dried desert tea he smelled heavier objects: the salty cured smell of old hides sewn into boxes bound in brass; the odor of old newspapers and cardboard, their dust smelling of the years they had taken to decay.

The old man pointed to the back of the circular room. "The west side is built into the hill in the old-style way. Sand and dirt for a roof; just about halfway underground. You can feel it, can't you?"

Tayo nodded. He was standing with his feet in the bright circle of sunlight below the center of the log ceiling open for smoke. The size of the room had not been lost in the clutter of boxes and trunks stacked almost to the ceiling beams.

Old Betonie pointed at a woolly brown goatskin on the floor below the sky hole. Tayo sat down, but he didn't take his eyes off the cardboard boxes that filled the big room; the sides of some boxes were broken down, sagging over with old clothing and rags spilling out; others were jammed with the antennas of dry roots and reddish willow twigs tied in neat bundles with old cotton strings. The boxes were stacked crookedly, some stacks leaning into others, with only their opposing angles holding them steady. Inside the boxes without lids, the erect brown string handles of shopping bags poked out; piled to the tops of the WOOLWORTH bags were bouquets of dried sage and the brown leaves of mountain tobacco wrapped in swaths of silvery unspun wool.

He could see bundles of newspapers, their edges curled stiff and brown, barricading piles of telephone books with the years scattered among cities—St. Louis, Seattle, New York, Oakland—and he began to feel another dimension to the old man's room. His heart beat faster, and he felt the blood draining from his legs. He knew the answer before he could shape the question. Light from the door worked paths through the thick bluish green glass of the Coke bottles; his eyes followed the light until he was dizzy and sick. He wanted to dismiss all of it as an old man's rubbish, debris that had fallen out of the years, but the boxes and trunks, the bundles and stacks were plainly part of the pattern: they followed the concentric shadows of the room.

The old man smiled. His teeth were big and white. "Take it easy," he said, "don't try to see everything all at once." He laughed. "We've been gathering these things for a long time—hundreds of years. She was doing it before I was born, and he was working before she came. And on and on back down in time." He stopped, smiling. "Talking like this is just as bad, isn't it? Too big to swallow all at once."

Tayo nodded, but now his eyes were on the ceiling logs where pouches and bags dangled from wooden pegs and square-headed nails. Hard shrunken skin pouches and black leather purses trimmed with hammered silver buttons were things he could understand. They were a medicine man's paraphernalia, laid beside the painted gourd rattles and deer-hoof clackers of the ceremony. But with this old man it did not end there; under the medicine bags and bundles of rawhide on the walls, he saw layers of old calendars, the sequences of years confused and lost as if occasionally the oldest calendars had fallen or been taken out from under the others and then had been replaced on top of the most recent years. A few showed January, as if the months on the underlying pages had no longer been turned or torn away.

Old Betonie waved his hands around the hogan. "And what do I make from all this?" He nodded, moving his head slowly up and down. "Maybe you smelled it when you came in.

"In the old days it was simple. A medicine person could get by without all these things. But nowadays . . ." He let his voice trail off and nodded to let Tayo complete the thought for him.

Tayo studied the pictures and names on the calendars. He recognized names of stores in Phoenix and Albuquerque, but in recent years the old man had favored Santa Fe Railroad calendars that had Indian scenes painted on them—Navajos herding sheep, deer dancers at Cochiti, and little Pueblo children chasing burros. The chills on his neck followed his eyes: he recognized the pictures for the years 1939 and 1940. Josiah used to bring the calendars home every year from the Santa Fe depot; on the reservation these calendars were more common than Coca-Cola calendars. There was no reason to be startled. This old man had only done the same thing. He tried to shake off the feeling by talking.

"I remember those two," he said.

"That gives me some place to start," old Betonie said, lighting up the little brown cigarette he had rolled. "All these things have stories alive in them." He pointed at the Santa Fe calendars. "I'm one of their best customers down there. I rode the train to Chicago in 1903." His eyes were shining then, and he was looking directly into Tayo's eyes. "I know," he said proudly, "people are always surprised when I tell them the places I have traveled." He pointed at the telephone books. "I brought back the books with all the names in them. Keeping track of things." He stroked his mustache as if he were remembering things.

Tayo watched him, trying to decide if the old man was lying. He wasn't sure if they even let Indians ride trains in those days. The old man laughed at the expression on Tayo's face. He wiped his mouth on the sleeve of his shirt.

"She sent me to school. Sherman Institute, Riverside, California. That was the first train I ever rode. I had been watching them from the hills up here all my life. I told her it looked like a snake crawling along the red-rock mesas. I told her I didn't want to go. I was already a big kid then. Bigger than the rest. But she said 'It is carried on in all languages now, so you have to know English too.'" He ran his fingers through his mustache again, still smiling as though he were thinking of other stories to tell. But a single hair came loose from his thick gray mustache, and his attention shifted suddenly to the hair between his fingers. He got up and went to the back of the hogan. Tayo heard the jingle of keys and the tin sound of a footlocker opening; the lock snapped shut and the old man came back and sat down; the hair was gone.

"I don't take any chances," he said as he got settled on the goatskin again. Tayo could hear his own pulse sound in his ears. He wasn't sure what the old man was talking about, but he had an idea. "Didn't anyone ever teach you about these things?"

Tayo shook his head, but he knew the medicine man could see he was lying. He knew what they did with strands of hair they found; he knew what they did with bits of fingernail and toenails they found. He was breathing faster, and he could feel the fear surge over him with each beat of his heart. They didn't want him around. They blamed him. And now they had sent him here, and this would be the end of him. The Gallup police would find his body in the bushes along the big arroyo, and he would be just one of the two or three they'd find dead that week. He thought about running again; he was stronger than the old man and he could fight his way out of this. But the pain of betrayal pushed into his throat like a fist. He blinked back the tears, but he didn't move. He was tired of fighting. If there was no one left to trust, then he had no more reason to live.

The old man laughed and laughed. He laughed, and when his laughter seemed almost to cease, he would shake his head and laugh all over again.

"I was at the World's Fair in St. Louis, Missouri, the year they had Geronimo there on display. The white people were scared to death of him. Some of them even wanted him in leg irons."

Tayo did not look up. Maybe this time he really was crazy. Maybe the medicine man didn't laugh all the time; maybe the dreams and the voices were taking over again.

"If you don't trust me, you better get going before dark. You can't be too careful these days," Betonie said, gesturing toward the footlocker where he kept the hairs. "Anyway, I couldn't help anyone who was afraid of me." He started humming softly to himself, a song that Tayo could hear only faintly, but that reminded him of butterflies darting from flower to flower.

"They sent me to this place after the war. It was white. Everything in that place was white. Except for me. I was invisible. But I wasn't afraid there. I didn't feel things sneaking up behind me. I didn't cry for Rocky or Josiah. There were no voices and no dreams. Maybe I belong back in that place."

Betonie reached into his shirt pocket for the tobacco sack. He rolled a skinny little cigarette in a brown wheat paper and offered the sack to Tayo. He nodded slowly to indicate that he had been listening.

"That's true," the old man said, "you could go back to that white place." He took a puff from the cigarette and stared down at the red sand floor. Then he looked up suddenly and his eyes were shining; he had a grin on his face. "But if you are going to do that, you might as well go down there, with the rest of them, sleeping in the mud, vomiting cheap wine, rolling over women. Die that way and get it over with." He shook his head and laughed. "In that hospital they don't bury the dead, they keep them in rooms and talk to them."

"There are stories about me," Betonie began in a quiet round voice. "Maybe you have heard some of them. They say I'm crazy. Sometimes they say worse things. But whatever they say, they don't forget me, even when I'm not here." Tayo was wary of his eyes. "That's right," Betonie said, "when I am gone off on the train, a hundred miles from here, those Navajos won't come near this hogan." He smoked for a while and stared at the circle of sunlight on the floor between them. What Tayo could feel was powerful, but there was no way to be sure what it was.

"My uncle Josiah was there that day. Yet I know he couldn't have been there. He was thousands of miles away, at home in Laguna. We were in the Philippine jungles. I understand that. I know he couldn't have been there. But I've got this feeling and it won't go away even though I know he wasn't there. I feel like he was there. I feel like he was there with those Japanese soldiers who died." Tayo's voice was shaking; he could feel the tears pushing into his eyes. Suddenly the feeling was there, as strong as it had been that day in the jungle. "He loved me. He loved me, and I didn't do anything to save him."

"When did he die?"

"While we were gone. He died because there was no one to help him search for the cattle after they were stolen."

"Rocky," Betonie said softly, "tell me about Rocky."

The tears ran along the sides of Tayo's nose and off his chin; as they fell, the hollow inside his chest folded into the black hole, and he waited for the collapse into himself.

"It was the one thing I could have done. For all of them, for all those years they kept me . . . for everything that had happened because of me . . ."

"You've been doing something all along. All this time, and now you are at an important place in this story." He paused. "The Japanese," the medicine man went on, as though he were trying to remember something. "It isn't surprising you saw him with them. You saw who they were. Thirty thousand years ago they were not strangers. You saw what the evil had done: you saw the witchery ranging as wide as this world."

"And these cattle . . .

"The people in Cubero called her the Night Swan. She told him about the cattle. She encouraged him to buy them. Auntie said that—"

The old man waved his arms at Tayo. "Don't tell me about your aunt. I want to know about those cattle and that woman."

"She said something to me once. About our eyes. Hazel-green eyes. I never understood. Was she bad, like Auntie kept saying? Did the cattle kill him—did I let the cattle kill him?"

The old man had jumped up. He was walking around the fire pit, moving behind Tayo as he went around. He was excited, and from time to time he would say something to himself in Navajo.

Betonie dug down into the cardboard boxes until dust flew up around his face. Finally he pulled out a brown spiral notebook with a torn cover; he thumbed through the pages slowly, moving his lips slightly. He sat down again, across from Tayo, with the notebook in his lap.

"I'm beginning to see something," he said with his eyes closed, "yes. Something very important."

The room was cooler than before. The light from the opening in the roof was becoming diffuse and gray. It was sundown. Betonie pointed a finger at him.

"This has been going on for a long long time. They will try to stop you from completing the ceremony."

The hollow inside him was suddenly too small for the anger. "Look," Tayo said through clenched teeth, "I've been sick, and half the time I don't know if I'm still crazy or not. I don't know anything about ceremonies or these things you talk about. I don't know how long anything has been going on. I just need help." The words made his body shake as if they had an intensity of their own which was released as he spoke.

"We all have been waiting for help a long time. But it never has been easy. The people must do it. You must do it." Betonie sounded as if he were explaining something simple but important to a small child. But Tayo's stomach clenched around the words like knives stuck into his guts. There was something large and terrifying in the old man's words. He wanted to yell at the medicine man, to yell the things the white doctors had yelled at him—that he had to think only of himself, and not about the others, that he would never get well as long as he used words like "we" and "us." But he had known the answer all along, even while the white doctors were telling him he could get well and he was trying to believe them: medicine didn't work that way, because the world didn't work that way. His sickness was only part of something larger, and his cure would be found only in something great and inclusive of everything.

"There are some things I have to tell you," Betonie began softly. "The people nowadays have an idea about the ceremonies. They think the ceremonies must be performed exactly as they have always been done, maybe because one slip-up or mistake and the whole ceremony must be stopped and the sand painting destroyed. That much is true. They think that if a singer tampers with any part of the ritual, great harm can be done, great power unleashed." He was quiet for a while, looking up at the sky through the smoke hole. "That much can be true also. But long ago when the people were given these ceremonies, the changing began, if only in the aging of the yellow gourd rattle or the shrinking of the skin around the eagle's claw, if only in the different voices from generation to generation, singing the chants. You see, in many ways, the ceremonies have always been changing."

Tayo nodded; he looked at the medicine pouches hanging from the ceiling and tried to imagine the objects they contained.

"At one time, the ceremonies as they had been performed were enough for the way the world was then. But after the white people came, elements in this world began to shift; and it became necessary to create new ceremonies. I have made changes in the rituals. The people mistrust this greatly, but only this growth keeps the ceremonies strong.

"She taught me this above all else: things which don't shift and grow are dead things. They are things the witchery people want. Witchery works to scare people, to make them fear growth. But it has always been necessary, and more than ever now, it is. Otherwise we won't make it.

We won't survive. That's what the witchery is counting on: that we will cling to the ceremonies the way they were, and then their power will triumph, and the people will be no more."

He wanted to believe old Betonie. He wanted to keep the feeling of his words alive inside himself so that he could believe that he might get well. But when the old man left, he was suddenly aware of the old hogan: the red sand floor had been swept unevenly; the boxes were spilling out rags; the trunks were full of the junk and trash an old man saves—notebooks and whisker hairs. The shopping bags were torn, and the weeds and twigs stuck out of rips in the brown paper. The calendars Betonie got for free and the phone books that he picked up in his travels—all of it seemed suddenly so pitiful and small compared to the world he knew the white people had—a world of comfort in the sprawling houses he'd seen in California, a world of plenty in the food he had carried from the officers' mess to dump into garbage cans. The old man's clothes were dirty and old, probably collected like his calendars. The leftover things the whites didn't want. All Betonie owned in the world was in this room. What kind of healing power was in this?

Anger propelled him to his feet; his legs were stiff from sitting for so long. This was where the white people and their promises had left the Indians. All the promises they made to you, Rocky, they weren't any different than the other promises they made.

He walked into the evening air, which was cool and smelled like juniper smoke from the old man's fire. Betonie was sitting by the fire, watching the mutton ribs cook over a grill he had salvaged from the front end of a wrecked car in the dump below. The grill was balanced between two big sandrocks, where the hot coals were banked under the spattering meat. Tayo looked down at the valley, at the lights of the town and the headlights and taillights strung along Highway 66.

"They took almost everything, didn't they?"

The old man looked up from the fire. He shook his head slowly while he turned the meat with a forked stick. "We always come back to that, don't we? It was planned that way. For all the anger and the frustration. And for the guilt too. Indians wake up every morning of their lives to see the land which was stolen, still there, within reach, its theft being flaunted. And the desire is strong to make things right, to take back what was stolen and to stop them from destroying what they have taken. But you see, Tayo, we have done as much fighting as we can with the destroyers and the thieves: as much as we could do and still survive."

Tayo walked over and knelt in front of the ribs roasting over the white coals of the fire.

"Look," Betonie said, pointing east to Mount Taylor towering dark blue with the last twilight. "They only fool themselves when they think it is theirs. The deeds and papers don't mean anything. It is the people who belong to the mountain."

Tayo poked a stick into the coals and watched them lose shape and collapse into white ash. "I wonder sometimes," he said, "because my mother went with white men." He stopped there, unable to say any more. The birth had betrayed his mother and brought shame to the family and to the people.

Old Betonie sat back on his heels and looked off in the distance. "Nothing is that simple," he said, "you don't write off all the white people, just like you don't trust all the Indians." He pointed at the coffeepot in the sand at the edge of the coals, and then at the meat. "You better eat now," he said.

Tayo finished the meat on the mutton ribs and threw the bones to a skinny yellow dog that came out from behind the hogan. Behind the dog a boy about fifteen or sixteen came with an armload of firewood. He knelt by the fire with the kindling; Betonie spoke to him in Navajo and indicated Tayo with a nod of his head.

"This is my helper," he told Tayo. "They call him Shush. That means bear." It was dark, but in the light from the fire Tayo could see there was something strange about the boy, something remote in his eyes, as if he were on a distant mountaintop alone and the fire and hogan and the lights of the town below them did not exist.

He was a small child
learning to get around
by himself.
His family went by wagon
into the mountains near
Fluted Rock.

It was Fall and
they were picking piñons.
I guess he just wandered away
trying to follow his brothers and sisters
into the trees.
His aunt thought he was with his mother,
and she thought he was with her sister.

When they tracked him the next day
his tracks went into the canyon
near the place which belonged
to the bears. They went
as far as they could
to the place
where no human
could go beyond,
and his little footprints
were mixed in with bear tracks.

So they sent word for this medicine man
to come. He knew how
to call the child back again.

There wasn't much time.
The medicine man was running, and his
assistants followed behind him.

They all wore bearweed
tied at their wrists and ankles
and around their necks.

He grunted loudly and scratched on the ground in front of him
he kept watching the entrance of the bear cave.
He grunted and made a low growling sound.
Pretty soon the little bears came out
because he was making mother bear sounds.

He grunted and growled a little more
and then the child came out.
He was already walking like his sisters
he was already crawling on the ground.

They couldn't just grab the child
They couldn't simply take him back
because he would be in between forever
and probably he would die.

They had to call him
step by step the medicine man
brought the child back.

So, long time ago
they got him back again
but he wasn't quite the same
after that
not like the other children.

Tayo stood up and moved around the fire uneasily; the boy took some ribs and disappeared again behind the hogan. The old man put some wood on the fire. "You don't have to be afraid of him. Some people act like witchery is responsible for everything that happens, when actually witchery only manipulates a small portion." He pointed in the direction the boy had gone. "Accidents happen, and there's little we can do. But don't be so quick to call something good or bad. There are balances and harmonies always shifting, always necessary to maintain. It is very peaceful with the bears; the people say that's the reason human beings seldom return. It is a matter of transitions, you see; the changing, the becoming must be cared for closely. You would do as much for the seedlings as they become plants in the field."[1]

The wind came up and fanned the fire. Tayo watched a red flame crawl out from under the white coals; he reached down for a piece of juniper and tossed it in. The fire caught. He rubbed pitch from the wood between his fingers and looked down at Gallup.

---

[1] **Note on Bear People and Witches**

Don't confuse those who go to the bears with the witch people. Human beings who live with the bears do not wear bear skins. They are naked and not conscious of being different from their bear relatives. Witches crawl into skins of dead animals, but they can do nothing but play around with objects and bodies. Living animals are terrified of witches. They smell the death. That's why witches can't get close to them. That's why people keep dogs around their hogans. Dogs howl with fear when witch animals come around.

"I never told you about Emo," he said, "I never told you what happened to Rocky." He pointed at the lights below. "Something about the lights down there, something about the cars and the neon signs which reminds me of both of them."

"Yes," the old man said, "my grandmother would not leave this hill. She said the whole world could be seen from here."

"Rocky wanted to get away from the reservation; he wanted to make something of himself. In a city somewhere."

"They are down there. Ones like your brother. They are down there."

"He didn't make it though. I was supposed to help him, so he'd make it back. They were counting on him. They were proud of him. I owed them that much. After everything that happened. I owed it to them." He looked at the old man, but he was staring at the lights down below, following the headlights from the west until they were taillights disappearing in the east. He didn't seem to be listening.

"There are no limits to this thing," Betonie said. "When it was set loose, it ranged everywhere, from the mountains and plains to the towns and cities; rivers and oceans never stopped it." The wind was blowing steadily and the old man's voice was almost lost in it.

"Emo plays with these teeth—human teeth—and he says the Indians have nothing compared to white people. He talks about their cities and all the machines and food they have. He says the land is no good, and we must go after what they have, and take it from them." Tayo coughed and tried to clear the tightness from his throat. "Well, I don't know how to say this but it seems that way. All you have to do is look around. And so I wonder," he said, feeling the tightness in his throat squeeze out the tears, "I wonder what good Indian ceremonies can do against the sickness which comes from their wars, their bombs, their lies?"

The old man shook his head. "That is the trickery of the witchcraft," he said. "They want us to believe all evil resides with white people. Then we will look no further to see what is really happening. They want us to separate ourselves from white people, to be ignorant and helpless as we watch our own destruction. But white people are only tools that the witchery manipulates; and I tell you, we can deal with white people, with their machines and their beliefs. We can because we invented white people; it was Indian witchery that made white people in the first place.

Long time ago
in the beginning
there were no white people in this world
there was nothing European.
And this world might have gone on like that
except for one thing:
witchery.
This world was already complete
even without white people.
There was everything
including witchery.

Then it happened.
These witch people got together.
Some came from far far away
across oceans
across mountains.
Some had slanty eyes
others had black skin.
They all got together for a contest
the way people have baseball tournaments nowadays
except this was a contest
in dark things.

So anyway
they all got together
witch people from all directions
witches from all the Pueblos
and all the tribes.
They had Navajo witches there,
some from Hopi, and a few from Zuni.
They were having a witches' conference,
that's what it was
Way up in the lava rock hills
north of Cañoncito
they got together
to fool around in caves
with their animal skins.
Fox, badger, bobcat, and wolf
they circled the fire
and on the fourth time
they jumped into that animal's skin.

But this time it wasn't enough
and one of them
maybe a Sioux or some Eskimos
started showing off.
"That wasn't anything,
watch this."

The contest started like that.
Then some of them lifted the lids
on their big cooking pots,
calling the rest of them over
to take a look:
dead babies simmering in blood

circles of skull cut away
all the brains sucked out.
Witch medicine
to dry and grind into powder
for new victims.

Others untied skin bundles of disgusting objects:
dark flints, cinders from burned hogans where the dead lay
Whorls of skin
cut from fingertips
sliced from the penis end and clitoris tip.

Finally there was only one
who hadn't shown off charms or powers.
The witch stood in the shadows beyond the fire
and no one ever knew where this witch came from
which tribe
or if it was a woman or a man.
But the important thing was
this witch didn't show off any dark thunder charcoals
or red ant-hill beads.
This one just told them to listen:
"What I have is a story."

At first they all laughed
but this witch said
Okay
go ahead
laugh if you want to
but as I tell the story
it will begin to happen.

Set in motion now
set in motion by our witchery
to work for us.

Caves across the ocean
in caves of dark hills
white skin people
like the belly of a fish
covered with hair.

Then they grow away from the earth
then they grow away from the sun
then they grow away from the plants and animals.

They see no life
When they look
they see only objects.
The world is a dead thing for them
the trees and rivers are not alive
the mountains and stones are not alive.
The deer and bear are objects
They see no life.

They fear
They fear the world.
They destroy what they fear.
They fear themselves.

The wind will blow them across the ocean
thousands of them in giant boats
swarming like larva
out of a crushed ant hill.

They will carry objects
which can shoot death
faster than the eye can see.

They will kill the things they fear
all the animals
the people will starve.

They will poison the water
they will spin the water away
and there will be drought
the people will starve.

They will fear what they find
They will fear the people
They kill what they fear.

Entire villages will be wiped out
They will slaughter whole tribes.

Corpses for us
Blood for us
Killing killing killing killing.

And those they do not kill
will die anyway
at the destruction they see

at the loss
at the loss of the children
the loss will destroy the rest.

Stolen rivers and mountains
the stolen land will eat their hearts
and jerk their mouths from the Mother.
The people will starve.

They will bring terrible diseases
the people have never known.
Entire tribes will die out
covered with festered sores
shitting blood
vomiting blood.
Corpses for our work

Set in motion now
set in motion by our witchery
set in motion
to work for us.

They will take this world from ocean to ocean
they will turn on each other
they will destroy each other
Up here
in these hills
they will find the rocks,
rocks with veins of green and yellow and black.
They will lay the final pattern with these rocks
they will lay it across the world
and explode everything.

Set in motion now
set in motion
To destroy
To kill
Objects to work for us
objects to act for us
Performing the witchery
for suffering
for torment
for the still-born
the deformed
the sterile

the dead.
Whirling
whirling
whirling
whirling
set into motion now
set into motion.

So the other witches said
"Okay you win; you take the prize,
but what you said just now—
it isn't so funny
It doesn't sound so good.
We are doing okay without it
we can get along without that kind of thing.
Take it back.
Call that story back."

But the witch just shook its head
at the others in their stinking animal skins, fur and feathers.
It's already turned loose.
It's already coming.
It can't be called back.

They left on horseback before dawn. The old man rode a skinny pinto mare with hip bones and ribs poking against the hide like springs of an old car seat. But she was strong and moved nimbly up the narrow rocky path north of Betonie's hogan. The old man's helper rode a black pony, hunching low over its neck with his face in the mane. Maybe he rode like that for warmth, because it was cold in those foothills before dawn; the night air of the high mountains was chilled by the light of the stars and the shadows of the moon. The brown gelding stumbled with Tayo; he reined it in and walked it more slowly. Behind them in the valley, the highway was a faint dark vein through the yellow sand and red rock. He smelled piñon and sage in the wind that blew across the stony backbone of the ridge. They left the red sandstone and the valley and rode into the lava-rock foothills and pine of the Chuska Mountains.

"We'll have the second night here," Betonie said, indicating a stone hogan set back from the edge of the rimrock.

Tayo stood near the horses, looking down the path over the way they had come. The plateaus and canyons spread out below him like clouds falling into each other past the horizon. The world below was distant and small; it was dwarfed by a sky so blue and vast the clouds were lost in it. Far into the south there were smoky blue ridges of the mountain haze at Zuni. He smoothed his hand over the top of his head and felt the sun. The mountain wind was cool; it smelled like springs hidden deep in mossy black stone. He could see no signs of what had been set loose upon the earth: the highways, the towns, even the fences were gone.

This was the highest point on the earth: he could feel it. It had nothing to do with measurements or height. It was a special place. He was smiling. He felt strong. He had to touch his own hand to remember what year it was: thick welted scars from the shattered bottle glass.

His mother-in-law suspected something.
She smelled coyote piss one morning.
She told her daughter.
She figured Coyote was doing this.
She knew her son-in-law was missing.

There was no telling what Coyote had done to him.
Four of them went to track the man.
They tracked him to the place he found deer tracks.
They found the place the deer was arrow-wounded
where the man started chasing it.
Then they found the place where Coyote got him.
Sure enough those coyote tracks went right along there
Right around the marks in the sand where the man lay.

The human tracks went off
toward the mountain
where the man must have crawled.
They followed the tracks to a hard oak tree
where he had spent a night.
From there he had crawled some distance farther
and slept under a scrub oak tree.
Then his tracks went to a piñon tree
and then under the juniper where he slept another night.

The tracks went on and on
but finally they caught up with him
sleeping under the wild rose bush.
"What happened? Are you the one
who left four days ago, my grandchild?"
A coyote whine was the only sound he made.
"Four days ago you left,
are you that one, my grandchild?"
The man tried to speak
but only a coyote sound was heard,
and the tail moved back and forth
sweeping ridges in the sand.
He was suffering from thirst and hunger
he was almost too weak to raise his head.
But he nodded his head "yes."

"This is him all right,
but what can we do to save him?"

They ran to the holy places
they asked what might be done.

"At the summit of Dark Mountain
ask the four old Bear People.
They are the only possible hope
they have the power to restore the mind.
Time and again
it has been done."

Big Fly went to tell them.
The old Bear People said they would come
They said
Prepare hard oak
scrub oak
piñon
juniper and wild rose twigs
Make hoops
tie bundles of weeds into hoops.
Make four bundles
tie them with yucca
spruce mixed with charcoal from burned weeds
snakeweed and gramma grass and rock sage.
Make four bundles.

The rainbows were crossed.
They had been his former means of travel.
Their purpose was
to restore this to him.

They made Pollen Boy right in the center of
the white corn painting.
His eyes were blue pollen
his mouth was blue pollen
his neck was too
There were pinches of blue pollen
at his joints.

He sat in the center of the white corn sand painting. The rainbows crossed were in the painting behind him. Betonie's helper scraped the sand away and buried the bottoms of the hoops in little trenches so that they were standing up and spaced apart, with the hard oak closest to him and the wild rose hoop in front of the door. The old man painted a dark mountain range beside the farthest hoop, the next, closer, he painted blue, and moving toward him, he knelt and made the yellow mountains; and in front of him, Betonie painted the white mountain range.

The helper worked in the shadows beyond the dark mountain range; he worked with the black sand, making bear prints side by side. Along the right side of the bear footprints, the old man painted paw prints in blue, and then yellow, and finally white. They finished it together, with a big rainbow arching wide above all the mountain ranges. Betonie gave him a basket with prayer sticks to hold.

en-e-e-ya-a-a-a!
en-e-e-ya-a-a-a!
en-e-e-ya-a-a-a!
en-e-e-ya-a-a-a!

In dangerous places you traveled
in danger you traveled
to a dangerous place you traveled
in danger e-hey-ya-ah-na!

To the place
where whirling darkness started its journey
along the edges of the rocks
along the places of the gentle wind
along the edges of blue clouds
along the edges of clear water.

Whirling darkness came up from the North
Whirling darkness moved along to the East
It came along the South
It arrived in the West
Whirling darkness spiraled downward
and it came up in the Middle.

The helper stepped out from the shadows; he was grunting like a bear. He raised his head as if it were heavy for him, and he sniffed the air. He stood up and walked to Tayo; he reached down for the prayer sticks and spoke the words distinctly, pressing the sticks close to his heart. The old man came forward then and cut Tayo across the top of his head; it happened suddenly. He hadn't expected it, but the dark flint was sharp and the cut was short. They both reached for him then; lifting him up by the shoulders, they guided his feet into the bear footprints, and Betonie prayed him through each of the five hoops.

eh-hey-yah-ah-na!
eh-hey-yah-ah-na!
eh-hey-yah-ah-na!
eh-hey-yah-ah-na!
eh-hey-yah-ah-na!

Tayo could feel the blood ooze along his scalp; he could feel rivulets in his hair. It moved down his head slowly, onto his face and neck as he stooped through each hoop.

e-hey-yah-ah-na!
e-hey-yah-ah-na!
e-hey-yah-ah-na!
e-hey-yah-ah-na!

At the Dark Mountain
born from the mountain
walked along the mountain
I will bring you through my hoop,
I will bring you back.

Following my footprints
walk home
following my footprints
Come home, happily
return belonging to your home
return to long life and happiness again
return to long life and happiness.

e-hey-yah-ah-na!
e-hey-yah-ah-na!
e-hey-yah-ah-na!
e-hey-yah-ah-na!

At the Dark Mountain
born from the mountain
moves his hand along the mountain
I have left the zigzag lightning behind
I have left the straight lightning behind

I have the dew,
a sunray falls from me,
I was born from the mountain
I leave a path of wildflowers
A raindrop falls from me
I'm walking home
I'm walking back to belonging
I'm walking home to happiness
I'm walking back to long life.

When he passed through the last hoop
it wasn't finished
They spun him around sunwise

and he recovered
he stood up
The rainbows returned him to his
home, but it wasn't over.
All kinds of evil were still on him.

From the last hoop they led him through the doorway. It was dark and the sky was bright with stars. The chill touched the blood on his head; his arms and legs were shaking. The helper brought him a blanket; they walked him to the edge of the rim-rock, and the medicine man told him to sit down. Behind him he heard the sound of wood and brush being broken into kindling. He smelled a fire. They gave him Indian tea to drink and old Betonie told him to sleep.

He dreamed about the speckled cattle. They had seen him and they were scattering between juniper trees, through tall yellow grass, below the mesas near the dripping spring. Some of them had spotted calves who ran behind them, their bony rumps flashing white and disappearing into the trees. He tried to run after them, but it was no use without a horse. They were gone, running southwest again, toward the high, lone-standing mesa the people called Pa'to'ch.

He woke up and he was shivering. He stood up and the blanket covering him slid to the ground. He wanted to leave that night to find the cattle; there would be no peace until he did. He looked around for Betonie and his helper. The horses had been tied by a big piñon tree, but they were gone now. He felt the top of his head where the cut had been made; it wasn't swollen or hot. It didn't hurt. He stood on the edge of the rimrock and looked down below: the canyons and valleys were thick powdery black; their variations of height and depth were marked by a thinner black color. He remembered the black of the sand paintings on the floor of the hogan; the hills and mountains were the mountains and hills they painted in sand. He took a deep breath of cold mountain air: there were no boundaries; the world below and the sand paintings inside became the same that night. The mountains from all the directions had been gathered there that night.

He heard someone come up from the west side of the ridge. He turned. Betonie looked even taller in the darkness. He motioned for Tayo to sit down. He sat down next to him and reached into his shirt pocket for the tobacco and wheat papers. He rolled a thin cigarette without looking down at his hands, still gazing up at the east sky. He lit it and took little puffs without inhaling the smoke.

* * * * *

The Scalp Ceremony lay to rest the Japanese souls in the green humid jungles, and it satisfied the female giant who fed on the dreams of warriors. But there was something else now, as Betonie said: it was everything they had seen—the cities, the tall buildings, the noise and the lights, the power of their weapons and machines. They were never the same after that: they had seen what the white people had made from the stolen land. It was the story of the white shell beads all over again, the white shell beads, stolen from a grave and found by a man as he walked along a trail one day. He carried the beautiful white shell beads on the end of a stick because he suspected where they came from; he left them hanging in the branches of a piñon tree. And although he had never touched them, they haunted him; all he could think of, all he dreamed of, were these white shell beads hanging in that tree. He could not eat, and he could not work. He lost touch with the life he had lived before the day he found those beads; and the man he had been before that day was lost somewhere on that trail where he first saw the beads. Every day they had to look at the land, from horizon to horizon, and every day the loss was with them; it was the dead unburied, and the mourning of the lost going on forever. So they tried to sink the loss in booze, and silence their grief with war stories about their courage, defending the land they had already lost.

18. Missionaries and the Religious Vacuum

VINE DELORIA, JR.

One of the major problems of the Indian people is the missionary. It has been said of missionaries that when they arrived they had only the Book and we had the land; now we have the Book and they have the land. An old Indian once told me that when the missionaries arrived they fell on their knees and prayed. Then they got up, fell on the Indians, and preyed.

Columbus managed to combine religion and real estate in his proclamation of discovery, claiming the new world for Catholicism and Spain. Missionaries have been unable to distinguish between their religious mission and their hunger for land since that time.

The first concern of mission work was land on which to build churches, homes, storehouses, and other necessary religious monuments. Like the men from New England in *Hawaii* by Michener, missionaries on the North American continent came to preach and stayed to rule. Or at least prepared the way for others to conquer and exploit.

Sacrifices often matched mistakes. Missionaries did more to open up the West than any other group, but in doing so they increased the possibility of exploitation of the people they purported to save. Land acquisition and missionary work always went hand in hand in American history.

While the thrust of Christian missions was to save the individual Indian, its result was to shatter Indian societies and destroy the cohesiveness of the Indian communities. Tribes that resisted the overtures of the missionaries seemed to survive. Tribes that converted were never heard of again. Where Christianity failed, and insofar as it failed, Indians were able to withstand the cultural deluge that threatened to engulf them.

The conflict between the Indian and white religions was classic. Each religion expressed the outlook and understanding of its respective group. Religious ideas of the two groups never confronted each other directly. The conflict was one of rites and techniques. Christianity destroyed many Indian religious practices by offering a much easier and more practical religion. It was something one could immediately understand, not a paving of the way for what ultimately confronted one.

The credal rhetoric of Christianity filled the vacuum it had created by its redefinition of religion as a commodity to be controlled. Although prohibited for several generations, Indian beliefs have always retained the capacity to return from their exile because they have always related to the Indian's deepest concern.

Indian religion required a personal commitment to act. Holy men relied upon revelations experienced during fasting, sacrifices, and visions. Social in impact, most Indian religious experience was individualistic in origin. Visions defined vocations in this world rather than providing information concerning salvation in the other world.

Formulas of faith were anathema to Indian societies. Debate over implications of the existence of God and creation of subtleties related to deity were unknown. The substantial doctrines developed by Christian theologians to explain, define, and control deity were never contemplated in Indian religious life. Religion was an undefined sphere of influence in tribal society.

Tribes shared with the Hebrews of the Old Testament the concept of the covenant of the People with God. The majority of tribal names, when translated into English, mean the People, First Men, or Original People. From the belief that the tribe is the People of God to the exclusion of other peoples, it usually follows that tribal customs and religious ordinances are synonymous.

Laws as such did not exist within tribal societies. Law was rejected as being force imposed from without, whereas peoplehood required fulfillment from within the individual. Insofar as there were external controls, Indians accepted only the traditions and customs which were rooted in the tribe's distant past. Time itself became irrelevant because custom prevailed long enough to outlive any knowledge of its origin. Mystery and reverence gradually surrounded rites and ceremonies, giving them the necessary *mysterium tremendum* by which they were able to influence social behavior.

Most mysterious was the Indian reverence for land. When told to settle down and become farmers, most Indians rebelled. For centuries they had lived off the land as hunters, taking and giving in their dances and ceremonies. Earth, they believed, was mother of all. Most important was the land which their particular tribe dwelt on. The Crow are a good example of the Indian religious love for land. The Crow have a long prayer which thanks the Great Spirit for giving them their land. It is not too hot, they say, and not too cold. It is not too high and snowy and not too low and dusty. Animals enjoy the land of the Crow, men enjoy it also. The prayer ends by declaring that of all the possible lands in which happiness can be found, only in the land of the Crow is true happiness found.

Even today I have watched Indian people look sadly over the miles of plowed ground of South Dakota, wishing that the land were returned to its primitive beauty, undefiled and giving to man and animal alike the life only land can give. Instead of beauty one sees a dust storm in the distance, ribbons of dirty highway going west, and the earth cut into a giant perverted checkerboard with no beauty and hardly even any symmetry.

Contrast this living, undefined religion, where man is a comfortable part of his world, with the message brought by the Christian missionary. The Reformation had divided the world into two arenas: church and state. Morality of one was not necessarily related to morality in the other. Often acts of the state, immoral by any standard, were endorsed by the church in an effort to gain political power and influence. Other times the church, in striving to protect its economic base, would encourage the state to undertake projects it dared not conceive of in its own moral terms.

There is, of course, an analogy in the contemporary role of the late Cardinal Spellman in supporting the United States in the Vietnam situation and the original encouragement by the churches of possession of lands the different European nations had *discovered.*

At one time or another slavery, poverty, and treachery were all justified by Christianity as politically moral institutions of the state. Economic Darwinism, the survival of the fittest businessman, was seen as a process approved by God and the means by which He determined His Chosen for salvation.

Exploitation of one's fellows by any means became a religious exercise. Law became a trap for the unwary and a dangerous weapon in the hands of those who understood how to use it. Public disclosure of wrongdoing was the only punishment society acknowledged either side of the grave, although religious sentimentalists talked vaguely about playing harps for an infinite number of years in some undisclosed heaven. Few mastered the harp before departing for that better life, however.

When the two religious movements came into conflict, the Christian religion was able to overcome tribal beliefs because of its ability to differentiate life into segments which were unrelated. When a world view is broken into its component disciplines, these disciplines become things unto themselves and life turns into an unrelated group of categories each with its own morality and ethics.

Missionaries approached the Indian tribes in an effort to bring them into western European religious life. Their primary message sought to invalidate the totality of Indian life and replace it with Christian values. Because Christian reality had been broken into credal definitions, all the missionaries could present to the Indians were words and phrases that had a magical connotation.

Missionaries looked at the feats of the medicine men and proclaimed them to be works of the devil. They overlooked the fact that the medicine men were able to do marvelous things. Above all, they overlooked the fact that what the Indian medicine men did *worked*.

Most activity centered on teaching and preaching. The thrust was to get the Indians to memorize the Large Catechism, the Small Catechism, the Apostles Creed, the Nicene Creed, the Ten Commandments, and other magic rites and formulas dear to Christianity. Salvation became a matter of regurgitation of creeds. In a very real sense, then, Christianity replaced living religions with magic.

And the white man had much magic. Blessed with the gun, the printing press, the iron kettle, and whiskey, it was obvious to many Indians that the white man's god took pretty good care of his people. Since there were no distinctions made between religion and life's other activities by the Indian people, the natural tendency was to adopt the white religion of recitation and forego the rigors of fasting, sacrifice, and prayer.

Missionary activity became an earthly parallel of what Christians thought was happening in heaven. Like the rich burghers of Europe, whom God bribed with earthly treasures, missionaries bribed their way into Indian societies. Once established, they began the laborious task of imprinting two thousand years of sterile dogmas on the unstructured Indian psyche.

Warfare between white and red solidified Indian religion in the persons of a few great leaders such as Sitting Bull, the Prophet (who was the brother of Tecumseh), Handsome Lake, and Wovoka, creator of the Ghost Dance. When these great leaders died, Indian religion went underground and became, like its white competitor, unrelated to the social and political life of the tribe.

By the middle of the last century few tribes were untouched by Christianity. When a tribe had been thoroughly subjugated, Army, trappers, and missionaries moved on and permanent personnel moved in to take control of Indian communities.

From 1860 to 1880, tribes were confined to reservations, as the West was in its death throes. Churches began lobbying early in the 1860's at the Indian Bureau in Washington for franchises over the respective reservations. Thus one reservation would be assigned to the Roman Catholics, one to the Lutherans, one to the Methodists, and one to the Episcopalians. Other churches were prohibited from entry on a reservation once it had been assigned to a particular church and could enter only with permission from the other church. It always bothered me that these churches who would not share pulpits and regarded each other as children of the devil, should have so cold-bloodedly divided up the tribes as if they were choosing sides for touch football.

Many times rations due Indians were mysteriously late in arriving, until the tribes responded to the pleadings of the missionaries. Other times outrageous programs designed to farm desert land were equated with Christian missions. A crop failure was sometimes seen as comparable to a decline in converts because the two harvests were inseparable in the minds of the missionaries.

Indian religious life was forbidden. The Ghost Dance movement, a last attempt to bring back the old hunting days, was enough to convince the Indian Bureau and the Army that the sooner the Indian was Christianized the safer the old frontier would be. Soon the only social activity permitted on reservations was the church service. Signs of any other activity would call for a cavalry troop storming in to rescue civilization from some nonexistent threat.

It always amuses me to hear some white missionary glamorize the reception of Christianity by the Plains tribes. He will tell how "two or three were gathered together and gladly heard the word of God preached." The simple fact is that had the two or three not been talking about the white god they probably would have been shot down for fomenting an uprising.

It was no feat, therefore, to convert Indians to a new religion. No missionary ever realized that it was less the reality of his religion and more the threat of extinction that brought converts to him. Or if he did realize it, he never acknowledged it.

Some churches patterned their work after existing social traits within the tribal culture. They were able to translate older Indian ceremonies and rites into Christian celebrations. Like the Gothic arches which took the place of the oak groves under which the European tribes had worshiped, the traditional gatherings of the tribes were made into annual meetings of the mission fields.

Particularly among the Sioux in the Dakotas, the Sun Dance was reinterpreted as the annual convocation of the missions on each reservation. And this type of accommodation to Indian life gave churches that used it built-in advantages over their competitors. But Christianity was presented in such a dogmatic form to the Sioux that it became frozen into a rigid structure. The religion, as it was presented in the 1870's, remains the religion of the Sioux today. This fact was brought home to me quite vividly in 1964.

That was the year that many church people became convinced that the Civil Rights movement was the only real Christian mission. Most of us secretly suspected that the opportunity for national publicity had more to do with this feeling than did God. But we accepted this message of the churches as valid.

Church officials from the East came out to the reservations to bring the new message and to get Indians involved in the struggle. A New Yorker attended a Sioux religious meeting in South Dakota and was treated to an evening of hymns and prayers sung in the Dakota language. And he was horrified.

Nowhere, he later stated, did he find the social concern for integration and equality which made up the bulk of the Christian message. God's number-one priority, he felt, was Civil Rights and here he had been overwhelmed with missionary hymns that had no relevance to the great struggle.

When this message was later related to the Sioux they were more outraged than was our friend from New York. They insisted that the missionaries had come out to them in the 1870's and taught them to sing "From Greenland's Icy Mountains" and had told them that this was God's word, and that, by God, they were going to keep on singing "From Greenland's Icy Mountains" regardless of what the rest of the world was doing.

Where, therefore, Christianity was accepted, it became so ingrained in the social life of the people that it often became impossible to change. And the tribes generally accepted what they felt was important and disregarded the rest.

Today it is fairly easy to tell which churches had which reservations by the predominance of members of a certain church among the older Indians. Nowhere was the validity of one denomination over another demonstrated. It always causes me to wonder why the various church bodies fight over doctrines today when a century ago they were willing to commit the souls of their red brothers to pernicious doctrines on one reservation in return for the exclusive preaching franchise on another.

Various Lutheran bodies do not share communions or pulpits today. The Roman Catholics and Episcopalians are always engaged in a brawl over the Apostolic pedigree of their ministry. Methodists, Presbyterians, and Baptists continually struggle over concepts of congregational sovereignty. Yet one hundred years ago these churches deliberately ceded various tribes to doctrines they considered heretical in order to gain a captive audience from the federal government.

What each denomination did share, however, was the Anglo-Saxon social forms. These modes of behavior were what they really taught and preached about on the various reservations. Churches struggled to make the Indians cut their hair because they felt that wearing one's hair short was the civilized Christian thing to do. After the tribal elders had been fully sheared, they were ushered into church meeting, given pictures of Jesus and the Disciples, and told to follow these Holy Men. Looking down at the pictures, the ex-warriors were stunned to discover the Holy Dozen in shoulder-length hair!

Often rows of sullen former warriors filled rickety wooden chapels to hear sermons on the ways of peace. They were told that the life of war was the path of destruction. Eternal hell, they were assured, awaited the man of war. Then the service would be closed with the old favorite hymn, "Onward, Christian Soldiers, Marching as to War."

An objective consideration of missionary efforts would indicate that the major emphasis was not religious conversion but experimentation with a captive culture. Western religion had failed to influence the society within which it was created. It had become a commodity for export long before Columbus discovered America. It had no choice but to attempt to gain a stranglehold on other cultures to reinstate itself. But its influence on Indian culture was comparable to that of other trade goods. Where it was useful, it was used.

Indian people obediently followed the way of the white man because it was the path of least resistance. The Great Spirit was exchanged for Santa Claus with some misgivings. Substituting toys for spiritual powers created a vacuum, however, and the tribes secretly preferred their old religion over the religion of the Easter Bunny.

The years from 1870 to 1930 were prosperous times, producing record harvests of red souls. Indian congregations were established in nearly every reservation west of the Mississippi. Many became self-supporting in a short time. By 1930 the majority of the Indian people had a tradition of three generations of church life behind them. Religious controversy centered on doctrinal differences unsolved by the denominations during Reformation days. Missionary work concentrated on such glamorous exploits as stealing sheep from another missionary's fold rather than the de-paganization which had characterized the early mission work.

The flower of tribal leadership served in the reservation chapels as laymen and helpers to the white missionaries. Many people hoped and expected that the mission status of Indian churches would soon be ended and they would receive full parish and congregational equality. Little did they realize that the Indian mission field had become a hobby in and of itself.

Church piety required that the "finest young men" take up the White Man's Burden and go abroad to save the heathen from their great darkness. Indian missions provided the only opportunity whereby young white clergymen could serve God after the mandate of Kipling and still enjoy the comforts of home. To release the Indian congregations to their own devices would have meant closing the only field in which traditional heroics could be achieved. A state of inertia set in.

The white missionaries of the Depression years and later frantically tried to duplicate the exploits of Whipple, Whitman, Father DeSmet, and Charles Cook. There was still glory to be gained by being identified as *the* missionary to a certain tribe. This struggle meant an absolute rejection of Indian people as candidates for the ministry. Recognition of an Indian as an equal or possibly a superior in the missionary venture would have acknowledged that the Indian people had already accepted Christianity. Paganism, per se, would have ceased to exist and there would have been no need for white missionaries.

The Depression missionaries were succeeded by a generation in which the mission field had been the glory spot of Christian work. Many arrived out West with the idea of finally completing the task started by the heroes of the faith two centuries ago. The new breed contemptuously announced that nothing had really been done by their predecessors. There were still Indians around and Indians meant pagans.

The new breed was something to behold. Almost universally they expected the Indian people to come to them for spiritual advice. The older missionaries had made the rounds of their chapels faithfully. After a time, most of the old timers were converted to the Indian way of life and spent their declining years ministering in an Indian way to the people.

But the new breed felt that the Indians were damn lucky they had come. Universally they downgraded Indian laymen. Often they changed patterns of worship and services that had been established for nearly a century. Quite a few had "days off," when they refused to do anything, and most spent a great deal of their time either on vacations or at conferences learning about the relevant new movements of the modern world.

The situation has not changed greatly over the past few years. Several years ago at a conference of missionary workers, a female missionary (somehow missionaries are able to achieve an asexual status) asked my advice on a problem she was having. It seemed that no matter how hard she tried, she couldn't get her little Choctaw pupils in Sunday School to understand the "technical side of being saved."

In her church, it turned out, there were seven steps to salvation. When one understood the seven steps to salvation and was able to recite the sequence correctly, he was saved. Then his task was to teach others the seven steps until Jesus came. Apparently the Lord would ask all people to recite the seven steps on Judgment Day.

Unfortunately I was not able to give her any insight into the task of getting six-year-old Choctaws to walk the seven steps to salvation, let alone memorize them. I asked her why, if it was so difficult to get them to understand, didn't she move to a field which the Lord had spent more time preparing. She replied that the Baptists had had the children for some time and had left them terribly confused. Her first task had been to correct all the heretical theology the Baptists had taught them. She said that she wouldn't dream of leaving and letting some other church come in after her and again confuse the children. On such incisive insights is Christian mission to the Indians founded.

The determination of white churches to keep Indian congregations in a mission status is their greatest sin. But it is more a sin against themselves than it is against Indian people. For the national churches do not realize how obsolete their conceptions have become and they continue to tread the same path they walked centuries ago.

The epitome of this blithe ignorance is the work of the Presbyterian Church among the Shinnecocks on Long Island. At a missionary conference two years ago, a Presbyterian minister, in charge of the Indian work for his denomination, described his church's work among this tribe. Then he asked for questions.

I asked him how long the Presbyterians intended to conduct mission activities among a tribe that had lived as Christians for over three hundred and fifty years. His answer to my question was representative of Christian attitudes toward Indian people today: "Until the job is done."

Christianity, which had laid the ancient world prostrate in less than three hundred years and conquered the mighty Roman Empire, has not been able in the same time period to subdue one hundred Indians huddled on Long Island. Needless to say, my faith was shaken to the core by this statement.

The impotence and irrelevancy of the Christian message has meant a return to traditional religion by Indian people. Tribal religions are making a strong comeback on most reservations. Only in the past few years have the Oglala Sioux and Rosebud Sioux revived their ancient Sioux Sun Dance. And this revival is not simply a re-enactment for tourists. The dance is done in the most reverent manner and with the old custom of piercing the dancers' breasts.

Pathetically, the response of the white missionaries has been to set up tipis and attempt to compete with the Indian religion by holding Masses and communions during the celebration. Nervously they try to convince the Indians that the Sun Dance and the Holy Communion are really the same thing and that Christianity is therefore "relevant" to the Indian people.

In the Great Lakes area the old Medicine Lodge religion has been making inroads with the Chippewas and Winnebagos. Two years ago at an annual conference of the Wisconsin tribes, a panel of Indians discussed native religions. Eagerly the younger conference participants listened to the old men talk. They left that conference with the conviction that Indian religion was for Indian people and Christian religion was for whites.

The Native American Church, famed for its use of the peyote button in its sacramental worship life, has doubled its membership in the last few years. It appears to be the religion of the future among the Indian people. At first a southwestern-based religion, it has spread since the last world war into a great number of northern tribes. Eventually it will replace Christianity among the Indian people.

When I was growing up on the Pine Ridge reservation before and during World War II, the Native American Church was something far away and officially "bad." Few adherents to this faith could be found among the two large Sioux reservations in southern South Dakota. Today a reasonable estimate would be that some 40 percent of the people are members of the Native American Church there.

Indian people have always been confused at the public stance of the Christian churches. The churches preached peace for years yet have always endorsed the wars in which the nation has been engaged. While the missionaries have never spoken about this obvious inconsistency, Indian people have been curious about it for some time. So the element of Indian people who believe deeply in pacifism have looked to other places for a religion of peace.

From the Hopi reservation has come a prophet of peace named Thomas Banyaca. He stands within the old Hopi religion and preaches to all Indians of their need to return to a life of peace and purity before the world ends. In 1967 Banyaca and some members of the Iroquois tribes traveled throughout the nation visiting the different reservations, bringing a message based on the prophecies of the Hopi and Iroquois. In June of 1968 Banyaca, "Mad Bear" Anderson, a Tuscarora prophet, and many of the traditional leaders of different tribes had two National Aborigine conventions in Oklahoma and New York to discuss prophecies of their religion.

Banyaca's message, and its ultimate influence, appears to me to be the most significant movement in religion in Indian Affairs today. Banyaca is very spiritual and highly traditional. He stands solidly within Hopi legend which looks at world history as a catastrophic series of events all of which the Hopi have been saved from. In the late fifties a Hopi delegation went to the United Nations to deliver a message of peace, as Hopi prophecies had required them to do. Legends said that should the Hopi delegation be refused entrance—as they were—the series of events foretelling the end of the world would begin. Banyaca's message to other Indian people is to orient them as to the number of prophecies now fulfilled.

The best statement of Hopi prophecy is contained in Frank Waters' *Book of the Hopi* in which the end of the world as we know it is foretold. There is great similarity between Hopi prophecy and Iroquois prophecy regarding the end of the white man and the restoration of the red man to dominance on this continent. Many people, especially whites, laugh when they hear the Hopi prophecy, feeling that they are so powerful that nothing can overcome them. They forget that Indian gods still roam these lands and do not realize that the Hopi have incredible gifts from their gods which cannot be duplicated by any Christian missionaries; not even, people tell me, by the Pope.

Even in the Northwest, Indian religions are on the move. The Northwest was supposedly converted by Marcus Whitman, early missionary to Oregon Territory. But those tribes, by and large, did not succumb to the word as easily as did tribes in other regions. People from Shoshone country tell me that the medicine men are more powerful there today than they were a century ago. Among the Yakimas the old religion still holds an honored place among the people. If and when native religion combines with political activism among the small tribes in western Washington, they are going to become extremely active in the coming Indian religious revival that many tribes expect in the next decade.

Perhaps only in eastern Oklahoma has Christianity been able to hold its ground. Among the Five Civilized Tribes, Cherokee, Choctaw, Creek, Seminole, and Chickasaw—called civilized because they were most like white men a century ago and have surpassed them in whiteness today—the Baptist denomination exerts great influence. This strength is due primarily to the large number of native clergy among the tribes. The Creeks particularly seem to have taken the Christian doctrines and made them their own. Native preachers exert tremendous influence among the Creeks and Cherokees. If Christianity is to have an Indian base of survival, it will be among the Creeks.

The dilemma of Christian missions today is great. National churches have committed two great mistakes, the solution of which depends upon their foresight and ability to reconcile themselves to what they have been preaching to Indian people for years.

The different denominations have, over the years, invested an enormous amount of money in mission buildings and property. In the closing years of the last century, churches could receive a piece of tribal land simply by promising to conduct certain operations such as a school, hospital, or mission station. Consequently many of them applied for and received a great deal of tribal land.

Now they are caught with property which is suitable only for religious use and with a declining religious following. What use has a church building other than as a church? National churches have continued to pour thousands of dollars annually into their mission programs simply to keep up the value of their investments. They must soon be prepared either to take a devastating paper loss as their congregations vanish or give the properties to the Indian people for their own use. Either solution is distasteful to the materialistic instincts of the churches.

Added to the question of property is the obvious racial discrimination of the denominations against the Indian people, which is becoming apparent to the reservation people. Try as they might, the churches cannot admit that an Indian minister speaking in his native tongue to his own people is more efficient and more effective than a highly trained white missionary talking nonsense.

The major denominations are adamant in their determination to exclude Indian people from the ministry. A number of devices, which skirt "official" pronouncements of concern for an indigenous ministry, are used to bar Indian candidates.

One church refuses to admit Indians to the ministry because it is afraid that someday an Indian priest or clergyman may want to serve in a white parish. Indian ministers would not, by definition, be able to serve in a white parish. Therefore, the reasoning goes, they are not suitable for work among Indian congregations either. While they are welcome, I have been told, they don't seem to be able to qualify.

Other churches are frightened that when the sacred doctrines are translated into the native tongue, the subtle nuances created by theologians of the Reformation will lose some of their distinctions. A perfect example of this attitude happened at an orientation session for new missionaries which I attended in 1963.

A Navajo interpreter was asked to demonstrate how the missionary's sermon was translated into Navajo. So the white missionary gave a few homilies and the interpreter spoke a few words of Navajo. The trainees cooed with satisfaction that meaning could actually be transferred into a barbaric tongue like Navajo.

One missionary was skeptical, however, and asked if there were specific words in Navajo that were comparable to English words. He was afraid, he said, that the wrong messages might be transmitted. So he asked what the Navajo word for "faith" was. Quickly the Navajo replied with the desired word.

"Yes," the missionary commented, "that's all very nice. Now what does that word mean?"

"Faith," said the Navajo smiling.

Nevertheless, many denominations are skeptical about letting Indians enter the ministry because of the possibility that doctrine may become impure. So they continue to send white missionaries for posts in Indian country to insure that the proper theological distinctions be drawn.

With the necessity of keeping large missions open and by refusing to bring Indian people into the ministry, churches have had great difficulty in filling their mission posts. The glory of intrepid pioneering is now gone, and the glory seekers as well as the devoted have long since written off Indian country as the place for service and advancement. Staff positions go unfilled for months and often the first white who comes wandering in across the desert is hired to operate the mission stations.

Some churches have an incredible turnover each spring and try all summer to fill their posts. Eventually they find some white who is a former basketball coach, a retired editor, an interested layman, or an ex-schoolteacher and promptly hand over the mission lock, stock, and barrel without further inquiry. The fact that the new appointee is white is sufficient to cover any theological or professional shortcomings.

Thus the quality of mission workers is at an all-time low. Most are not interested in their work and regard it as a job rather than a calling. Generally they have great contempt for the Indian people they are supposed to be helping.

But probably worse, much mission work is done by white clergymen who are not capable enough to run white parishes. In most cases, the Indian field is their last stop before leaving the ministry altogether. They are hauled from pillar to post by frantic church officials desperately trying to shore up the sagging fortunes of their mission fields. A great deal of money is spent covering up disasters created by these white misfits. When they cause too much controversy in one place they are transferred to another and turned loose again. More money is spent on them than on recruitment and training of Indian people for church work.

Pay is not high in mission work for either white or Indian workers. But it is universally higher for whites than it is for Indians. In the past there was some justification for a pay difference. Many Indian workers were only part-time workers and had another source of income. Gradually, however, Indian clergymen were assigned to remote areas and received less compensation.

Often the pay scale is based primarily upon whether a man is white or Indian. Indians receive less pay, even with seminary training. And Indians are still assigned to the remote areas with the poorest housing and least facilities. Go out to any mission field today and examine the placement of church workers and clergymen. You will discover that white workers have the best assignments, the best houses, the best fringe benefits, and receive the most consideration for advancement from their superiors.

No other field of endeavor in America today has as much blatant racial discrimination as does the field of Christian missions to the American Indian people. It is a marvel that so many Indian people still want to do work for the churches.

Documentation of discrimination and favoritism would be fairly easy were it not for the fantastic ability of the churches to cover their tracks. Instead of forcing resignations from the ministry, church officials transfer incompetents from station to station in order to protect the good name of the church. Thus some tribes are visited with a problem missionary who should have been sent on his way years ago but who has managed to hang on to his ministerial status by periodic transfer and the lack of moral courage by church officials to take action.

The Indian people have come a long way in the last generation. For a long time they accepted the missionary because he seemed to want to do the right thing. But there has always been a desire for the Indian people to take over their own churches. Now they no longer have the expectation that there will be native clergy in their churches. More and more they are returning to Indian dances and celebrations for their religious expressions. They now wait only for a religious leader to rise from among the people and lead them to total religious independence. Thomas Banyaca or Frank Takes Gun, leader of the Native American Church, or someone yet unknown may suddenly find a way to integrate religion with tribalism as it exists today and become that leader.

Indian religion appears to many of us as the only ultimate salvation for the Indian people. Religion formerly held an important place in Indian tribal life. It integrated the functions of tribal society so that life was experienced as a unity. Christianity has proved to be a disintegrating force by confining its influence to the field of formula recitation and allowing the important movements of living go their separate ways until life has become separated into a number of unrelated categories.

Religion today, or at least Christianity, does not provide the understanding with which society makes sense. Nor does it provide any means by which the life of the individual has value. Christianity fights unreal crises which it creates by its fascination with its own abstractions.

I remember going to an Indian home shortly after the death of a child. There was a Roman Catholic priest admonishing the mother not to cry because the child was now with

Jesus. Automatically, he insisted, because it had been baptized. Grief, he declared, was unnatural to man ever since Jesus had died on the cross. He went on to tell how God had decided on a great mission for the child and had called it home to Him and that the mother could see the hand of God in the child's death and needn't wonder about its cause.

In fact, the mother had not wondered about the reason for the child's death. Her child had fallen from a second-story window and suffered internal injuries. It had lingered several days with a number of ruptured organs and had eventually and mercifully died.

I could never believe that the priest was comforting the mother. It seemed rather that he was trying frantically to reinforce what had been taught to him in seminary, doctrines that now seemed shaken to their roots. The whole scene was frightening in its abstract cruelty. I felt sorrier for the priest than for the mother. His obvious disbelief in what he was telling her and his inability to face death in its bitterest moment made *him* the tragic figure.

That is why I believe that Indian religion will be the salvation of the Indian people. In Indian religions, regardless of the tribe, death is a natural occurrence and not a special punishment from an arbitrary God. Indian people do not try to reason themselves out of their grief. Nor do they try to make a natural but sad event an occasion for probing the rationale of whatever reality exists beyond ourselves.

Indians know that people die. They accept death as a fact of life. Rather than build a series of logical syllogisms that reason away grief, Indian people have a ceremony of mourning by which grief can properly be expressed. Depending on the tribal traditions, grief is usually accompanied by specific acts of mourning, which is then ended by giving a feast for the community. After the feast, there is no more official mourning. When expression of grief is channeled into behavioral patterns—as it is, also, in the Jewish religion—it can be adequately understood and felt. When it is suppressed—as it is in the Christian religion—death becomes an entity in itself and is something to be feared. But death also becomes unreal and the act of an arbitrary God.

When death is unreal, violence also becomes unreal, and human life has no value in and of itself. Consider the last talk you had with an insurance salesman. Remember how he told you that you would be covered "if" you died. An Indian salesman would have said "when," but then an Indian would have known how to die and both "if" and "when" would have held no terror for him.

Many tribes have kept their puberty ceremonies, and these ceremonies are very much alive today in the Southwest. Childhood and adolescence are marked off by these ceremonies so that the natural growth processes are recognized and young people growing up will be sure of their place in society.

Contrast the value of these ceremonies with the confusion of suburban America where children are pushed into imitations of adults in their younger years and then later denied the privileges of adults. Certainly the pressures on boys in the Little League are comparable in intensity and form with those professional ballplayers face. But after ten years of being treated like adults, young people begin to demand adult status and they are clubbed into submission by police at Columbia University and in Chicago.

The largest difference I can see between Indian religion and Christian religions is in interpersonal relationships. Indian society had a religion that taught respect for all members of the society. Remember, Indians had a religion that produced a society in which there were no locks on doors, no orphanages, no need for oaths, and no hungry people. Indian religion taught that sharing one's goods with another human being was the highest form of behavior. The Indian people have tenaciously held to this tradition of sharing their goods with other people in spite of all attempts by churches, government agencies, and schools to break them of the custom.

Christianity came along and tried to substitute "giving" for sharing. There was only one catch: giving meant giving to the church, not to other people. Giving, in the modern Christian sense, is simply a method of shearing the sheep, not of tending them.

Several years ago a Roman Catholic priest on the Wind River reservation complained bitterly about the Indian custom of sharing as being "un-Christian" because it distributed the wealth so well no middle class could be established. Hence "bad" Indians dragged the "good" ones down to a lower economic level and the reservation remained economically static.

The initial object of the Roman Catholic priest's outburst was an Indian woman who had a telephone and let all her neighbors use it. The bill ran as high as one hundred dollars some months. Often the woman was behind on her bill. But she didn't mind letting her neighbors use the phone when they wanted to.

The priest was furious when he reminded himself that of a Sunday the collection plate was not filled by the Indians. He felt that was intolerable and he wanted to teach the Indians "stewardship." Stewardship meant saving money and giving a percentage of the savings in the plate.

There was no difference, for the missionary, between sharing one's goods with the community and squandering resources. He preferred that the people give their money to the church, which would, in turn, efficiently define who was in need of help. Indians looked at the missionary's form of sharing as a sophisticated attempt to bribe the Great Spirit.

The onus is not on the Roman Catholics alone. The Protestants have devised a scheme whereby sharing is reduced to a painless sixty minutes a year. It is called One Great Hour of Sharing. Once a year they remind themselves how lucky they are to be Protestants and call for an outpouring of money so that others might receive the same privilege. Tough social problems always go unsolved.

Sharing, the great Indian tradition, can be the basis of a new thrust in religious development. Religion is not synonymous with a large organizational structure in Indian eyes. Spontaneous communal activity is more important. Thus any religious movement of the future would be wise to model itself on existing Indian behavioral patterns. This would mean returning religion to the Indian people.

The best thing that the national denominations could do to ensure the revitalization of Christian missions among Indian people would be to assist in the creation of a national Indian Christian Church. Such a church would incorporate all existing missions and programs into one national church to be wholly in the hands of Indian people.

Such a church would include all ordained Indian clergymen now serving as church workers in the Indian field. The actual form of the ministry would not be determined by obsolete theological distinctions preserved from the middle ages, but would rather incorporate the most feasible role that religion can now play in the expanding reservation societies.

Each denomination that has been putting funds into Indian work would contribute toward the total budget of the new church. Existing buildings and church structures would be evaluated by the new Indian church and the tribal council of the reservation on which the property is located. Congregations of the various denominations would be consolidated and reservation-wide boards of laymen would direct activities on each reservation.

With the religious function integrated into the ongoing life of the tribe, the Indian church would be able to achieve self-support in a short time as the role of religion clarified itself to the reservation communities. Religious competition, which fractures present tribal life, would disappear and the movement toward ancient religions might not be so crucial.

Such a proposal is too comprehensive for most denominations to accept at the present time. The primary fear of turning over the sacred white religion to a group of pagans would probably outrage most denominations, too few of whom realize how ridiculous denominational competition really is.

The best example I can mention of denominational competition existed at Farmington, New Mexico, a couple of years ago. The situation has probably changed since 1965. But that year there were twenty-six different churches serving an estimated Navajo population of 250. That's less than ten Indians per denomination! Assuming each church had a choir of eight, the congregations must have totaled one or two people per Sunday. Which does not indicate a field ready for harvest.

I estimated that the total mission budget for the Farmington area that year was in excess of $250,000. Christianity, not tourism, was Farmington's most profitable industry in 1965.

Churches face literal dissolution on the reservations unless they radically change their method of operation. Younger Indians are finding in Indian nationalism and tribal religions sufficient meaning to continue their drift away from the established churches. Even though many churches had chaplaincies in the government boarding schools, the young are not accepting missionary overtures like their fathers and mothers did.

As Indian nationalism continues to rise, bumper stickers like "God is Red" will take on new meanings. Originally put out at the height of Altizer's "God is Dead" theological pronouncements, the slogan characterizes the trend in Indian religion today.

Many Indians believe that the Indian gods will return when the Indian people throw out the white man's religion and return to the ways of their fathers. Whether or not this thinking is realistic is not the question. Rather the question is one of response and responsibilty of the missionaries today. Will they continue to be a burden or not?

Can the white man's religion make one final effort to be real, or must it too vanish like its predecessors from the old world? I personally would like to see Indians return to their old religions wherever possible. For me at least, Christianity has been a sham to cover over the white man's shortcomings. Yet I spent four years in a seminary finding out for myself where Christianity had fallen short.

I believe that an Indian version of Christianity could do much for our society. But there is little chance for such a melding of cards. Everyone in the religious sphere wants his trump to play on the last trick. In the meantime, Banyaca, Mad Bear Anderson, and others are silently changing the game from pinochle to one where all fifty-two cards are wild. They may, if the breaks fall their way, introduce religion to this continent once again.

19. The Presence of Isanaklesh: The Apache Female Deity and The Path of Pollen

INÉS M. TALAMANTEZ

Facing an unknown yet profound transformation in their young lives, Mescalero Apache girls run vigorously at the first light of the rising sun during their female initiation ceremony. Isanaklesh, the Apache female deity, will meet the young initiate as she runs toward the eastern direction and then the young girl will bring her back once again to be present with the Mescalero people at yet another yearly ceremony celebrating the life of a young Apache girl who has reached puberty. Girls are prepared since their menarche and sometimes even earlier to enter into the sacred ceremonial tipi for four days of ritual in which they are transformed into Isanaklesh, given her name and healing powers, and instructed in Apache religious history, philosophy, and ethics. It is in these teachings that Apache culture bestows upon its women authority in leadership roles and religious ceremonial rules. Apache religious traditions consider women to be in a very special place within the culture as it seeks to establish balance and harmony in its historical continuity.

Women, especially those who are blessed and initiated into womanhood, are a powerful cultural influence. They inspire appropriate behavior by their own everyday examples as compassionate mothers, wise elders, grand-mothers, wives, and political and religious leaders. From a woman's point of view, Apache ethnohistory provides an excellent paradigm that exemplifies and demonstrates the powerful ideals that are still practiced today in spite of Christian missionization and American assimilation campaigns. Concerns ranging from family to extended family to community, and from ecology to peace and justice are often expressed by Apache women. They are skilled at handling whatever comes their way, by living moral and unselfish lives. Isanaklesh, the Apache female deity, is the leading religious authority for most of the women. Even Apache Christian women often speak of her as the one that they pray to in times of need. Isanaklesh exemplifies compassion; she always understands us and the need for peace and justice in our lives. Oral tradition informs us that Isanaklesh brought knowledge and especially the healing arts to the people when, in the creation myth, she taught her son, *Tobasishine,* Child of Water, how to acquire and use medicines for the needs of the people.

It is Isanaklesh's power, her *diye,* ultimate spiritual strength, that makes her the perfect example of virtue and strength for the culture. It is clear that oral tradition throughout Apache history has provided the framework for female identity. Women in this culture have followed Isanaklesh's teachings and have worked toward a balanced sense of power whether as tribal chair, healer, teacher, council member, forestry worker, or in any other profession. Naturally, no culture is perfect, so here too there are those women who for many different reasons did not have a ceremony. Some of these women have expressed regret that they did not receive the guidance, support, ethics and philosophical teachings which the ceremony offers. Some have dreamed the ceremony, even though they themselves did not have it.

Dreams and power-visions can come from natural phenomena through the help of a supernatural being such as Isanaklesh or Child of the Water. Such dreams can be considered a vehicle of transmission of divine wisdom from Isanaklesh to a woman.

The Dream

I dreamed Isanaklesh about twenty years ago, during a ceremony held for the daughter of a friend on the Mescalero Apache reservation in New Mexico. I had worked during the day before my dream, helping the women in the cooking arbor to prepare food for the guests. For many hours, I listened silently as the women told of their own ceremonies and those of their daughters and granddaughters. That evening, my friend invited me to sleep with the initiate's female relatives in the family's tipi. Gazing up the smoke hole, I could see the night sky, clear and filled with glittering stars. Although we were all tired after a long day of work, we talked on, perhaps for several hours. Then I fell asleep. During that peaceful night, the dream began. The images are so sharply printed on my memory that it seems as though everything were happening today. . . .

I am walking near the river, towards the very center of Mescalero, following an old animal path. Slowly a female figure approaches, stirring the pollen dust on the path with every gracefully placed step. I sense that she wants something from me. I wonder who she is and why she is here. The air has become so quiet that only the rippling river can be heard. The green meadows disappearing behind me as I pass are covered thickly with grasses, fragrant with wild onions, and ferns. Fresh-smelling blue flowers are scattered here and there, and dropped evergreen needles make the ground soft underfoot. The entire landscape spread out before me is suffused with yellow pollen. Pollen falls like a soft rain from heavy boughs of nearby evergreen trees; the wet meadow grass shimmers, mirage-like with the yellow dust. The sunlight filtering under the pollinating trees, the forested mountains and misty passes under the slow-moving clouds all appear undisturbed, as they were at the world's beginning.

I know I am dreaming. Feelings and memories fuse together. I know why I am here; yet everything I see appears to be mysterious, veiled, hidden. As I approach, the mask pulls away, and I see what is actually there. Am I seeing the essence of the trees and grasses and wildflowers? Or am I remembering what I once knew—what I was always told?

I suddenly feel alone and anxious, disturbed without knowing why. The path ahead is clearly marked and the sunlight that filters through the trees has become quite bright; my shadow moves along beside me. The trees shimmer with yellow pollen that gently falls in the breeze. Suddenly I see Her again, walking toward me. All at once she is standing in front of me, tall and dark-skinned, with smooth black hair flowing to the ground. It too is covered with pollen. Her deerskin dress is carefully stained the same green as the evergreen pines. Hanging from her neck is an abalone shell that contains the pollen of the ocean floor. Her eyes are like shining obsidian, and her beads sparkle, catching the sun. I look down at her moccasins, beaded with crystals, and covered with small pieces of turquoise. At first I cannot speak; I take a deep breath and raise my head slowly. She is still looking at me. I wonder what I should say. I hear my own words, coming as if from a distance.

"What are you doing here?"

"I've come to do a ceremony for you."

She turns and points with her lips in the Apache way, beckoning me to follow. As she walks away, I see pollen flowing from the fringes of her dress. Slowly she walks further and further away. I known that this is Isanaklesh, Mother Earth, the woman who never grows old because she is revitalized by the young initiate's life during our ceremony, she who witnessed creation and gives us what we need for life. I feel awed, yet balanced and peaceful, fearless, protected by a power that no outer source can penetrate. I have reached the place of meeting on the pollen path.

In Mescalero Apache culture, to dream the goddess Isanaklesh is to be ritually bound to her just as her myth is bound to the ceremeny that initiates young Mescalero girls into womanhood. Whomever she touches and enriches through a yellow cattail pollen vision or dream must always work for her, for she is asking for something; she wants something from the dreamer. Her power and beauty, utterly beyond that of earthly women, compel the dreamer to search always for the meaning of this wondrous vision.

I therefore told my dream to several spiritual advisors, for the Apaches feel that seeking such advice is proper when one has experienced such a powerful dream. One elder woman respected for her knowledge explained the general significance of dreams to me. She told me that understanding our dreams helps us to understand the world around us. Dreams, she said, reveal the many things that we do not apprehend during our waking lives. By reflecting on our dreams and their meaning, we learn to develop our senses and heed spiritual signs. Apache elders use this method of dream interpretation to see and study the world more carefully, and especially to locate the connections between the natural and supernatural realms.

Dreams full of color, like mine, are said to reveal nature and the spirit world. Others may lead one to understand a certain person or object, or they may yield sacred traditional knowledge about plants or animals.

In my dream, Isanaklesh showed herself amidst yellow pollen. Cattail pollen, *tadidine*, is the essence of *diye*, supernatural power. The quest for *diye* is at the very heart of the Apache religious system. Most traditional Apaches seek *diye* for protection, healing, and spiritual knowledge. *Diye* assures one of a long and fruitful life. A second advisor and old friend interpreted my dream's imagery in the following way:

All that pollen, the fir trees must be in their fourth year; that is when they drop their pollen. The bright light means summer is coming and you have to be alert and ready. If you look closely at everything, if you look inside, you can see what's going to happen ahead of you. For the next four years you must think about this dream. The more you pray about it the better it comes every time. It will stick with you because it is important. You were up about 10,000 feet in the forest; if you were walking on softness, you were among the clouds. These are the springtime clouds pushing under your feet. The breeze is behind you so you are going down canyon as the pollen falls from the trees and all around you. Walking towards the center means any place where you go it is with you. It is a good day when you see all of these things around you. That good strong feeling means you will be around for a long time. There is a lot of motion, a lot of feeling, as I have told you before; a good day is when you move around, when you accomplish something.

Still another spiritual adviser, a woman at Mescalero, told me about Isanaklesh.

We must always remember Isanaklesh, her name means, "our mother," she is sacred Mother Earth. We depend on her for all of our needs. We ask her for our food both from the plant world and the animal world, as well as for shelter and healing. Because of her power, we have been given life, we are shaped and molded by her. All of our life we are protected by her; we experience her as we see with our eyes, hear with our ears, smell with our nose, as we touch, as we grow old, and become wise like her. If she appeared to you she wants you to work for her, you must do this or things could go wrong for you. Now you are tied to her. You must pray to her for diye, *which will protect you and keep you to a healthy old age.*

The Mescalero Apache preserve an extensive oral mythology about Isanaklesh. She is a living reality, as well as the creative Earth Mother. She *is* the earth; her name literally means "Woman (isana) of Earth or Clay (klesh)." She wears the earth's white clay on her face when she is seasonally painted with it during Isanaklesh Gotal, the girls' puberty ceremony. Because of our belief in her, and because the ceremony again and again renews her, Isanaklesh, the Woman of Earth, never grows old.

The Myth of Isanaklesh

In Mescalero Apache sacred stories about the beginning of the world, Isanaklesh is said to be one of the five great deities who were present when the world was made. The bottom half of her face was painted with white earth clay, and her body was completely covered with yellow cattail pollen. Wearing a necklace of abalone shell on her chest, she watched over all things growing on earth. She used her *diye* to ripen trees and fruits, flowers of the fields, all plants and herbs. Her compassion and creative wisdom as healer gave aid from the beginning of time to those who suffered from distress, injury, or disease.

An older woman friend told her clan's version of this myth to me (I recorded it in Apache and then together we translated it into English). She took about five hours to explain the following portion of the myth to me. This segment depicts Isanaklesh as the mother of the culture hero, and as the one responsible for our knowledge of healing.

Isanaklesh hid her son, Child of the Water, and raised him with great care so Giant would not find him. When he was old enough, she made four sacred arrows for him and he went out to find Giant. Giant, as it is said, had a coat of hair that was four layers thick, and for that reason he was not afraid of anything. Child of the Water finally came upon Giant. He took aim and quickly shot the first sacred arrow, and the outer layer of Giant's thick coat first came off. Child of the Water then took aim again, and the second arrow took off his second coat. The third sacred arrow took off his third coat and left his heart still beating. Child of the Water then shot the fourth sacred arrow and pierced the Giant's heart. After this, the Earth became safe and Isanaklesh and Child of the Water taught Apaches how to live on this earth. This all happened on Sierra Blanca at the time of Creation.

Child of the Water spoke in sacred language while he was creating all of the things we need for life. But at one point in the story he stopped and asked his father Life Giver to look at all he had made for the people, and to tell him of anything that might still be needed. His father approved of what he saw around him, but said that the people would be exposed to disease; therefore, they must have something that they could prepare to cure it. Child of the Water said that he would ask his mother Isanaklesh for this. Isanaklesh then appeared and told him how to create the many herbs and minerals that would cure diseases. She gave him the names for sacred plants and taught him how to use them properly, explaining that:

> some they will have to gather and then boil them, some they will chew and swallow, some they will ceremonially paint on their bodies in very special ways, some they will burn and use for their healing smoke and ashes that will be used to heal the skin, some they will drink as medicine, and some they will breathe in for healing vapors.

Medicine from all the herbs that we know will be used to cure if it is breathed in four times in a ceremonial manner. Among Apaches, as among other Native American peoples, things of a sacred or ceremonial nature, for example blessings or healings, are usually repeated four times, facing in each of the four directions. One starts with the east, where the sun rises, then turns to the south, where the sun travels, then to the west, where the sun sets, and then to the north where it does not appear at all until it rises again in the east.

Isanaklesh then gave the ritual prescriptions for the use of cattail pollen, also known as the "pollen of the earth," which symbolizes the earth's life-giving powers as these powers go out to the four directions to bless all people. To live "in the pollen way" means to live in balance and harmony, like the balance and harmony that we see in nature. In this way, one will live to be old. If anything is even mixed with pollen, then Isanaklesh will give the added substance the power to heal.

Thus Isanaklesh spoke of all the herbs, trees, and minerals that are sacred to the Mescalero—everything needed to sustain life and heal humankind, so that people can live in a peaceful way, celebrating the goodness and beauty of life. In this version of the creation myth, she also gives the Isanaklesh ceremony to counteract diseases and imbalances that provoke disharmony and suffering for all women and all of humanity. This ceremonial gift, focused on the life of the Mescalero girl who is passing through puberty, is the ritual that Apaches still celebrate. By honoring each girl with these rites, Apaches honor Isanaklesh as well. They hence win for themselves a long full life by drawing upon Isanaklesh's healing power and wisdom.

The Ceremony

In southern New Mexico, east of the great White Sands, stands Dzil gais'ani, or Sierra Blanca. This 12,000 foot sacred mountain is the home of Isanaklesh, who has been revered as a powerful female deity since oldest Apache memory. At the time of creation, after the world was made safe for people, Apaches gathered together in small bands to receive *diye* and to learn the traditions. Isanaklesh then spoke and proclaimed her special ceremony:

We will have a feast for the young girls when they have their first flow. Many songs will be sung for them, so that they will grow strong and live a long life.

This eight-day ceremony, called Isanaklesh Gotal, is celebrated in recognition of the significance of a young Apache girl's first menses. According to Apache myth, the ceremony was founded by Isanaklesh as a means through which the girl might temporarily experience herself as a manifestation of the goddess and be honored as such by the people. The first four days of ceremony are marked by elaborate ritual detail and festive social activities. The ceremony's songs, stories, and images combine to leave a powerful imprint of Isanaklesh both on the girl herself and on the relatives, friends, and family members who attend. Throughout the final four days the girl secludes herself to reflect on her ritual experiences.

The name given to this ceremony, Isanaklesh Gotal, literally means "Ceremonial Song for Isanaklesh." The Apache term *gotal*, "ceremonial song," suggests not only a festive celebration, but also a raising of supernatural power to accomplish the many moments of transformation that the young girl experiences. Not only is the girl temporarily transformed into the goddess during this rite of passage; she is also permanently transformed into a mature Apache woman by the end of the ritual.

This transformation into womanhood is accomplished by ceremonially awakening the initiate to the world around her. For some girls, the ceremony is said to calm their adolescent imbalances. The Mescalero conceive of "fixing" the young initiate, ridding her of her baby ways and helping her through the door of adolescence, for at this young age the girls are said to be soft and moldable, capable of being conditioned and influenced by their female kin and others around them. Timid girls may need to be awakened to their powerful female identities, while others may need to be taught to settle down and be more sensible and feminine. This sense of awakening female potential is expressed in the words of a twelve-year-old, recalling her ceremony:

While we were at my sponsor's house, she told us about how the feast would help me to be good, healthy, and keep the Apache tradition in its full swing. On Friday, she washed my hair in the soap suds of a yucca plant. Before she did it, she blessed it with pollen. She prayed in Indian while she washed. She said she would be here at 5:00 Saturday morning. Saturday morning, I woke up about 5:15 and washed up. She came and we began to build a small fire in the cooking arbor. She put four rocks in the four main directions around the fire. We waited until the fire got started. Then she put my hands in the flames and told me this was to keep me from being afraid of any kind of fire. That morning we waited until Willetto Antonio, my medicine man, had come so she could dress me. He came and we went into the white tent. She laid my buckskin dress and boots and jewelry down on the rug. She blessed it all, and just before she put it on, she pushed it towards me four times. Then she put the dress on me. After I was all dressed, people came into the tent to be blessed. . . . They went outside so I could do my run. She told me to turn to the east. Some more people came to be blessed. As Willetto Antonio started to sing, she told me to lie down so she could rub me (massage me for strength). After she did that, they laid a buckskin down and Willetto put four half-moons on it, two of yellow pollen and two of red ochre outlined with black galena. Just before I was to run, I had to step on these moons. Then they told me I was to run my hardest so that I could run my babyhood out of me. I ran around the basket four times. But each time they would move it farther. After the ceremony outside, we went into the tipi so I could bless people. My sponsor showed me how to bless little kids and babies.

This initiate was well aware that she had undergone special teachings during the ceremony and that she had emerged somehow different. Analysis of the ceremonial procedures and their religious implications helps us to understand the transformative aspects of the ceremony. There is no single moment at which the transformation of girl to goddess, or of goddess to woman, occurs. It is the fusion of all the ceremony's elements, over the eight-day period, that produces the desired goals. During the ceremony, great attention is paid to the ritual details, and the meanings of the symbols are carefully explained to the girls. As the Singer and sponsor explain these teachings to the initiate, the girl begins to understand important elements of Apache culture that from now on she will be charged to maintain. After her ceremony, she will be a keeper of Apache traditions and the pattern of everyday living in which they will continue to endure. Thus she is not only taught and protected by this ceremony; like Isanaklesh, who gave it, she will also teach and protect her tribe.

Sometimes it is not easy to convince young girls to participate in Isanaklesh Gotal. Many are intimidated by the prospect of becoming such a center of attention. Thus the mothers and grandmothers of the tribe's young girls try to prepare them psychologically for the ceremony long before the girls reach their menarche. The women try to convince the girls that they will change in a positive way if they participate fully—and that the ceremony will bring them a good and healthy life. Older women will often encourage pre-pubescent girls to observe the ceremonies of other initiates closely so they will know what to expect. I have heard mothers or other female kin say to a girl: "Go up toward the front of the Big Tipi where you can see and hear everything better."

The family begins preparations for the ceremony several years in advance of their daughter's menarche. They begin collecting the necessary ritual objects, including the sacred pollen which can only be gathered during the season when cattails are ripe. It is no less important to gather relatives' support, because the ceremony will be a tremendous burden on family resources. When the proud day of the girl's first menstruation arrives, her family celebrates with a small private dinner. Soon after, a male Singer and a woman sponsor are secured in the proper ritual manner: four gifts must be given, and the proper words must be exchanged.

Throughout the year following menarche, the girl's women kin and female sponsor then teach her the proper Apache ways. These include the use of medicinal herbs and healing skills. The women also prepare her deerskin dress, like Isanaklesh's dress, with elaborate symbolic beadwork; attached to the ends of the fringes are the tiny metal cones that now replace deer hoofs, which will gently jingle when she walks or dances. If the girl is to have a private ceremony, or "feast" as it is called today, her family and kin will usually host it at a carefully selected site well away from congested areas. The girl also has the option to join the several girls honored at the annual public Feast; in this case, her ritual will occur on the ceremonial grounds of the Mescalero tribal headquarters on whatever weekend falls closest to the Fourth of July. In either case, friends and family gather, supplies are stored, temporary tipis and cooking arbors are assembled, and preparations are made to feed all who come to the first four days of the ceremony.

Prior to dawn on the first day of the ceremony, the girl is placed in her own private tipi and carefully attended by female kin and her sponsor. The sponsor blesses the initiate with pollen, and ritually bathes and dresses her for the ceremony. She reminds the girl of how good it feels to be cared for, so that the girl will learn to care for others. The girl's hair is washed with *Izhee,* yucca suds; she is fitted with leggings and moccasins; she is ritually fed traditional Apache foods. She is given a special reed, or *uka,* through which she will sip water, since water is not allowed to touch her lips for fear that this will bring floods; she also receives a scratching stick, or *tsibeeichii,* for she is not to scratch with her fingernails.

Meanwhile, outside on the ceremonial grounds, the Singers and the girl's male kin begin to construct the sacred tipi. This will be the central structure where most of the rites take place. It is called the ceremonial home of Isanaklesh. According to Apache sacred songs, only when this tipi's four main poles are properly erected can the goddess reside there; then the power of the songs will go out from the tipi to carry the ceremony's benefit out to all of the people on earth. To raise these poles, four rocks are first used to mark the sacred place which was touched by the first rays of the sun. Then, at this spot, the four poles are sung into place. A song is sung for each pole as it is placed into the earth and tied to the others at the top of the structure. Thus the Apache sacred number four is established musically as well as visually. Ideally the first songs should be sung approximately at dawn, as the sun rises to the east, where the opening of the tipi must face. This way both song and sunrise mark the beginning of sacred time. Since the voice of the Singer can only carry so far in an outdoor setting, the songs also serve to mark off a sacred space for the circle of participants, who must move close enough to hear as well as to see.

The sacred tipi is now completed and readied for Isanaklesh, who has been approaching from the east with the early dawn light. The tipi's upper portion is wrapped with a clean white canvas cloth, and its lower portion is filled in with branches. The eastward opening is built out to the sides, in order to let the sun's light inside. After the tipi is in place, the initiate in her ritual garment appears with her sponsor and family. She is freshly bathed and dressed and carries a blanket and white deer-skin to be unfolded and placed in front of the tipi. The initiate, now taking on the sacred role, then blesses with pollen members of the tribe who come forward, and the people in turn bless the initiate. An essential component of this rite is the *tadodine,* the cattail pollen, which is the pollen that Isanaklesh used in the creation myth. The girl motions in the Apache way to the four directions and then applies the yellow life-giving substance over the bridge of the person's nose, moving from the right to the left side; she may also apply it to other parts of the person's body. This blessing assures the people of a good long life; it also prefigures the healing powers of this young deity-to-be. Hence, to remind the girl of her role as healer, the sponsor now tells her:

> *When you become Isanaklesh in the ceremony, you will have her power to heal because it is Isanaklesh who handed this knowledge to us. There is a sacred story about this. Since you will be Isanaklesh, you will be asked to heal and bless people who come to see you. You must always remember how you felt during your ceremony, when you were the living goddess; then later in life, you can call on her for help whenever you have problems; you will remember how you felt when you were her, when you became her.*

The initiate's young soft body is next "molded," that is, massaged and aligned by her sponsor to insure the transformation of girl to Isanaklesh, as well as for continuing health and strength and a long, productive life. The Singer then draws four naturally paced footprints on the deerskin with pollen. While a sacred basket is put in place to the east of the tipi, the initiate steps on the pollen prints and is then gently "pushed off" to run around the basket and return to the tipi. This sequence symbolizes walking on the pollen path, again to bring the initiate a long, healthy life. The initiate runs around the basket four times, as four verses of the ritual song are sung. Before each run, the basket is moved a little closer to the tipi. Meanwhile, the girl's female sponsor makes the "ritual marker," a long high-pitched sound, to draw the attention of the supernaturals. For as she runs, the initiate meets the approaching Isanaklesh and escorts her back to the Apache people.

After the first morning's rituals, the initiate appears in public only during the next four nights. During the day, she may not have any ordinary social contact; only relatives, close friends, and those who wish to be blessed or healed may visit her in her private tipi.

When dusk arrives on the first night of the ceremony, male dancers appear to bless the young initiate and the central ceremonial fire. These dancers have been ritually transformed into *hastchin*, supernaturals who live inside the mountains near Mescalero. They wear buck-skin kilts with long fringes finished with tin-cone jingles; above the waist, they are painted front and back with bold designs. Black cloth masks cover their faces and hide their human identities; yucca headdresses and ceremonial staffs complete their ritual dress. The *hastchin* dance in teams of four, each with its own drummer and group of singers. Trailed by one or more ritual clowns, or *libaye,* who are usually apprenticed *hastchin,* they also bless the ceremonial tipi. They bow toward it and back up four times from all four directions, making owl-like sounds. Then they return to the ceremonial grounds to dance around the central fire until the young initiate arrives.

At about 10 P.M., the initiate, her sponsor, and the Singer appear at the sacred tipi. The Singer leads the girl into the home of Isanaklesh by extending an eagle feather which he holds in his right hand. The girl takes hold of the other end of the feather and follows as he takes four steps into the tipi; each step is accompanied by the verse of a song that refers to the tipi as home of Isanaklesh. Inside, facing the fire at the center of the tipi, the initiate and her sponsor sit on deer hides and blankets. The Singer kneels in front of the girl with his back to the fire and prays and blesses the initiate, whom he now calls Isanaklesh.

As other songs are sung in groups of four, the initiate dances back and forth across a deer hide, looking always just above the fire or at the Singer's rattle, as the ritual rules prescribe. Accompanied by the light, regular pulse of the Singer's deer-hoof rattles, each song and dance lasts for about four to six minutes. Between songs, the girl rests for three to four minutes. Sometimes the Singer and sponsor will talk, but usually they are silent. As each group of four songs ends, a short formula is sung to mark its conclusion. Then the Singer lights hand-rolled cigarettes of ritual tobacco, and a longer break is taken, during which Isanaklesh is sometimes offered water through her drinking tube. During nights two and three, the same pattern occurs, with no morning or daytime activity. Only the content of the songs varies with each nightly performance.

A closer look shows that this seemingly endless repetition is a tightly structured and deliberate ritual form. The repetition establishes a stable place, quite literally when combined with the dancing, which is restricted to the area of a small deer hide. In the matrix of this stability, thoughts are free to wander. The young Isanaklesh appears to be in a trance-like state as she dances more vigorously each night. The Singer tells her to think in images about the tribe—to visualize troubles and illness and to send them over the mountain and away from the tribe. She is to set her mind and spirit in motion, even as her physical space is confined.

Similarly, the repetition also alters the sense of time. All necessary elements for a good life are said to be present in the ceremony; all the important symbols of Apache culture and of the world of women are contained in the songs that are sung each night. By calling on these symbols with the songs' powerful words, participants evoke images that are sometimes literally seen in the sacred space. The mind can travel between these images. When similar tunes are used, it is as if no time has elapsed between one set of songs and the next—or between the present ceremony and the first ceremony ever sung. Ishanaklesh is *there;* and her *diye,* her healing power, is present, as it was during the first moments of the world's creation.

The ceremony lasts almost until dawn on the fourth day. Songs are counted by wooden markers that are driven into the ground around the fire. Then, on the fifth and final morning of the ceremony's public segment, the ceremonial circle is completed by actions that reverse the pattern of the first morning. The sponsor and the Singer assemble in the tipi just as dawn is about to break. Isanaklesh has again been freshly bathed. The sacred basket is beside them, holding pollen, the eagle feather, tobacco, a gramma grass brush, several kinds of clay, and galena, a shiny black lead ore found in the mountains at Mescalero. Using the galena, the Singer paints an image of the sun on the palm of his hand. As he sings, he holds his hand up to the sun, so that the galena glitters as the early sun's rays hit it. When the song is finished, the Singer turns to Isanaklesh and touches his sunpainted hand to her shoulders and chest. Then he touches each side of her head and rubs the sun-image into her hair.

Singing another song, the Singer paints her with white earth clay, covering all the exposed skin on her arms and legs, as well as the lower half of her face. As this is happening, other participants remove the cloth and branches covering the sacred tipi, so that only the four main poles remain. Within this skeleton structure, the ritual blessing and healing of the tribe again take place. Taking red clay from a basket beside him, the Singer blesses every member of the community (and anyone else seeking blessing) by marking them with the clay, taking special care for young children, the elderly, and the sick. This period for blessing can last for over an hour.

The next and final ritual sequence occurs very quickly. Isanaklesh is led out of the tipi to the same tune that led her in; she walks on pollen footsteps, which are again painted on the deerskin. The sacred basket is once again placed to the east of the tipi, at the same distance from the tipi as it had been during the final run of the ceremony's first morning. Once again, she takes the four ceremonial pollen footsteps and runs off, accompanied by the four verses of her running song. This time, after each run, the basket is moved further to the east. On the last run, she runs to the basket—now very far to the east. She picks up her eagle feather and, while running back, begins to rub the white clay from her face as she returns to her private tipi, where she will stay during the next four days. During the past four days she has symbolically left behind her childlike youth and has been ritually transformed into Isanaklesh. After the next four days of quiet reflection, the initiate will emerge from her tipi as an adult Apache woman and Isanaklesh has departed.

As the girl performs her last run, the Singer chants as the rope that tied together the tipi poles is loosened and undone. Now the tipi's last four poles fall to the ground with a great crash. During all this excitement, the Singer has continued to sing, accompanied by his rattle. However, the crowd, which knows the traditions of this ceremony, has by now moved towards the cooking arbor. Here pickup trucks have driven in, loaded with candy, fruit, and household goods. These are thrown to the crowd as gifts from the family sponsoring the feast. The effect of the final run, the dismantling of the sacred tipi, and the giveaway with all of its accompanying excitement are meant to decisively break the sense of sacred space and time. The music also ends at this point, appropriately, after the Singer has sung over 100 songs during the total five-day period. Except for the girl, the participants now return to normal tribal life. In a traditional ceremony of incomparable beauty and coherence, another girl has reached womanhood, guided by the women of her culture and reassured of both her female and her Apache identity.

Isanaklesh is a potent symbol for Apache women. This deity whom the initiate has *been* for a while is also everything that a woman can hope to be. She is wise; she is powerful; she heals; she provides effective tools for living a life of harmony and balance. She is creative and fertile. As earth, she is the ultimate mother; but she also exemplifies ideal human motherhood by protecting and teaching her own child.

The ceremony of Isanaklesh Gotal constantly brings these female images to consciousness. All a woman has to do when she meets obstacles in her life is to remember how she felt during her ceremony when she was Isanaklesh. For the women who experience Isanaklesh, she becomes a deeply engrained model and source of empowerment. For men, knowing that women's lives are closely entwined with such a being implies that women must therefore be treated with respect and esteem. Moreover, the shared reverence for Isanaklesh that is focused in this ceremony forges a strong sense of Apache community. Thus Isanaklesh indeed brings power to the Apache; she helps us to find balance in our lives, and knowledge of our identity.

Further Readings

Basso, Keith H. *The Gift of Changing Woman*. Bulletin of American Ethnology Anthropological Papers, No. 196. Washington D.C.: U.S. Government Printing Office, 1966.

Hoijer, Harry. *Chiricahua and Mescalero Apache Texts*. Chicago: University of Chicago Press, 1938.

_____. "The Apache Verb." *International Journal of American Linguistics,* Vols. XI: pp. 13–23, 193–203; XII: pp. 1–13; XIV: pp. 2147–259; XV: pp. 12–22 (1945–1949).

Mescalero Apache Tribe. *Mescalero Apache Dictionary,* complied by Evelyn Breuninger, Elbys Hugar, Ellen Ann Lathan, Scott Rushforth. Mescalero, New Mexico: 1982.

Nicholas, Dan. "Mescalero Apache Girl's Puberty Ceremony." *El Palacio* 46: pp. 193–204. Originally published 1939.

Opler, Morris E. *An Apache Life-Way: The Economic, Social and Religious Institutions of the Chiricahua Indians*. New York: Cooper Square Publishers, 1965. Originally published 1941.

_____. "Adolescence Rite of the Jicarilla," *El Palacio* 49: pp. 25–38. Originally published 1942.

_____. *Childhood and Youth in Jicarilla Apache Society*. Publications of the Frederick Webb Hodge Anniversary Publication Fund, Vol. 5. Los Angeles: Southwest Museum. Originally published 1946.

Talamanetz, Inés. *Ethnopoetics: Theory and Method: A Study of 'Isanaklesh Gotal with Analyses of Selected Songs, Prayers, and Ritual Structure, and Contemporary Performance*. Ph.D. Dissertation, University of California, San Diego, 1977.

_____. "Dance and Ritual in the Study of Native American Religious Traditions," *New Scholar* 8 (1982): pp. 535–50. [Reprinted in *American Indian Quarterly* 6, no. 3–4 (fall-winter, 1983): pp. 337–57.

_____. "The Mescalero Apache Girls' Puberty Ceremony: A Consideration of the Role of Music in Structuring Ritual Time and Transformation," with Ann Dhu McLucas, *Yearbook of the International Council for Traditional Music* 18 (1986).

_____. "Images of the Feminine in Apache Religious Traditions," in *Feminist Transformations of the World's Religions,* Paula M. Cooey, William R. Eakin, and Jay B. McDaniel, eds. Maryknoll, NY: Orbis Press, 1991.

Turner, Victor W. *The Ritual Process: Structure and Anti-Structure*. Chicago: Aldine Publishing Co., 1969.

Van Gennep, Arnold. *Les Rites du Passage*. Translated by Monika B.Vizedom and Gabrielle L. Caffee as *The Rites of Passage* (Chicago: University of Chicago Press, 1960). Originally published 1908.

20. The Native American Church of Jesus Christ

EMERSON SPIDER, SR.

First of all, I'm very thankful that you boys could come to the Native American Church of Jesus Christ, which was built here at Porcupine not too long ago. I am Emerson Spider, Sr., and my title is Reverend of the Native American Church. I'm the headman of the Native American Church of Jesus Christ in the state of South Dakota.

Our church began to come into South Dakota during the early 1900s. There was a man named John Rave, a Winnebago Indian. This was before I was born. I guess this man was very smart. He was in the Catholic Church. Then he ordained another man named Henry White, also a Winnebago, as a minister in the Native American Church. That man came to the Sioux in the community of Allen, on Pine Ridge Reservation. So we got our ordination by rights.

At first we weren't organized as a church. It was a Sioux man named Jim Blue Bird who organized this peyote way of worshipping as a church and put the Bible in there to be the head instrument in our church. Then he said that we should have ministers. So in 1924 we organized as a church with ministers, like any other church. Last June we had our fifty-eighth annual convention. My grandpa on my mother's side, Reverend William Black Bear, was the first headman of the church in South Dakota. Then after he was gone, my dad took over. He was sixty-six years old when he passed away. For the past seventeen years I have been head of the church.

We started out as a traditional church. We didn't have the Bible or practice Christianity. Among the Indians, we always say that it is the oldest church in the world. Gradually we learned about the second coming of Christ, and finally we accepted the Lord as our personal savior, just as in any other church. Originally, the Native American Church followed the Half Moon way. Then the Winnebagos adopted the Cross Fire way. The fireplace on their altar looks like a half-moon, but instead of tobacco smoke they use the Bible.

The Native American Church started out with the Half Moon way of the Peyote religion. They use what they call the "Generation Fireplace." On the altar they mound the earth like a half-moon, and they put a little road on that mound which represents your life from the time you were born until you come to the center, and on to when you get old and go from there to death. They put the Generation Fireplace at the altar within the tipi, and at the center of the road they place the peyote.

We know that this Generation Fireplace pushes souls to Christ. The Cross Fire way comes in after believing on the Lord Jesus Christ. In this way we put the cross at the center to represent the place where Christ gave his life for each and every one of us. So it begins with this Half Moon way and then comes into the Cross Fire way, where you believe in Christ and pass to believing on the Lord. I'm not saying that the Cross Fire way is better, but as we come along we learn about the second coming of Christ. We put the peace pipe aside and we put the Bible in its place.

When I was becoming a Christian, I heard some people say, "I'm worshipping the same God as my forefathers." I thought that was real good, but now I think our forefathers must not have had the right kind of god. I hate to say this, but it is so. In the olden days, when people from different tribes came around, they killed them. We said they were enemies because they didn't speak our language. They had the same skin as we had, but we killed them. In those days they prayed to the Great Spirit, but I don't think that's the right god. The God we found is love. He loves us all. If in the olden days they prayed to that God, why is it they killed each other as enemies?

Also, in the olden days, one tribe believed that the souls of the departed went east, riding white horses. The Happy Hunting Grounds were supposed to be over the fourth hill to the east. Other tribes said the departed souls went south, riding sorrel horses. Every tribe had different beliefs. If they prayed to the same Great Spirit in the early days, they should all have had the same belief. Christ gave His life and made a road for us to go on. That's one way: towards heaven.

Right now some traditional Indian people say this Bible doesn't belong to the Indians because the white man made it. But I never thought of it that way. I thought this Bible belongs to any wicked man, any man with a living soul in him, so that through this Bible he would be saved. This is the way I think. It wasn't for just the white men alone but for every man, every person who has a living soul within him. It's the food for that person.

I'm not saying the traditional ways are bad, but it tells in the Bible, "Choose you this day whom you will serve, whether the gods of Amorites our forefathers served; but as for me and my house, we will serve the Lord." These are not my own words; I always like to use the words of God. Some people say they are real traditional men, but Christ is also a traditional man. He's been here almost two thousand years. That's traditional; that's a long time. I was thinking that we didn't use this peyote until after 1900, but Christ was in the world two thousand years ago. I think that's more traditional than what we have been trying to do here.

In the traditional way of worshipping in the Native American Church, the leader is called a *road man*. We still have our traditional way, especially in this area. In the traditional way we pray with the tobacco and corn-shock cigarette in place of the peace pipe. I held a service like that the other night, a back-to-school meeting. I prayed for the little ones who are going back to school. So we still have our traditional way as well. I ordained some of the traditional road men as ministers of the church. I did this because if we don't it will just be tradition, and we won't be recognized as a church.

The peyote that we use is classified as a drug by the state of South Dakota. We use it in the Native American Church as a sacrament. Because we are organized as a church, the government can't take the peyote away from us. Our church is the last thing we have among the Indian people, the peyote way of worshipping. We call it *Pejuta yuta okola-kiciye*, "medicine-eating church." The Native American Church is organized among the Sioux in South Dakota on three reservations: Pine Ridge, Rosebud, and Yankton. I have some ministers working on all three of these reservations. We are supposed to keep records, but I really don't know how many members there are. The other tribes still hang onto the traditional way of worshipping. They don't want to organize as a church, but the Sioux organized as a church. I think this is good, because other churches will recognize us as a church.

My grandpa and my dad told me that when they first started using peyote in the community of Allen, the Indian police would sneak up on them and stop them. They would take away the drum and the peyote. At that time my mother was real small, and she was going to the boarding school at Pine Ridge. While she was there, they found out that she had tuberculosis. In those days it was considered incurable. They placed my mother in the hospital, in a little room all by herself. No one was supposed to go near her because the disease was contagious. So they kept her there.

One day a grandma of mine was visiting the sick ones in the hospital. The door to my mother's room was open just a little bit. Her eyes were swollen nearly closed, and her body was swollen up; she was dying. As she lay there, she was looking towards the door, and she recognized the lady who went by. Mother called her name, so that lady came into the room. Although she was my mother's aunt, she didn't recognize my mother for awhile. Pretty soon she recognized her. "Is that you?" she said. "Yeah, that's me."

"Why are you lying here like this? Did you let your dad know that you're here?" My grandma on my mother's side passed away when my mother was real small, so she grew up with no mother, just my grandpa. I don't know what had happened, but the hospital hadn't notified my grandfather. So this grandma of mine said, "As soon as I get home I'm going to go to your dad and I'm going to tell him that you are here." I guess that made my mother feel real good. She said, "You do that."

Sure enough, in a few days my grandpa went after her. In those days there were just buggies, no cars. My grandpa really got mad because he had not been notified that my mother was sick. But the doctor told my grandpa not to take my mother because she had that contagious disease and was going to die anyway. Still, my grandpa took her home.

When they got home, my mother started taking that medicine, the peyote. They started giving her the medicine. My mother told me that it was towards springtime. All through that summer they would give her medicine, put her on a horse, and let her go out riding. She'd be on that horse most all day long. When she came back in the evening they would give her some more medicine. After a few months she was well. She was all right.

About that time they were caught while they were holding a Native American Church service. The man who ran the store at Allen at that time was against peyote, and he was the one who caught them. They called him *Nape Blaska,* "Flat-handed," because his hands were deformed. All of them got caught, including my mother, so they took them to Deadwood for trial. The court said that peyote was a narcotic, that it was no good. The judge asked, "Why are you using that?"

My mother's dad said: "This is good. This peyote's good. It is good medicine and I can prove it."

"What have you got to prove it with?"

"This girl here." So they had my mother stand up. "This girl had tuberculosis. The doctors gave up on her. She was placed in the sanitarium. I got her away from there. Now she's alive today."

Luckily, the doctor who had cared for my mother was in the courtroom. He asked her if she was Jessie Black Bear. "Yeah, it's me," she said.

He said, "How did you get well?"

"Through the peyote, through what we have here. I got well through that."

I guess the doctor got up and shook her hand, saying: "I thought you were gone a long time ago. I thought you were dead."

So right away the judge said, "I have nothing to do with this." "These mescal beans must be good," he said. (In those days they called peyote mescal beans.) "These mescal beans are yours; they don't belong to the white man. Give them back to them." So they gave the whole thing back, a wooden barrel full of peyote.

This is the reason that people say my mother is the one who saved the peyote. If she hadn't been there, they would have had a hard time proving that this medicine was good. After this happened, that man *Nape Blaska* went back and got into some kind of trouble. I guess he was in debt and couldn't pay, so he killed himself in the garage—committed suicide.

My dad was from Porcupine community. His family lived right across the road from here. My dad was born and raised here. He belonged to the Episcopal Church. My grandpa on my dad's side was a minister in that church. And my mother was from Allen, where the peyote church originated. They didn't tell me how they met, but anyway they got married. But my dad didn't like this medicine. He didn't believe in it. So whenever he went to Allen, and they started tying a drum for a service, he would take off. He didn't like to hear the drum or the songs. He would get on his horse and go way over the hill someplace. When they were through, he would come back. He did that for four years, I think.

My dad didn't believe in the peyote, but at the same time he was always thinking about it. He wondered, "What does it do for these people when they eat it?" Some people told him that when you ate it you got high, just like drinking. My dad never drank and never smoked. I guess he grew up like that. So he was wondering; he had it in mind all the time. But at the same time he was scared to use it because some people said it was dope.

Finally one day, when my mother and dad were alone, he said to my mother, "Jessie, I wonder if you could give me some of that medicine you eat?"

"Sure," she said. So she picked out four dried ones. She gave them to my dad and he started to eat one. This medicine is very bitter, so as he started to chew on it, he quickly took it out of his mouth. "This is awful," he said. "I don't see how you could eat it and why you would eat it. It's no good, not fit to be eaten." Then he got up. "This is not a thing to eat," he said. He started towards the stove, and although my mother tried to stop him, she couldn't. He opened that stove, threw the peyote in there, and burned it up.

Four days later, all of a sudden my dad couldn't pass any water. It stopped completely. His kidneys were swelling up, so he came back to Porcupine. His father sent for a doctor from Rapid City. That doctor came in a hurry; the Indians called him *Wasicu Wakan Witkokola*, "Crazy Doctor." He came and got his bag out and examined my father all over. I guess he told my grandpa: "If I wanted to, I could give your boy some medicine, but I want to tell you the truth. That boy's not going to live four days. You'd better get ready for it. There's no medicine that will cure him."

So my grandfather heard that. Then he wrote out a note and gave it to my father. "You take this to your father-in-law," he said. So they got in a buggy and rushed back to Allen, about twenty miles on the cut-across. When they got there, they gave that note to my grandpa on that side. He said, "Yeah, I got good medicine for that." My dad wanted to find out what kind of medicine he had. I guess he kept asking my mother, "What kind of medicine does your father have?" Finally my mother told him. "It's the same medicine that you burned here not too long ago." My dad said: "Well, that's it. If that's the medicine they are going to give, I don't want any. I'd rather die. I'm not going to eat it." "I'm not going to take it," he said.

My dad's older brother went with them on this trip. He's still alive today, over ninety years old. My dad was real young in those days. And I guess my uncle said to my father, "Brother, you're a coward." He said: "You're a coward. I'll eat it. You're scared of it. I'll eat it first," he said.

You know how young men are. When my dad heard that about being a coward and being scared, he got mad. "Well, bring all you got," he said. "I'll eat everything you got. Bring everything." So right away they told my grandfather. "Okay," he said. They got everything ready in no time. They boiled some of the powdered medicine in water to make tea, and they started giving my dad some of the dried medicine to eat. My dad said he didn't know how much he ate. "A lot of it," he said, "and I drank a lot of tea." His stomach and his kidneys were so swollen he could hardly walk. "I could hardly move," he said.

They were beating a drum, but it seemed to my dad that they were very slow to begin. My grandpa went after some boys, and pretty soon they came back and started their service. That morning my dad had to be excused, so he went out. There was no longer anything wrong with him. Back there about three gallons of water came out of him, I guess.

This is the way my dad told it. He said, "That's good medicine—real good medicine. It could cure anything. But the way they're praying with it, that's another thing." He grew up in the Episcopal Church, so he didn't believe in the Native American Church. "How can they pray with that peyote? How can they say that it is holy and leading a man to Christ? How could it be?" My dad kept going to church. Then one day he took some medicine, and I guess it showed him. Although he never brought out what happened, he learned that those who were weak in faith could benefit from using the peyote, that it was put here for the Indian people to lead them to Christ.

Now some of us are Christians—you might say born-again Christians. That's what we are. As we come along, we try to do whatever other churches are doing. In the past we had the Half Moon way of worshipping, and we used the peace pipe in our services, because the peace pipe is the traditional way of worshipping among our Sioux Indian people. As we came along, we put the peace pipe away, and in place of it we now use the Bible, so that we may be saved in the end. I know and believe that the Great Spirit in heaven did this for the Indian people, so that through this medicine we would find Christ.

In my own life I have experienced this, and I've told a lot of people about it. Indians from all tribes went out to hunt for roots to use as medicines, so God put this peyote here for the Indians to find. They call it peyote, but we say *pejuta,* which means "medicine" in our language. All the different tribes call it "medicine" in their own languages. Because God loves all of us he put this medicine in the world so that the Indians would find it and through it they would come to Christ.

Today I am well-known among other tribes as a good person because I have the fear of the Lord and I love God and I love Jesus Christ. If you live this way you'll get somewhere. I went to school as far as the fifth grade at Holy Rosary Mission at Pine Ridge, South Dakota. Some of the teachers there talked against our church and said that I was a dope eater. The boys I played with got scared of me. They said, "Don't go close to Spider cause he's going to poison you. He's a dope eater. He's no good." Sometimes I cried in the classroom, or on the playground, because I wanted to have friends but the boys didn't like me. They always said things like that to me as I grew up.

About two years ago they called me to that same place where I went to school. The people there used to hate me for using this peyote, but now they wanted to find out more about it. I didn't refuse them, because I have the love of God. I went back and told them about what the peyote had done for me.

To start with, we had our services in a tipi, with a fire burning inside. Our instruments were the drum, rattle, and feather fan. And we used God's plant, the Divine Herb. Through that, some of us—not all of us, but some of us—have become Christians. We're walking hand in hand doing the Christian walk. It's pretty hard to put in words; I think it's a mystery of God and no one can bring it out in words. But I'm going to try my best to explain some of what happened to me.

One time, before I became a Christian, I was sick. At that time I used the Divine Herb and I was healed by Christ. I got hurt when I was fifteen years old. The sickness I had was osteomyelitis. The doctors told me that it's incurable. There's no medicine on earth that will cure it, they said. And sure enough, the peyote eased my pain, but it didn't kill the disease. They said it's in my bones. I got hurt when I was young, and it started from there. When I was sick, I got double pneumonia, too. I was on my deathbed. I overheard the doctor talking to my parents, and he said if I didn't make it through that night, I would die. The doctor was telling my dad and my mom to be ready.

That day a preacher came into my room, passing out tracts. He gave me one, but I couldn't read it. I had poor eyesight, so I couldn't read it. So I just put it on the table. I was lying down. I couldn't get up from bed. I couldn't sit up, and I could hardly talk. That morning—I think it was a Sunday—it was coming daylight, and I remembered that the old people used to tell us that that's the time to talk to God. If you tell Him something, He'll hear you, they said. So that morning I was praying on my deathbed that if it's at all possible, I wanted to live longer.

God must have pitied me, because that morning He called me by my name. It was real loud. It was the first time I heard something like that, and it really hit me hard. The voice said, "Emerson!" real loud in the room. I couldn't get up from the bed but I answered that call. I said: "What? I am over here. I'm lying here." I thought it was one of the other boys in the room with me. There were about four other patients who were about to die, too, so they were placed in the room. But when I looked around they were all in bed asleep. I just started to go back to sleep again when I heard it a second time. It got me out of bed, sitting up. I noticed I was sitting up as I said, "Hau! I'm over here. What do you want?" But there was no answer, so I lay back down again.

The third time the voice got me to my feet, standing up. I knew that I was on my feet standing up. I walked towards the aisle and looked around, and here it was, the high calling of God; and it seemed like cold water on my face that morning, like it tells in the Scriptures about spiritual baptism. And that morning Christ healed me from my sickness. So I rejoice in the Lord every day of my life. Every time in the morning, ever since then when I get up I praise the Lord. I give Him thanks every day of my life. That's the life I'm leading now.

When I came back to the bed, I noticed the tract that had been given to me. I picked it up and read it, and it said, "Come as you are." Christ was speaking. "Come as you are." I knew it meant me, because I was a real sinner. I was no good, but it said *as I am*, He wants me to come to Him. And it says in there, "If any man comes unto me, I shall in no ways cast him out." So I know Christ called me by my name to be a leader of our church. I was supposed to stop sinning and try to be a good person because I was going to be the leader of the church. I was married when I was twenty-one, and when I was twenty-three years old I stopped drinking and smoking.

While I was coming along, there were some Christians who said to me: "You should come to our church where you won't be shedding tears for your people. Although you try to tell them right from wrong, they don't listen to you. Our church will listen to you," they said. But God wanted me to go where the church wasn't doing right, to tell them about the second coming of Christ. So actually God sent me to this Native American Church. He used me as a tool of the church to be the head man to try and guide them in the right way.

In our church we have leader helpers who can hold a service if there is no leader present. I remained a leader helper for a long time. Then I became a candidate leader. And then I became the chief leader. I gave information on how to hold a service. Gradually I became the headman of the community; you might say a minister of the community, the headman of the local branch. Then pretty soon, when the assistant man who sat next to my dad passed away, they appointed me his assistant. So I came to it step by step, and then when my dad passed away, I became the high priest.

Before my dad passed away, he said: "This is my best. I want you to make it right for me." So that's what I'm doing now. I'm trying to make the other non-peyote people see that I can lead a Christian life in the Native American Church. I stand up for my church and say that it is a good church.

By rights we can hold our church services most any time. During the summertime we can have our services any time of the week, but during the wintertime we have to have services on Saturday because the kids have to go to school Monday. And lately some of the church members have been working, too, so we have to consider them. Also, the cost of the medicine we use is getting real high. Usually we go and harvest it ourselves, but the trip is very expensive. I know just lately there are people selling land to get the money to go and harvest peyote and bring it back.

It takes four persons to run a service: the leader, the drummer, the cedar man and the fire man. They don't pick out just anybody for these positions.

The man who takes care of the drum is supposed to be a certain kind of man who knows how to hit the drum. He can't live a wicked life and handle the drum. It's sacred to the Indians. Indians really like the drum. It is made into a great big drum which they use at powwows and things like that. We use that same drum, but we make it into a real small drum, and we use it to praise and sing unto the Lord. For that reason the drummer has to be a certain kind of person to hit that drum. He has to know how to sing, how to hit the drum, and how to live a good life. He must know how to make instruments in the church.

The man who takes care of the cedar throughout the night has to be a man who knows how to pray to the Great Creator, to the Great Spirit. He has to take care of the prayers. Every time a person prays, he burns cedar. We use the cedar smoke as incense, just like the Catholic Church. We were told that a long time ago the old people made smoke signals in order to send messages to others far away. We were told that we're doing that. That's the reason they used the peace pipe to pray to the Great Spirit, making smoke signals to pray with. During our church services in the tipi we burn that cedar whenever somebody prays, so that the smoke goes up. Our understanding is that we are making smoke signals to the Great Spirit so that He will hear our prayers. That's what we have been told.

The fire man is supposed to know how to build the fire; they don't just throw the wood into the fireplace. This man has to know how to chop and gather wood, how to build a tipi, and things like that. We have a fire going inside the tipi all the time, so this man takes care of it, he watches it. He's the only man who moves in the church, like an altar boy in the Catholic Church. He goes out, brings wood in, and keeps that fire burning. In our church building we have lights, but when we hold traditional services in the tipi, we have to keep the fire going all night.

In the traditional way our services started at sundown and continued until sunrise. That's the way it used to be. But nowadays the people come late. When the leader, drummer, cedar man, and fire man all arrive, then we start our service.

There are different instruments that we use in our services in order to praise the Lord. To start with we use this staff, which we call *sagye*. That means "cane" in our language. Each man, when he sings in the service, holds onto this cane.

We use this small drum, tied in a certain way, with water inside. Only a few men know how to tie and beat the drum. We call it a holy drum.

We use this drumstick, which can be made from all kinds of wood. One kind is called snake wood. It makes a really good-looking stick.

We use this gourd rattle, which each man holds when it is his turn to sing.

We use this sage. From the beginning of our church, the Half Moon way, we have used this sage. It was used as a traditional way of praying. They were told that they should use it to refresh themselves, to cleanse themselves, before going into a ceremonial like the Sun Dance or sweat lodge or fasting. If you wipe yourself with it there is a good fresh smell and it cleans you. That's the reason they used it all over the body in the sweat lodge. For that reason the traditional way of worship in our church uses sage. They hit themselves all over with that sage to clean themselves. Then they partake of the Divine Herb.

We use this bone whistle, made from the wing bone of an eagle. The leader blows it in a ceremonial way during the service.

We use this fan, made from different kinds of bird feathers, to perform holy orders. To start with, they used to use a feather fan made from two swift hawk tails, twelve feathers on each bird, a total of twenty-four. These feathers are arranged to form a circle. On the outside are four eagle feathers, and inside, at the center, is an eagle plume. They say this swift hawk is the swiftest bird in the world, and they say the eagle is the fiercest bird. The plume inside the fan represents the living soul that's in a person. We were told that the tail feathers are there for the swift hawks to try to catch the living soul, the spirit of a man, the soul of each person. They can surround him and catch that living soul. The eagle plume is there so that if any bad spirit comes, the eagle will fight that spirit away. This is the way we were taught by our elders. We should use this type of feather fan to come out of the traditional way into a Christian way of worship.

Today they make fans from red and blue macaw feathers, and what they call scissortails—real pretty feathers. They bring all these different feathers into the church. They're good, they're God's creation, but it didn't come to us like that from the start.

Finally, we use the Divine Herb. When a person takes the peyote in a service, if he has teeth, he usually eats it dry. When I was young, when I had teeth, I could eat it dry. Sometimes they grind it up. Then a person can put the powder in his hand and eat it like that. Or he can mix it with water and make it into a kind of gravy and eat it like that. We also make tea out of the powdered peyote, using warm water. The peyote is very bitter. If you can eat four of them it is good, and if you can eat more, it will do you a lot of good.

When peyote first started to come into our area, we used our native tongue all the time to preach the word of God. I have a Bible that's written in our language, and I can read it well. Gradually our young people have gone to school and gotten a good understanding of English. The man who had this church building built is half Sioux and half Shoshone, but he was raised in a city, so he didn't learn either the Sioux language or the Shoshone language. He speaks just this whiteman language. So when we have our services and there's no person who doesn't speak our language, we usually talk in our own native tongue. But when somebody who doesn't understand our language comes into our church, we try to perform everything in English so it will be understandable. But some things we can't do in English, because we were brought up in a certain way and it has to be that way. It doesn't have to be understood by other men, just so the Great Spirit will understand us, listen to us, hear us. We believe that way.

During the service we sing songs in groups of four. Some are in Lakota and others are in English. These are the words to one set of songs. I composed the first song using words from my favorite gospel hymn; the words of the third song are in English, and the other three are in Lakota:

(1) I have decided to follow Jesus.
     No turning back.

(2) Jesus I love your words
Because your words are eternal life.
Give me life.
I love your words.

(3) Praise our Lord Savior Jesus.
Did you know that our Lord Savior Jesus died upon the
cross for our sins?
Praise our Lord Savior Jesus.

(4) God, look upon us Indians,
We want to be saved.

After the service we eat a breakfast of four symbolic foods. They are sacred to the Indians and are eaten not for the body but for spiritual strength.

The first is water. They say everything lives by water, so in the morning we have a woman bring in water and pray over it. This is because in the beginning it was a woman who first found the peyote. Later, when the Indians learned to read the Bible, they found out about the well of Jacob, and about Christ saying "I am the living water." They found where Christ says: "The water you will give me, I'll be thirsty again, but the water I'll give you, you will never be thirsty. You will become a spring within yourself." This is what it tells in the Scripture, so they pray over the water for spiritual strength.

The second is corn. Usually at this time of year they have fresh corn on the cob, but in the wintertime they used dried corn, which they cook so it comes out just like it was fresh. We have been told that before the white men ever came across, the Indians knew how to plant corn. They already had that here and they lived by it. They use this to pray that their gardens will be good; they pray over the corn that in the summertime everything will grow real good.

The third is meat. A long time ago they used only dried meat, but today they use any kind of meat, usually beef. They boil it and serve it with soup, although some pass around just the meat itself. In the olden days the Indians used to have a lot of livestock, cattle, and wild animals like deer and buffalo. So they prayed over the meat that the hunting season would be good, that their children would have good food.

The fourth is fruit. The old people prayed over the fruit so that the wild fruits along the creeks would grow for the Indians to use. They pounded the fruit up and dried it so it would keep.

All the church services we have are not alike. We have services for birthdays, healing, marriage, baptism, prayers, funerals—anything, we have it all. Every service is different. That's the mystery of God.

One time we had a healing service here which pretty much surprised us. We had a man who was going to have surgery for gallstones, and we had a healing service here and gave him medicine. He was seated right near the altar. A girl suffering with arthritis was seated across the room, against the east wall. We performed their healing. Lately we're trying to get the healing of Jesus Christ. We don't give sick people a whole bunch of medicine like in the olden times, but we just give them so much. One Scripture I used was, "Any man sit among you, let him call the elders of the church that they anoint him with oil, pray over him that he may get well, and if he commits any sin, it shall be forgiven." These are the Lord's words, so I used them. That man was healed right there that night. And the girl, even though she wasn't out in the center of the church, was also healed. So things like this happen. It's altogether different than the works of the peyote.

I might put it this way. When people come to a service and partake of the Divine Herb, it works on them in different ways. That's the mystery of God. Sometimes, even if a person is no good, the peyote will work for him. Through the peyote he will throw away the evil and give himself to Christ. In this way some of our church members have put away alcohol, become Christians, and gotten good jobs again. And they help other people in the church, too.

One time my dad went to a prayer ceremony. He must have eaten a lot of medicine, and the service was going on and on. And all at once he saw the door open, so he looked over there and here was a man coming in. It seemed like nobody else noticed that man coming in. But my dad kept watching him, and that man came up to him and said: "I've been looking for you all over. I couldn't find you. I heard that you were in a meeting someplace. I went to one meeting but you weren't there, so I came over here." He sat beside my dad and said, "Tonight I'm going to pray with you, sing with you." So my dad was happy. My dad wasn't a drummer, but he was a good singer, had a good voice. And my dad was a minister and a good man. The visitor had a box with him, so he took his instruments out. Everything he had was perfect. When the singing came to them, the visitor sang first. He sang good songs, real pretty songs. Then he hit the drum for my dad, but he made that drum sound different, a good sound. Then he talked and prayed, prayed real good, prayed so interestingly that the people started crying. He was really good at everything.

My dad was watching him, but he never did see the man talking. Then he saw that the man was going around to every person in there, looking at their prayer instruments, opening their boxes up and taking a good look at their instruments. Then, finally, he came to where the altar was, and he looked at everything there. They had this Divine Herb there, which they were partaking of. My dad saw him open it, and suddenly it seemed like somebody had hit the man in the face and knocked him toward the door. When he landed by the door, my dad could see his tail and horns. As he was going out, he looked back at my dad and said: "I'm going to come back and visit you again. Someday I'm going to come back again."

From this we know that the Evil One can come into any place, even a church. The Evil One can read the Bible, he can talk, he can pray, but he doesn't believe in Christ. He says he believes in Christ, that he knows Christ, but doesn't believe it. He's that powerful, fooling people all over the world. So a man should be aware that the Evil One can come anywhere.

Through my work in the church I came to know many things. One thing I wanted to find out for sure is where the souls of our departed ones are. I went around to different ministers, different churches. "I want you to tell me the truth of it," I said. "Where is paradise?" But no one could answer me. So I came back to my church and finally learned that the departed souls are here. They're not going any place. When we pray in the prayer service, and we are thinking about our departed loved ones, they come near us. They come right close to us. The only thing I found out about it in the Scriptures is that the departed souls are just like they are behind glass. They're on the other side, we're on this side. They see us, but we can't see them; they hear us, but we can't hear them. That's how it is. I found this out in our church and by reading the Scriptures, that the departed ones are always here with us. I thought this was real nice.

We are Indian people, and we still have some of our traditional ways. One thing we have, which the Indians grew up with, is what we call the spiritual food for our departed ones. Long ago, when people were eating something good, they would think about their loved ones who had gone beyond. Then they would take a little bit of the food they were eating and throw it outside, saying, "*Wanagi le iyakiya*," which means, "Spirit, find this." When my grandpa and my grandma were alive, I saw them do this, and we still have this. We couldn't part with the things that the traditionals had, so we still have them.

They prayed for these departed ones, too, and they talked to them. They grew up with that. The Bible says that when a person dies he knows nothing, he can't hear, he can't see. But the Indians say that for four days that body is holy. It can see you, it can hear you, they say. One time I went to a gospel mission. The preacher was a white man. His wife had just died, and they were having a wake service. I said: "This lady is not dead, she's sleeping, I think, resting. So she sees you." And that man started crying. He said to me, "Those are comforting words that you brought here, words we never heard before."

"That's the way I was taught," I said, "and that's the way it is." So I prayed over her, and I talked to that dead body, because that's how I was brought up.

There are some traditional things that we still have in the Cross Fire way, things we still hang onto because we grew up with them and we're Indians. But actually I don't know about the next generations, the coming generation. I notice that every generation changes. Things are changing.

I was told that God created all men equal, so this was the reason He put the peyote here for the Indians. Some of us didn't find out about it for a long time. But it is a good thing that my grandfather and my father found out about it, because it helped us to find Christ. Lately I have been going around to other churches and to schools telling about what our church is doing for us Indian people. For this reason I am happy to put my talk in a book so that people will read it and learn about our church. The days are getting short. The second coming of the Lord is at hand and we're getting ready for it. People will not be judged according to their beliefs, or according to which church they belong to. God will not say, "What kind of church do you belong to? What ways do you have?" It's not going to be that way. The bad things we've done and the good things we've done shall be weighed; and if we do good we'll be in the arms of Christ. It doesn't matter what church we belong to—the church will not save us. These are things I want to bring out to people, especially to the younger generation.

I would like you to understand that the fear of the Lord is the beginning of all knowledge. It says in the Scriptures that it doesn't matter if you gain the whole world's knowledge if you don't have the fear of the Lord. You have to be good in every way and put Christ ahead of you all the time so you won't go wrong. If you put your beliefs or anything else ahead of Christ, you'll be wrong. This world will come to an end. Everything must be stopped. So you need to have the true love of God to be saved.

Some people tell me that the knowledge of this world is the key to tomorrow. That's what they say. This earthly knowledge is good; it's necessary to get by in this world. I wish that the boys and girls will stay in school and learn—but put Christ ahead of your schooling. Read your Bible and you'll be safe in the arms of Christ. There is no other way to salvation.

If you come to the Lord, no matter what sickness you have, you can be healed. I was healed and now I'm a born-again Christian, and I'm working for my church. It used to be that when we had the traditional way of worshipping, we believed in earthly life. Now we believe in the second coming of Christ, although we still have our traditional ways. We still believe in them. I believe in the Sun Dance and fasting and all the traditional ways. I believe that they are sacred and I believe that they are good. But they are earthly, so by them alone no man will be saved.

The second coming of Christ is the only way to salvation. So I want you to know me and I want you to understand my church. There are some Christians who don't know our church, who may even think we are uncivilized. I want the Native American Church to be recognized by other churches. And I want people everywhere to pray for us, too.

21. Who Can Sit at the Lord's Table? The Experience of Indigenous Peoples

ROSEMARY MCCOMBS MAXEY

The purpose of this essay is to explore the place of indigenous peoples' religions within and without the diverse theological stances of the United Church of Christ. Indigenous people are those who today are called American Indians or Native Americans. I intend to recall briefly the history of the Euro-American Christian movement and the indigenous peoples' responses in early "American" history thereby creating a basc for a deeper understanding of Native American particularization of their perspectives as they relate to Christian churches today. The major thrust has to do with relationships, not with classical definitions of ecclesiology as proposed by European and Euro-American scholars. Relationships link the present with past and future and link people with all creation. Theologically, environmentally, and in their holistic understanding of human nature, indigenous people have much insight to offer to those who seem to have garnered the best seats for themselves at the Lord's Table. The United Church of Christ, which carries as its motto "That They May All Be One" and proclaims its unity in diversity, should be especially receptive to the voices of indigenous people who desire room at the table.

Historical Survey

Beginning with the "discovery" made by Christopher Columbus, Christians have struggled with the issue of what should be done with the original inhabitants of the New World. When Columbus returned from his first voyage in 1493, a squabble arose between the kingdoms of Castile and Portugal over possession of the lands of the New World. The Pope intervened with four papal bulls in 1493 and one in 1506, in them demarcating lands, giving most of the New World to Spain, which would convert the pagan indigenous inhabitants. Other European countries denounced or ignored the Pope's bulls, but throughout the sixteenth century theologians, jurists, historians, friars, and administrators debated what to do with the indigenous people. In 1550 the issue was debated by the Catholic Church's Council of Fourteen. Two theological camps emerged. Bishop Bartolome de las Casas debated one side: that the noble savages were developed in the arts, languages, and government. They were gentle, eager to learn, and quick

"Who Can Sit at the Lord's Table?: The Experience of Indigenous Peoples." by Rosemary McCombs Maxey. Reprinted by permission of the author.

to accept Christianity. The other side, represented by Gines de Sepulveda, argued that these creatures were savage-like, slaves by nature, pagan, uncivilized, incapable of learning, and unable to govern themselves.[2] The issue was what to do with the aboriginal inhabitants, whether they were entitled to the soil, and what could be done to them if they refused the beneficence of "lumbre y doctrina" ("light and doctrine" or "light and teaching"). The debate ended in Las Casas's favor, but when missionaries came from Europe, the results were more closely tied to Sepulveda's argument.[3] And for five hundred years, the primary mission strategy of many mainline denominations has followed or paralleled that early approach.

Common historic interests have always existed between the indigenous people of North America and the forebears of the United Church of Christ. In 1629 the Congregationalists began efforts to include indigenous people in the Christian fold. With well-intentioned, dedicated missionaries, the general thrust was to "wynn and invite the Natives . . . [to] the onlie God and Savior of Mankinde."[4] Missionaries from that time to the present have consistently tried to make indigenous people participate in the church as acculturated Euro-American Christians. Indigenous people have resisted, reacted, and responded in a variety of ways to Christianity as presented by the missionaries. A monograph in the United Church of Christ Heritage Series, *Two Spirits Meet*, traces the process of cultural change and conflict:

> *Prof. Robert Berkhofer, in* Salvation and the Savage, *demonstrated that when missionaries successfully converted part of the tribe, they set off a sequence of events through which the tribal unit frequently crumbled. Berkhofer studied Protestant mission history of the one-hundred-year period prior to the Civil War. He outlined a sequence of four stages. After missionaries converted some members of a tribal group, either the traditional or the Christian group was ostracized. The ostracized group usually moved and separated physically from the other members of the tribe. However, both groups frequently reunited physically in the face of common military threats. After they reunited and reestablished common government, political factions emerged, usually based on religion, which prevented the tribe from taking totally effective actions.[5]*

The same continues to be true today. Three patterns of participation can be discerned among the indigenous people who relate to the United Church of Christ. The first, occurring in the earliest relationships with the missionaries, was the development of native churches. Using their tribal language in worship and church polity, single tribal churches developed along family, clan, and community lines. These churches exist today among the Dakotas and the Winnebagos.

Second, in 1982, a multitribal congregation was started in Minnesota, called All Nations Indian Church. Incorporating some of the symbols of their ancestors and their native languages, this church worships and provides services to the community. The third pattern involved other indigenous people over the years who joined Anglo churches and became involved in them to varying degrees, sometimes minimizing their identity with the indigenous community, sometimes assimilating in terms of worship but maintaining an identity with the tribal community.

My own relationship with the church as a Muscogee (Creek) Indian Christian has taken me through all three relationships. Three generations of my family have been Christian in a tribal community church affiliated with the Southern Baptist Convention. The Muscogee language is spoken in worship and business. During college and seminary, and immediately thereafter, I attempted to assimilate with the Anglo churches by working in new church development. It was not until I was a member of a multiracial church in New York City that I began to question the Euro-American nature of all Christian churches and to search for a new church relationship where the attempts at pluralism were more intentional. My search ended when I moved to Westminster, Maryland, and became friends with the leaders of a United Church of Christ congregation. In the tradition of my grandfather, who said, "I will be a Baptist because I have met a real good one," I became a member of the United Church of Christ because I met some "real good ones" who shared with me convincing evidence of the United Church of Christ's genuine interest in pluralism and ecumenism.

Since joining this congregation I have been privileged to sit with those in conference and association-level consultations who are serious about theology and serious about ecumenicity. But even they are more apt to cling to investigating "the unity." With furrowed brows, members of theological consultations and study groups pore over an array of theological position papers looking for that shred of evidence that enables them to proclaim, Aha! We are alike after all! Let's celebrate our unity. The fact that the United Church of Christ cannot declare a single or at least a four-strand theological position bothers even the most progressive theologian. The nameless "they" seem to push the panic button. "Other denominations make fun of the United Church of Christ because it is too diverse to take a theological position. . . . The UCC has been accused of a murky Christology," wailed two theologians in my presence recently.

From an indigenous person's perspective, I raise some questions about the denomination's proclaimed inclusivity. One must ask, What exactly is the criteria for sitting diversely together at the Lord's Table? What conditions and limits are placed on such an invitation? Do the indigenous peoples' ways of living and believing keep them marginalized in the United Church of Christ because there is no Euro-American theological or ecclesiastical category for them at the Lord's Table?

Can indigenous people, in their diversity, and others in the United Church of Christ, in their diversity, sit side by side in wholeness to strategize and pray for a realization of an eschatology that restores the unity of a fragmented world? Can we, in our united particularities, prepare our human communities for the wholeness that is more than people, and includes the entire cosmos?

There are difficulties in addressing these questions. In the first place, there is no way of presenting a single homogeneous view of the indigenous peoples. We are as varied and diverse as the United Church of Christ claims to be. We are many tribal groups and nations who vary in culture, thought, government, and language. However, some tribal and national commonalities exist in theological beliefs about the deity, ceremonies that celebrate the relationship between the Creator and the created, the origins of humankind, and the relationship and responsibility for living within the created order.[6] We also have many symbols and rituals that are common to us and parallel those of the Christian church. We often practice parallel Christian/Traditional rituals and rites simultaneously.

The second difficulty is our loss of pure culture. What was ideal and complete culturally cannot be entirely regained. Exploitation, relocation, assimilation, loss of sacred land bases, and loss of many of our languages (our roots of understanding) hinder us from achieving our cultural and religious goals, our ways of being. Most of us have become "diaspora people" in our own homeland.

The third difficulty in presenting the indigenous peoples' perspective is the "majority" audience who will read this essay. Conveying ideas in our common language of English is incomplete and misunderstood because of our differing world views, which remain largely unexplored and foreign to one another.

The motivation for listening to each other should, however, point to our mutual need for understanding, respecting, and living with each other. Indigenous people need the help of Christian churches in advocacy for justice and survival as distinct peoples. Christian churches need the indigenous people to help the church reclaim the activity of a particularly significant and faithful community of believers. That is, Christian people need to undertake their specific mission in the world, understand their possession of a sacred history, and live out their sacred duty to humankind and to the cosmos.

Further, the church needs to hear the indigenous peoples' voices regarding place in the universe and care for the created order. The United Church of Christ is just now doing its exegetical work on environmental theology and stewardship and coming to the same conclusions that the Ancient Ones have proclaimed all along.

Identity versus Assimilation

In December 1978, the Native American Project (now called the Indigenous Peoples Project to avoid confusion of "Native Americans" as a reference to second and third generations of others who have staked a claim in "America") of Theology in the Americas worked out a position paper to describe and analyze the commonalities that exist for indigenous peoples in their religions and the effects Christianity has had on them. The uniqueness of this project lies in the sixty-five indigenous people who participated. They included Catholic and Protestant Christians and traditionalists (those who practice only their tribal religions) from urban and reservation dwelling places and represented some fifteen tribal nations.

The common beliefs or themes that emerged follow:

We are an ancient people whose religious oral traditions declare that we have lived and evolved in these lands since the beginning of time. Examining our history, our traditions and our beliefs, we find creation stories that point to a time of birth from out of the earth and a covenant relationship with a Creator Spirit that is unique to this part of the world. We know that we have always been integral to this part of the world; we did not come from anywhere else. We know that our covenant with the Life Giving Force did not end and was not negated with the arrival of Christopher Columbus, the Mayflower or any other foreign vessel that has ever come to this continent. Many of our tribal people have clung tenaciously to the ancient beliefs and ritual ceremonies of our people even under persecution: therefore, we have survived as distinct peoples with a history and a place in the cosmos.[7]

With the introduction of Christianity to the tribes, some of our people, regardless of tribal affiliation, found the teachings of Jesus similar and compatible to the ancient moral and ethical teachings of our people. Jesus' teachings were accepted by many who did not give up their understanding of their place in the universe as taught in traditional instruction prior to missionary influence. Indigenous peoples have started churches of their own and conducted the business of the church from a tribal perspective, that is, using the same style of selecting a minister as was used in designating a chief and designing the worship according to the model of traditional religious ceremonies. Accepting "civilization" and Christianity from this orientation was an attempt to maintain separate sovereign nations in the face of Western expansion. Ultimately, the "Indian Church" did not help maintain tribal sovereignty, but it did provide indigenous expression in a Christian mode.

Assimilation attempts by the U.S. government, working in concert with the Euro-American church, have had an impact on many of our people as well. This triumphal church approach led many of us to join the Anglo church and we often find ourselves accepting Americanized Christianity as a way of believing and living. I find that, for me, this is a dangerous way to live. The different perceptions of the ministry of the church and the Euro-American's view about humankind's place in the universe and the: church's efforts to universalize and impose its beliefs on all peoples of earth create difficulty and confusion for many indigenous people.

In spite of Christianity's doctrine of original sin and the virtue of humility, the European perception and attitude about their place ("a little lower than the angels") is quite lofty. This is the irony of a pessimistic view of sinful humanity. The contradictions between stated beliefs and the actual life style leave one to compromise and compartmentalize daily living into incompatible units. The belief that Jesus came "that all may have life" and the actual practices of genocide to indigenous peoples are strange bedfellows indeed.

Granted, the United Church of Christ has adopted an impressive and new missiology. It has become common to affirm that "the gospel is in the people and we go to them and discover the gospel in their lives." Evangelism has become more of a witnessing/inspecting mechanism to see the gospel at work and respond with awe. Is this another name for "fact-finding missions" where the church checks to see if God is at work and is surprised to find out that it is so? This missiology may have been slow in coming, but it does make way for cultural diversity within the church and may be welcomed by indigenous people who are outside the church.

Those indigenous people outside the church who maintain their tribal religious ceremonies and ways of being are referred to as the traditionalists. Indigenous people within the church who adore their heritages must express gratitude to those who in the face of adversity have held to the ancient beliefs of our peoples. It is through the efforts of the traditionalists that indigenous Christians stand a chance of regaining identity as a distinct and covenanted people. We must reconsider our old values if not our old practices, even as we take our places at the Lord's Table.

To promote greater understanding and cross-cultural exchanges, traditionalists have invited Anglos to share in ceremonials such as the Vision Quest and Sweatlodges. Recently, some of our brothers and sisters in the United Church of Christ have explored these experiences of Native Americans. Ordinarily, one would welcome these cross-cultural opportunities but two suspicions arise. These ceremonials are about the essence of survival as a covenanted people. When nonindigenous persons bypass the hardships of reservation life and what it means to be Indian in this country and move into the ceremonials for filling a personal spiritual void, are they not exploiting the religious experience for personal gain? What are they contributing back to the survival of a people and our beloved Mother Earth? Another question concerns people like those in the New Age movement. The New Age movement people who have explored Native American spirituality have turned a nice profit by writing and lecturing on Native American spirituality.

I find it odd/interesting that while some Anglos learn and experience Native American roots of spirituality, the United Church of Christ affirms and supports indigenous Christians in their efforts to learn about scripture, tradition, and reason in order to provide leadership for indigenous peoples' church community. Such engaging issues are prime topics for opening dialogue for all of us. Consider Joshua 24:25-28, where God made a covenant with the tribes of Israel:

> *So Joshua made a covenant with the people that day, and made statutes and ordinances for them at Shechem. And Joshua wrote these words in the book of the law of God; and he took a great stone, and set it up there under the oak in the sanctuary of the Lord. And Joshua said to all the people, "Behold, this stone shall be a witness against us; . . . lest you deal falsely with your God."*

Some of the psalms likewise speak of God's power in created nature. Psalm 96 says, "Sing to the Lord, all the earth! Let the heavens be glad . . . let the sea roar . . . let the field exult, and everything in it . . . the trees of the wood will sing for joy."

Perceptions of the Deity

In the Muscogee (Creek) language, the name of the creator-spirit deity is *Hesaketvmese*, that is, "Breath Holder." Other meanings include Creator (earth), Sustainer (air), Redeemer (water), Intervener (unexpected events), Lover, Intimate Confidant, and Fun-Loving Friend (gentle breezes and small whirlwinds). The deity is accessible and present throughout the entire cosmos.

The scriptures, in remarkably similar ways, attest to the presence of the deity in what are considered by the Euro-Americans to be inanimate objects. In the Gospel according to Luke, when Jesus was making the triumphant entry into Jerusalem amidst the palm waving and praise, the Pharisees in the crowd spoke to Jesus, saying, "Teacher, rebuke your disciples." He answered, "I tell you, if these [disciples] were silent, the very stones would cry out" (Luke 19:40). Passages such as these resonate vibrantly in the essence of indigenous peoples.

In the history of the church there have been a few individuals, Francis of Assisi, St. Anthony, and Julian of Norwich, for example, who have been especially spiritually alive to the Creator in the created world. In the indigenous peoples' history Black Elk is recorded as a spiritual holy man attuned to the created order, and there are many others, including women, who are known to us by oral tradition.

But greater than the enchantment of mystery in the created order and stones that shout is the recognition that nature is an active participant with human beings and has feelings. Nature may have immortal and inexhaustible qualities, but it can die and it can die at the hands of human beings if human beings are not attuned to the voices and feelings of nature.

Indigenous people call for the recognition of the Breath Holder who through the act of creation permeates all life forms. Native thought has always embraced the philosophy enculturated through our oral traditions that all of the created elements are to be revered as an elder and nurtured as a child. What creation provides is to be cared for and used by all.[8] All of creation is sacred.

Perceptions of Humankind

The stories of many tribal nations concerning the creation of human beings are not unlike the Genesis account (2:4a-23). We are created from the earth, made last, not as a hierarchical culmination, but in a more humble position.

The human being is considered the weakest of creation, entirely dependent on all other created life forms for mere existence. Gratitude, nurture, and equality are to be accorded all creation.[9] The Genesis story of the fall from grace and expulsion from Paradise (Genesis 3) should humble us, not make us proud and possessive. Christian faith aims to restore the state of grace with God and creation but Christians have alienated themselves too far from nature, making reconciliation in universal wholeness difficult.

Only in recent biblical scholarship have theologians begun to see that the Hebrew words for dominion (*radah*) and subdue (*kabash*) are antithetical to universal harmony and order.[10] Some ancient manuscripts can be read as either *radah* or as *mashal*. Could it be that substituting the Hebrew verb *mashal* for *radah* would clarify human beings' place in the created order? While the root word of *mashal* is difficult to trace, one of the verb's meanings is "to pattern one upon the other" as in speaking in parables. If humankind could pattern its relationship to the created order in the way the Creator is related to creation, humankind could be cocreators with God in God's world. God-likeness would generate harmony and order rather than dominion and subjugation.

Contrast that to the Euro-American distortion of the concept of "man" naming, subduing, and having dominion over the earth. This forces the earth to produce rather than allowing the earth to flourish under the rhythm of life. Western European technological arrogance has jarred the harmony of the cosmos and thwarted the Creator's intention. The drive to possess the land, rather than act as God's cocreators, further adds to the imbalance. Christianity's influence in this regard affects all humanity. The earth and every living entity have been objectified, depersonalized, and made inanimate. The concept of humankind being patterned after God, the Breath Holder and Gardenkeeper, is lost.

The United Church of Christ has exhibited concern for the environment and a desire to uphold a theology of stewardship rather than dominion. It seems, then, that one of the areas that indigenous peoples have in common with the United Church of Christ is the goal of restoring harmony with each other and the natural order. But how do we overcome our diverse perceptions of what that means?

I had the privilege of attending the first Theodore Roosevelt Environment and Conservation Symposium (Fall 1986) sponsored jointly by Grace Reformed Church in Washington, D.C., the United Church Board for Homeland Ministries, the Central Atlantic Conference of the UCC, the UCC Office for Church in Society, the Stewardship Council, and the National Wildlife Federation. While the goal of preserving creation was common to all, the contrast in approach between the United States Forestry Service and the United Church of Christ was interesting. The theological approach was that the problem is people taking over the function of God instead of recognizing that God is at home in God's world, and that God has shared God's home with nature and humankind alike as a household. The Forestry Service representative called for persons to exercise their responsibility to be God's stewards and use and renew resources as appropriate to the technology that has been developed by humankind. In other words, to the Forestry Service it seems that people have found a way to care for the world in God's absence.

The perspective of the UCC theologian is in harmony with indigenous peoples' goal of restoring and maintaining harmony with each other and the natural order. But we have a lot of work to do to overcome our diverse perceptions of what that means. Over a century ago, Chief Seattle spoke of the indigenous peoples' perspective of our human relationship to earth and the environment, the indigenous sense of harmony and the problem with the Euro-American world view. In 1854, at a time when the president of the United States was trying to negotiate a treaty, Chief Seattle said,

> *So we will consider your offer to buy our land. But it will not be easy. For this land is sacred to us. . . . We may be brothers after all; we shall see. One thing we know, which the white man may one day discover, our God is the same God. You may think now that you own him as you wish to own our land, but you cannot. He is the God of man, and his compassion is equal for the red man and the white. This earth is precious to him and to harm the earth is to heap contempt on its Creator. Continue to contaminate your bed, and you will one night suffocate in your own waste.*[11]

A Perception of Harmony

For God so loved the world that God gave God's only Son, that whoever believes in him should not perish, but have eternal life. (John 3:16, RSV adapted)

This famous verse that the missionaries taught us, but often neglected to analyze or assess for themselves, contains real truth in the word "world." The Greek word is *kosmos*, or universe. The intention of the deity seems to be to offer salvation to all of creation. The offered salvation is not limited to the people in the church, to those who have strands of unity, but salvation is opened to the entire cosmos. Cosmic balance, harmony, and longevity belong to all of the created order in their particularities and even when there seems to be no common thread among them! Justice, ethics, and morality flow from the intertwined, interdependent, and intimate relationships of Creator and created.

Genocide, extermination, exploitation, pollution, contamination, and oppression are the acts that most upset the natural order and upset the deity. When harmony is disrupted, the

Creator is sad, hurt, angry, and vengeful (in the sense that the disrupters must suffer the natural consequences of their deeds). Sometimes the deity turns away from, does not favor, those who are disruptive. Sometimes, in a manner reminiscent of Jesus' Beatitudes, the deity intervenes with those least likely to appear worthy and orthodox.

Learning the lessons of restoring harmony involves individuals and their community as they participate in the ceremonies of the tribe. It is in the seasonal, temporal, geography-centered, rigidly followed ceremonies that one learns the ways of worship, gratitude, and well-being.[12] Ceremonies always begin with prayer. Many tribes use a sacred pipe filled with special tobacco. First, offering the pipe to the four directions, then to the sky and the earth, then to "all my relatives" symbolizes the inclusion of all creation. Then, the smoking of the pipe by every person in the circle symbolizes communion and accepting the gift from the Creator and Mother Earth. Dances, such as the hoop dance of the Ojibwe, represent the circle of the universe. Other dances remind the tribe of its dependency on and relatedness to the Creator and the created.[13] In the ceremonies harmony is restored and perpetuated for the future. In the ceremonies indigenous nations express their connection with primordial time and space, with cosmic reality.

Yet the very ceremonies that ground our beings were hindered and outlawed with the arrival of Europeans. The attacks on our ways of life are unparalleled in human history and our ability to regain and restore these ceremonies in their fullest sense is all but lost.

What Can we Do at the Lord's Table?

Vine Deloria, Jr., says, "Tribal religions have a very difficult time advocating their case (in the courts) . . . They may have to wait for the radical changes now occurring within Western religious institutions to take root and flourish before much progress can be made. Protestantism is increasing its ceremonial/ritual life, and Catholicism is becoming more secular, so that behavior comparable to tribal ceremonial behavior among Christians may not be far off."[14]

The United Church of Christ is noted for its diversity within the Euro-American theological tradition, in its historic pluralism and flexibility, its ecumenical interest, and its being on the cutting edge of social issues as a prophetic voice in the world. If this church can relinquish its defensive power posture and assume a listening posture, then we can sit at the Lord's Table as I believe God intends us to do. Let the United Church of Christ forthrightly say, We don't see one strand of commonality on which to base our unity, but let's be our unique selves at the Lord's Table. At the Lord's Table there is room to be, to be included, to be fed, to be forgiven, to be acknowledged, and to be at home in God's world.

At the Lord's Table, there is a theology of listening toward mutual hearing. Our various voices, the voices of all creation, and the voice of the Creator can speak and be heard. In mutuality, we can examine our motives for listening, our motives for hearing, our motives for talking—if we can risk being heard. Indigenous peoples' ceremonies and ceremonial grounds and the worship centers of the United Church of Christ have community-building opportunities that are mandated by our sacred histories and sacred obligations.

Each of us, indigenous peoples and the United Church of Christ, must learn how to authenticate our relationships with our own people. It is one thing to stand on the side of justice in Central America, South Africa, the Philippines, and the "uttermost parts of the earth" (Acts 13:47), but it is quite another to do justice with the victimized of our own people and the contamination of the environment in which we are blessed to dwell. Community building and living requires rebirth and relinquishment in the present in this place as well as in other lands and in the future so that "all may have life" at the Lord's Table. Paulo Freire wrote,

> *Those who authentically commit themselves to the people must re-examine themselves constantly. This conversion is so radical as not to allow ambiguous behavior. To affirm this commitment but to consider oneself the proprietor of revolutionary wisdom—which must then be given to (or imposed on) the people is to retain the old ways. The [person] who proclaims devotion to the cause of liberation yet is unable to enter into communion with people, whom he [or she] continues to regard as totally ignorant is grievously self-deceived. Conversion to the people requires a profound rebirth. Those who undergo it must take on a new form of existence; they can no longer remain as they were.*[15]

May it be so.

Notes

1. J. Leitch Wright, Jr., *The Only Land They Knew* (New York: MacMillan Free Press, 1981), 29.

2. *Ibid.,* 30–33.

3. Vine Deloria, Jr., *God Is Red* (New York: Delta Books, 1973), 3.

4. Stuart Lang, *Two Spirits Meet,* Heritage series, ed. Edward A. Powers (Philadelphia: United Church Press, 1976), 3.

5. *Ibid.,* 18.

6. Position paper of the Native American Project of Theology in the Americas, 475 Riverside Drive, New York, N.Y., 1978.

7. *Ibid.*

8. *Ibid.*

9. "Recalling, Reliving, Reviewing," a report on a religious dialogue sponsored by the Native American Theological Association and the Minnesota Humanities Commission, October 1979.

10. David Jobling, "Dominion Over Creation," in *Interpreter's Dictionary of the Bible,* supp. vol. (Nashville: Abingdon Press, 1976), 247–48.

11. The words of Chief Seattle were quoted by Adam Cuthand, in "The Spirituality of Native Americans," a speech given at the Toronto World's Future Conference (July 1980).

12. Deloria, *God is Red,* 262ff.

13. *Ibid.*

14. Vine Deloria, Jr., "Indians and Other Americans: The Cultural Chasm," *Church and Society* (Presbyterian Church U.S.A.) (Jan.–Feb. 1985): 11–19.

15. Paulo Freire, *Pedagogy of the Oppressed* (New York: Seabury Press, 1969), 47.

22. The Native Church: A Search for an Authentic Spirituality

LAVERNE JACOBS

One memorable Saturday morning in May of 1959 I "committed my life to Jesus Christ." Thus began a very convoluted spiritual journey. This commitment was preceded by a searching question posed several weeks earlier by my pastor. His question as I lay on a hospital bed was, "Laverne, are you saved?" I knew he was asking about my relationship with God. I also knew I was not satisfied with that relationship. Several weeks later on the side of a road I prayed the "sinner's prayer," guided by my pastor, and began a new relationship with God.

Christian Roots

The stability and identity I needed as a Native youth growing up in the late fifties and early sixties was provided by that experience. The social and economic conditions of my reserve community caused me tremendous shame. I struggled with all the stereotypes of the lazy, drunken, irresponsible Indian. As a new Christian, I gained a status which I did not enjoy as a Native person. I became a "child of God," an "heir of God and joint heir with Christ," and a "fellow citizen with the saints and members of the household of God" [Romans 8:16, 17; Ephesians 2:19]. Following high school and two years in the work world I entered an Anglican theological college.

I grew to appreciate the devotional life of the Church during my seminary years. I learned about the church fathers, the history, and traditions of the Church. I read the writings of Tillich, Kierkegaard and others. I learned the songs of the Church and embraced its rituals. I studied Greek. This was my formation for the priesthood. I accepted this process willingly and acknowledged western thought and theology as normative and absolute in my preparation for life as a priest and as a Native Christian. These were happy years. The Christian traditions which I had embraced brought meaning and purpose to my life.

"The Native Church: A Search for an Authentic Spirituality" by Laverne Jacobs. Reprinted by permission of The Rev. Laverne V. Jacobs.

Resurgence of Traditional Native Spirituality

I was convinced that Native traditions and spirituality were inherently evil and pagan. Such traditions were contradictory to the Christian faith. I was warned about the dangers of syncretism and told I must not compromise my faith as a Christian. Deeply concerned about the centrality of Christ, I resolved that I would not bring dishonour to Christ by seeking after other gods.

In 1975 I returned to my home community to pastor both the Anglican and United congregations. During this period I and members of the faith community struggled with the resurgence of traditional Native Spirituality. Younger members of the reserve in their search for identity were exploring their Native heritage. These young people travelled to powwows throughout North America. They brought back ways and cultural traditions foreign to our community.

Years of Struggle

The years that followed were difficult years marked by religious zeal and conflict. "Born again" members of my parish burned their Native symbols and quit making Native crafts. Christian members of the community boycotted powwows. Followers of the Traditional Ways lobbied to have Native Spirituality taught in the school. Anxious church members launched a counter campaign. Confusion and conflict struck to the core of people's beings. A funeral exacerbated the turmoil. Once a faithful church member, the deceased person left the Church and embraced the Traditional Ways. At death the body was prepared in the Traditional Way with painted face and the use of traditional symbols and rituals. Community members were torn between their desire to support the bereaved family and their fear of Native Spirituality. As the parish priest, I did not know what an appropriate pastoral response should be. I was just as confused and fearful as everyone else.

The Journey

These years of turmoil and religious conflict were the beginning of a long and painful journey. Early on I attended a conference, enrolling in a workshop by Father John Hascall, a Native Roman Catholic priest. Father Hascall was a Pipe Carrier and spiritual leader in the Midewiwin Lodge. I was deeply disturbed and troubled by his address. In sharing his spiritual journey he seemingly equated Native Spirituality with Christianity. His whole story evoked my worst fears of syncretism.

Within that same period I attended a United Church conference for Native peoples. Two Traditional Elders led sessions on Native Spirituality. The Elders talked about the Pipe and Sweetgrass ceremonies. Provision was made for people to participate in a Sweat Lodge.

People chose either to participate in or to observe the Sweetgrass Ceremony. Those actively participating in the ceremony formed an inner circle; those choosing to observe formed an outer circle. All were permitted to talk about the choices they had made. I remained in the outer circle anxiously observing the ceremony. I deliberately chose the outer circle because I did not understand the ceremony and was afraid of compromising my Christian beliefs. There was no way I would join the group in a Sweat Lodge! Engaging in a Sweat was just asking too much of me. I was fearful of aligning myself with the Evil One.

I put these experiences aside determined to devote my energies more fully to the Christian faith. As a part of this new commitment I went to confession and sought forgiveness for delving into pagan rituals. I resolved to refrain from any involvement with Native Spirituality.

This renunciation of Native Spirituality seemed to provoke more confrontation and struggle. Again I sat in the presence of Father John Hascall, the Medicine Priest. On this occasion, I attended a service of the Native community in my home diocese. This service, held in the cathedral, began with Father Hascall praying with the Pipe in the Four Directions. He began the ceremony with a brief explanation saying that certain people would be invited to share the Pipe with him. His assistant called me to come forward. Time stood still. I struggled with the implications of this request: *Was it right for me, as national staff, to share in this ritual? What would such action say to people? Would I be compromising my Christian beliefs? Would it be right to refuse something which was sacred to others and offered to me as a symbol of honour and trust?*

In my turmoil and anxiety I placed the Pipe to my lips and drew upon the sacred substance not knowing what would follow, but trusting and hoping that somehow God was present in this action and praying that I would be protected from that which I did not know or understand. I returned to my seat and watched as the ceremony continued. I looked at the young men, just barely in their teens, who had been invited to be "helpers" to Father John. They were engrossed in the ceremony and service; their faces reflected a deep sense of pride in their Native heritage. As I pondered the whole experience I had the sensation of One saying *"This is you."*

Years later I attended a World Council of Churches assembly in Korea on *Justice, Peace, and the Integrity of Creation*. I was the only First Nations person from Canada in a gathering of several thousand. The process was so European and overwhelming. I felt alienated and alone. I desperately wanted to be back home. In my loneliness, I was approached by four Native Americans who asked me to join them in prayers. I felt relieved to be with my own people. The next morning we gathered on a mound outside the conference hall. As we stood in a circle, one of the men beat a drum and sang a prayer song. Another man prepared the Sacred Pipe for our prayers. Again, I wondered if I should be there. I was torn between my desperate need for support and my fear of Traditional Ways and the possibility of compromising my Christian principles. As the Pipe was handed to me, I asked for protection and prayed to the God that I knew and to Jesus my Brother. During and following this ceremony I felt a certain peace of mind and heart and was assured that I had not compromised my Christian values. In the remaining days of the conference, the daily prayers with the Pipe—the very thing which I feared—sustained me.

A Sacred Time

Of all Native ceremonies in my ken, the one I feared most was the Sweat Lodge. It is a ceremony I was determined to avoid. In the summer of 1992 I attended a Native gathering sponsored by the Roman Catholic Church. The program included healing circles and the Sweat Lodge. As I read the program I had the ominous feeling that this time I would not be able to run away and that I would participate in a Sweat which filled me with anxiety and fear. I attended the seminar on the healing circle and the Sweat Lodge. I still did not know what to do. After the seminar, a deacon told me of his first experience of praying in a Sweat Lodge, a dramatic and wonderful experience. His glowing account did not allay my fears. It was only at the last moment, comforted by the knowledge that a close friend would be with me, I decided to join in the Sweat. The presence of my friend and the fact that the Elder leading the ceremony was one I trusted enabled me to go forward. Following the example of other men I took a pinch of tobacco and offered it at the Sacred Fire as I entered the Sweat Lodge, crawling on hands and knees behind other participants. When all had entered, the Elder ordered the flap of the lodge closed and began the ceremony. The intensity of the prayers matched the intensity of the heat from the steaming rocks. After several rounds and hours of prayer the ceremony came to a close. As we emerged from the lodge into the coolness of the night, we sat or lay on the ground knit together by the sacred bond of men who had shared a sacred journey. As I lay gazing up into the starlit sky I felt a tremendous sense of restfulness and peace. It was a truly sacred time. There was nothing that was contradictory to the Christian gospel which I embraced.

Both Native and Christian

Through these and many other experiences I gained an openness to faith journeys different from mine. I listened to stories of others whose ways are different, but in whose stories I have found the Christ of the Christian gospel. I learned to put aside my fears and step out in faith; and in that step of faith experienced the vastness of God, the Creator. I hear the sounds of many voices, each with a tenor and beauty of its own, but which together sing the praises of God the Creator and Jesus the Son in one great symphony of creation. In the midst of that glorious sound rings the phrase *"This is you—both Native and Christian."* The meaning of that phrase will be a lifelong dialogue with self. Each new experience and each year will uncover different aspects of that reality like the many facets of a precious gem. This dialogue is a dialogue shared by many First Nations people and which must continue in the midst of a changing world.

Index